Seventeen Sisters

Tell Their Story

∾

By Barbara Barlow & Virginia Webb

ISBN 978-0-9895523-5-6

This is a work of creative nonfiction. The events herein are portrayed to the best of each sister's memory. While all the stories in this book are true, some names and identifying details have been changed to protect the privacy of the people involved.

Publishing services provided by ScrivenerBooks.com.

Printed in the United States of America.

Table of Contents

Introduction

————————— ○○ —————————

IN THIS BOOK are the personal experiences Seventeen Sisters had growing up in polygamy, how it shaped each one and how it affected their
choices in life. How do you bring 17 stories with 17 different writing styles
and personalities into a cohesive book? We hope we have done that and
made it not only interesting but also offered each reader something that
may touch his or her own life.

We begin with excerpts about Albert E. Barlow from a book written
about him, the father of these seventeen women. From his childhood to
the ultimate choice he made, polygamy and then to continue living that
lifestyle no matter what the cost. He was bigger than life to his children
and to his wives.

We have included a family tree after the stories to help keep up with
the 34 children born into this family from three different women.

Albert E. Barlow

∽

CHAPTER I

1912

W HEN I WAS NINE, I went with my sisters, Alice and Clara, to get
milk from our Uncle Edmund's house. On our way back home,
we walked through his wheat fields. The next day, out of nowhere, Papa
suddenly cuffed me on the head.

"What's the matter with you?" he said. "You knocked the heads off all
the wheat everywhere you walked. You know better than that!"

"I didn't do it!" I cried.

"Don't lie to me." Papa yelled, smacking me again. "Edmund told me
the ground was covered with heads of grain. He was ready to give you a
beating himself." Papa slapped me a few more times, just for good measure.

I choked back sobs as I said, "Alice was doin' it. I told her not to."

But Papa would have none of my attempts to explain. As he stomped
away, he shouted over his shoulder, "I don't want to hear any more."

Even though Papa was a large man, Mama was not in the least
intimidated by him, but respected him enough that she never interfered
or contradicted him. As was normal during Papa's bad tempers, Mama
watched with respectful silence until he had left the room. She then hugged
me and said, "It's all right. Uncle Edmund was mad, and your father had
to punish someone."

She wiped my face. "Don't worry. I'll take care of Alice."

Just knowing that Mama believed me made things better. It seemed
like Papa blamed me for everything.

1915

My father's voice roared through the early-morning air, drilling into my head where dreams had been.

"Bert, giddup. You have to take True's team back to him this morning."

I was sleepy, but that wasn't the worst of it. The thought of going up Wild Cat Canyon was like a splash of icy water. The panic washed over me as I remembered my experience of a year earlier in that same canyon.

Papa was already out of the tent by the time I moaned, "Why can't Win go?" Struggling into my outgrown overalls and worn flannel shirt, I burst through the door of the kitchen.

"Why can't you go, Win?"

Mumbling something through his hot mush about cutting the wood, thirteen-year-old Win kept his eyes on his bowl. Frantic, I raced outside to find Papa hitching up Chub.

Shivering in the early-morning air, I cried, "Win's been there and knows the way. I can stay here and cut the wood."

Papa turned and looked me in the eye. Quietly but firmly, he said, "YOU will take the team back." I knew he meant business. I also knew it was his way of telling me to stop. There would be no further discussion.

The panic drove me on. "But Win's older and he's been there. I'm strong enough to cut the wood." Slowing a little, I pleaded, "Please make Win go."

In only a matter of seconds, my pleading turned to fury. I faced down my father, something any of us rarely did. "He always gets the soft jobs; he can talk you into anything."

I'd gone too far. Papa swung at me with lightning speed and cuffed me so fast I couldn't avoid the blow. But still I couldn't stop. "We're the same size but you make me do all the dirty work."

Did I say that?

"You made me go to Black Pine alone."

Why couldn't I shut up?

His fists clenched, Papa said through a tight jaw, "Put both harnesses on the mule, put the collar on the horse." With that, he stomped off through the dusty yard.

My stomach was in knots as I followed his instructions. As I was ready to climb on the horse, Mama emerged from the cabin and walked over to where I struggled with the horse.

"You'll be fine, Son," she said, handing me a small bundle with food in it. My mother was never disrespectful of my father but sometimes I could tell if she felt sorry for me, and I took advantage of that to argue more. Today her look was blank; any courage I had left....dissolved.

"Just head straight south, up the mountain and back down again," she advised.

"You'll be fine," Papa muttered as he passed me on his way back into the cabin.

Mumbling, I thrust myself up on the horse, jerked on the reins, and headed both animals toward the mountain. My legs hung around the horse's belly, pushing my pants almost to my knees. I had to curl my toes to keep the handed-down boots on my feet. The laces had broken long before.

As the sun peeked over the mountain my stomach groaned, reminding me of the biscuits Mama had tucked into the bundle. I wolfed down breakfast, wondering how long it would be before I reached the mouth of the canyon. There was no trail to follow, but the sun served as my compass. I knew the sun came up in the east, so I knew I was headed south.

There was a comfortable sense of community property at that time. It was common practice that a traveler could stop at any dwelling and eat. It didn't even matter if no one was there. The traveler was welcome to fix himself some food as long as he cleaned up after himself. If he used the fire, he was expected to clean it up and prepare it for another fire. What comfort I felt when I saw what looked like a dwelling in the distance—my salvation.

The sun beat down on me, and my thick hair was plastered against my face. The short shadows indicated it was mid-day, and my stomach bawled for food. How could it be possible that I had already eaten all the food Mama had sent with me? I gulped down the last of my water, hoping against hope for a friendly welcome at the ranch I had seen from a distance. I needed to eat—and my team needed to rest.

As I approached the ranch, an old man hobbled out of the barn. "Hallo" he hollered to me. Then, turning toward the house, he bellowed, "Ma, we got company."

I could see the man was about the same age as Papa, but his legs looked like they had grown around a tree trunk. The wrinkles around his eyes when he laughed immediately eased my worries, and his voice, though scratchy, warmed my stomach. "Ma" approached, wiping her hands on her apron.

I jumped down. Shaking both their hands with what I hoped was a manly grip. They overlooked my smooth cheeks and the squeak in my voice, treating me like a man.

A smile spread quickly across Ma's face. "Now, Harold, you feed his animals while I fix him a bite, where ya from, Son?" She kept up a steady banter, never waiting for answers.

I washed up while she piled a plate high with salt pork and beans. Thick slices of bread appeared as fast as I could eat them. As I mopped up the last of the beans with a slice of bread, she chuckled, "Haven't eaten for days, eh?" With that she slid a large piece of apple pie in front of me. A thick slice of melted cheese oozed down the sides of the slice. Food had never tasted so good.

I thanked her and headed toward my team as Ma rushed after me. She thrust a bundle into my hands and said, "This oughtta keep you from git'n too hungry."

I thanked them both, but my words seemed empty in proportion to their kindness.

I headed south again; I felt better, and the animals were easier to prod after their food and rest but as I approached the mouth of the canyon, my anxiety from earlier that morning returned.

There was no trail through the thick trees and brush. I pulled off my oversized hat to mop my brow, and I tried to hurry the team. My stomach churned at the thought of being in the canyon after dark, and tangles of branches from the thick brush scratched my legs as I pushed ahead. I prayed silently for help to keep me headed in a southward direction.

Suddenly a strange, high-pitched moan broke through the stillness. I clutched the reins tightly and froze in place, looking intently through the tangle of brush. When the sound shattered the silence again, goose bumps erupted all over my body, despite the heat of the relentless sun. I tried pulling my sleeves over my wrists.

Then I saw it—off to the right, in a small clearing, the young sheep was still alive and bleating weakly, its hindquarter chewed away. Fear went through me like a bucket of ice water. I knew that getting off my horse was not an option, so I kicked my boots into his sides and hurried on. A hundred yards up, another sheep lie dead, covered with fresh blood. Fear strangled my heart. I forced myself to look ahead, afraid of finding tracks.

My father knew the danger of Wild Cat Canyon, and he sent me anyway. Win could have offered to trade me jobs. Even Mama hadn't said anything. If I never came back, who would care?

A large lump grew in my throat and tears carved a path down my cheeks. I prayed again—this time for courage—and wiped the wetness away with shame. I clenched my jaw, kicked the horse, and hurried on. I forced myself to think of Mama—her gentleness, her devotion to her children, and her understanding. I began to forget my fear as I struggled to find my way. A chipmunk stared at me as I passed.

The sun was dancing along the horizon as I reached the top of the mountain. I knew it would be dark soon, and without a trail, I'd be lost.

I cried in a fervent, loud voice, "Father, I need help." Within seconds I noticed a trail. The mist from a light rain highlighted the dust on the trail and—oh, wonderful, precious tracks, not those of a wildcat, but of a wagon and team going down, going south. I couldn't believe it.

My voice was choked with emotion as I cried, "Oh, Heavenly Father, thank you, thank you."

The clouds became a bright orange as the sun slid behind the mountain. In the dusk I noticed all of the amazing colors, like someone had taken every shade of red, yellow, orange, and green and splashed it across the hillside. My melting fear enabled me to see what was all around me, and I knew I'd never see fall colors the same way again.

The night air became cooler as the sun set behind the mountains, so I pulled my coat out from behind me and put it on. The moon was full and the stars were bright. My voice cut through the stillness as I enthusiastically sang, "We-e Thank Thee, O Go-od, for a Pro-phet."

By the time I reached Dove Creek, it was close to midnight, and the Hatch place—home to Papa's Sister Alice and her husband, True—was still an hour away. They had always been nice to us, and I wondered as I pressed on through the darkness if Aunt Alice and Uncle True would let me work for them. I had decided I was not going home.

So what if I didn't come back? My father would have to make Win work harder, and that was fine with me. He didn't care about me anyway. I could work for my keep in Dove Creek until I could think of something else to do. I was a good worker; just this summer I overheard Aunt Alice tell mother that I was as good as her hired man.

As the horses clopped up to Hatch's house, their dogs started leaping all around us. Close on their heels was Aunt Alice. She gave me a big hug, took me inside, and insisted that I eat something before hitting the bunk. The large bowl of bread and milk topped with a slice of raw onion was just right.

Aunt Alice peppered me with questions as I ate. "How's the family? Any sickness? Is everyone in school? Oh, yes, little Mable and the baby are home yet. And your mother, is she all right?" She scarcely came up for air, and I was nodding in response to each question.

His voice startled me. "What time'd ya leave home, Bert?" Uncle True asked as he came in from bedding down the team.

"Just before dawn." Was my proud reply.

"Made good time, Son. Go climb in with Barlow. Good night." He good-naturedly rumpled my hair as he strode past my chair. (Note: Aunt Alice gave her oldest son her maiden name, Barlow.)

"Good night, Sir."

I listened to the heavy breathing of Barlow and wondered if I really did make good time. If I did, maybe Uncle True would give me a job. I wasn't going home. I'd show Papa. He'd see that I did most of the work while

Win just talked about it. I'd miss my little sisters and Mama, but I wasn't sure they would miss me.

I slept fitfully between nightmares of wildcats chasing my sisters and those of Mama laboring over huge pieces of wood with a tiny hatchet. I woke early feeling a little weak about my decision to stay in Dove Creek, but my youthful stubbornness won. The delicious aroma of bacon, eggs, and hot biscuits and gravy drew me to the kitchen.

"Up already?" Uncle True asked as he sat down for his breakfast.

I screwed up my courage as I asked, "Can you use an extra hand around here? I'll work hard for my keep, and I'll stay out of trouble." I focused on lowering my voice so I sounded more like a man. "If you can't use me, I'll go into Dove Creek and see if I can find work there."

Aunt Alice turned and stared as True shot her a quick glance.

"Win will help Papa. I'm big enough to be on my own now." I hoped I sounded more confident than I felt.

It seemed like hours while Uncle True kept his eyes on his food, shoveling one biteful after another into his mouth. Finally finished, he stood up and looked me steady in the eye. "Sure, we can use a good man. After you eat, come out and I'll git you started diggin' potatoes. We'll have a good harvest this year."

I was grateful that there were no questions asked. My plate was piled high with the steaming food and Aunt Alice touched my shoulder lightly as she left the room.

Time passed quickly as I dug potatoes, plowed, and brought in wood for Uncle True. My thoughts were always racing. If I worked real hard, maybe I could get work on a ranch near Dove Creek. Uncle True paid me very little, but I managed to buy a warm coat, some shoes, and some new underwear. Next I would get a horse. Then I could get a job on a ranch. I'd ride my own horse home. Papa would finally be proud of me, treat me with respect.

I worked hard; I had to prove myself not only to Uncle True and Aunt Alice but also to my parents—and to myself. Every day at dinnertime I gratefully dropped into a kitchen chair and gulped down the hot stew, thick pieces of bread, and slices of cheese. In my determination to work like a man, I was bone weary. By evening, after a bowl of bread and milk, I crawled into bed too tired to think—at first. But soon my heart began to ache for the tender kindness of my mother.

Aunt Alice was wonderful. She treated me like I was one of her brood of ten children but I missed Mama. It had been two months since I'd seen her. Why had I heard nothing? Could it be that they really didn't care? For all they knew, I could be dead in the canyon. Maybe Win worked harder than I thought. Maybe Mama was sick again—or maybe little Hazel, my precious baby sister, was suffering.

My brother Thomas was just a baby when he died. Then, when we all got whooping cough, Bryant died. He was only six weeks old. Poor Mama had suffered so much. Was I adding to that suffering? I began to pray that Heavenly Father would watch over my mother.

Then I wondered why Uncle True didn't have family prayer. Papa always had family prayer in the evening, a practice that was taught and encouraged by the leaders of the Mormon Church. We would all kneel in a circle as a family, and on the days when Papa didn't say the prayer himself, he called on one of us to offer it. As I started to think about the differences between my home and this one, my two months at Uncle True's seemed more like a year.

One day as I finished dinner and headed back out to the field, I saw a rider on horseback approaching the ranch. As he got closer, I recognized him as Harley Dudson, a neighbor of ours from back home.

He slid easily off his horse and strode toward me. I had a moment of real anxiety . Harley was pleasant enough, but when he got stirred up, his powerful fist had landed more than one boy on his back.

"Your father is in Rosette, and he wants you to come home," he said.

"I'm not goin' home," I answered with more defiance than I felt.

He looked out over the fields, up at the mountains, over at his horse, and finally directly at me. "Well, your dad said I was to bring you. I can carry you, or you can ride behind me, your choice."

That was it. I followed Harley to his horse. As I turned to look at the house, Aunt Alice ran toward us with a bundle. Handing it to me, she gave me a hug. "Here's something to chew on. Be careful and tell Chloe hello."

Had this been planned? Was the bundle of food ready because Aunt Alice knew I was leaving?

It took us several hours to reach Rosette. Papa had just finished loading his wagon as we trotted up to him. He glanced at me and climbed onto his horse without a word, so I jumped into the back of the wagon. He didn't seem angry, but I was rarely able to read his moods accurately. It was going to be a long ride.

When we got home, the girls came running out, happy to see us. Nine-year-old Clara grinned at me. Five-year-old Mable hugged me. Mama clutched little Hazel tight to her breast as tears streamed down her cheeks.

I had hurt her. She had been worried. I should have known. I helped unload the wagon and resolved right then to try harder to get along with my father and to be more obedient. Heavenly Father had guided me and protected me in the canyon—just like Papa knew He would.

It was good to be home, and I was proud of my new shoes and coat. I liked school and worked hard to catch up. I did well when I attended, but after spending two months away, I was far behind the kids who were my age.

Mama had given birth to another baby girl while I was gone. Her name was Mary. I was awed by the soft, tiny white fist clutching my big brown finger.

1920

It was early spring. I had worked like a man, ten to fourteen hours a day from the first tilling to the last harvest, for what seemed like as long as I could remember. Although I was only sixteen, I could do anything any grown man could do. That included drive a six-up—a six-horse hitch that combined six powerful horses into one unified team. But instead of taking pride in my work, resentment and anger continued to build in my heart. No matter how hard I worked, it was never good enough to please my father—and I never received any money.

I was self-conscious about my outgrown clothes, and I wanted other things that most of the other boys my age had, such as their own horse and saddle. Dad was able to buy a 1918 Model T stem-wind and stem-set automobile of which he was very proud. If he could have a car, I reasoned, there should have been enough money to let me have just a little something.

Exhausted from stuffing my feelings inside, one morning I started telling Dad how I felt as we were on our way out to start chores. With astonishing speed, he slapped me—hard—across my mouth.

Glaring at him, I wiped the blood off my mouth and said, "If it makes you feel better, then do it again."

Accepting my invitation, Dad doubled up his fist and knocked me so hard I flew off the porch and out into the yard. As I picked myself up, I swore I would never come home again.

Nursing my injured jaw, I walked into Burley, asking for jobs all along the way. "I'm sorry, I don't have anything for you to do," one man said, "but if you stand in the labor line downtown every morning, the farmers come in and pick up anyone who is willing to put in a good day's work."

I thanked him for the tip and figured I would at least make enough to eat.

It was harder than I thought—the farmers always picked the older men first. Many days I didn't get chosen at all, so I barely scratched out an existence. The room I rented cost a dollar a day, and there were some days when I had nothing but a dollar.

I had been away from home only a few weeks when the crew I was working with took me with them to a party. It was prohibition time, and there wasn't supposed to be any liquor available. But Russ Langton had some.

"Here, Bert." he said. "Have one on me."

It burned all the way down, but I managed to maintain a cool nonchalance. With the warmth spreading through my stomach, I grinned foolishly and told Russ, "I'd like to find out what it feels like to be drunk."

"Oh, yeah?" he said. "Have you got three dollars?"

Filled with foolish pride, I handed him the only three dollars I had. "Follow me."

I followed him for about a block until he stopped and started combing through the grass behind a bush. He stood up and thrust a full bottle of whiskey at me. I proceeded to drink myself into a stupor.

Someone at the party had a car, and we all piled in. I couldn't see very well, so I climbed out and sat on the hood. The marshal saw me and stopped us.

Sizing me up, he observed, "You've had a lot to drink."

"S-s-s-o-o, throw me in jail!" I stammered at the double vision in front of me. He did exactly that. I woke up in a basement on a bed with no mattress. The awful taste in my mouth reminded me of dry dandelions. My head pounded with every beat of my heart. I hollered, but no one heard me.

The next thing I knew, there was Win. He had been looking for me, and by asking around, he found me—and got me out of jail. The minute we were outside, I said, "Let's get a drink somewhere."

"No," he said. "Let's get out of town." He was pulling me alongside him as he quickly put distance between the jail and us.

"What's your hurry?"

"I was lucky to get you out of there, and I gotta git back to my job."

We finally reached the farm where Win had a job. He thought maybe they would let me work too, but as it turned out, they didn't want either of us.

That was our one-way ticket back home. I was stunned. Dad acted like nothing had happened—like I had never left. Mama gave us both a hug and quietly admitted, "I've been worried. I'm glad Win found you."

"I'm sorry, Mama," I said, and I meant it. I was glad she didn't know where Win had found me.

Later that year, Dad was promoting the building of a movie house in town and took me with him one Sunday afternoon to see the building. By the time we got back home, Win had already gone to the granary where we slept.

Mama pulled me aside. "Bert, you'd better go downstairs to bed. Don't go out where Win is. He's plenty mad."

"Oh, I'm not afraid of him, and never will be," I said as I shut the door behind me. The afternoon with Dad had relaxed me, and the crisp October air felt good as I headed out to the granary.

Four-year-old Roy was snuggled under a blanket on my cot. I smiled as I asked, "You gonna sleep with me tonight?"

"He came out here to sleep with me!" Win snapped. He was sullen, looking for a fight.

For as long as I could remember, Win and I had been the same size, and hard work made us both strong. We were now both just over six feet tall. Lately his attitude had gone from annoying to intolerable. I wondered if he was jealous because I was still attending school while he had finished the year before and had to work from sunup to sundown.

I slipped off my clothes and lay on my cot, ignoring him. "Come on, Roy, you can sleep with me if you want to."

Win lunged at me so fast I didn't see him until he nailed me. We fought fiercely for what seemed like an hour but was more likely about fifteen minutes. Win was fueled by alcohol—I could smell the booze on his breath. When he finally started losing his wind, I pinned him. "Say uncle." I said, holding him down.

He glared at me. "Okay, I'll say uncle."

I raised off him and rolled onto the floor. I stretched out, extremely fatigued and very relaxed. Suddenly Win, wearing his work boots, jumped onto me from the top bunk, landing with all his weight on my short rib.

I thought I was going to die. I had never been in such pain in my entire life.

"There, damn you," he said as he lay down to sleep.

I didn't sleep at all that night. When I heard the rooster crow, I forced myself to get out of bed and dress for school. I could hardly stand up, but complaining would only bring ridicule from Win. Grabbing a couple of biscuits, I gave Mama a kiss on her soft cheek and headed for the door.

"You didn't eat, Son."

"I'm not hungry. I'll just take these biscuits."

Her look told me she knew I was not okay. "Let me look at you."

"Him an' Win were fightin'," Roy said.

"I'm late for ball practice," I said, gently pushing Mama away. "I gotta go. I'm okay."

Avoiding her eyes, I ducked out the door, knowing she would worry.

I didn't go to practice. I could hardly ride the horse to school. I tried to concentrate on what the teacher was saying, but the pain kept getting worse until I couldn't even think. The ride home seemed endless. I was doubled over with pain. Stumbling into the kitchen, I landed in a chair before passing out. As I opened my eyes a few minutes later, Mama was wiping my forehead with a cool cloth.

"What is the matter with you?" she asked, alarm in her voice.

"I don't feel good." I tried to act normal.

"I'll get you some tea." She helped me into the living room, lowered me onto the sofa, and hurried to the kitchen. I didn't like Mama's herb tea, but I was ready to try anything if it might help me feel better.

"Were you sick last night? Why did you go to school if you were sick?" Her voice was shaking.

I couldn't answer. "Bert, what happened last night?" Her voice was quiet but insistent.

I was vaguely aware that Dad had come in. "Clara said Bert was sick. What's the matter?"

"I don't know; he won't talk to me. Where's Win?"

I was doubled up with pain, sweat streaming from every pore. "Mama. . . ."

I vaguely heard Dad's somber voice through the wall of pain that gripped me. "We'll have to take him to the hospital in Burley. He's bad."

Dad had never taken one of us to the hospital, and he had very little faith in doctors. But he knew something was very wrong with me. On the way to the hospital, I passed out several times. Finally Dad said, "Son, we need to know what happened last night to cause this pain." At that moment, doubled over with pain and, fearing I might die, I felt a love from him I'd never felt before.

"Win—jumped on me. He meant no harm, Dad."

Dad swore under his breath. And even through my gut-wrenching pain, I could hear him begin to offer a prayer. He prayed the rest of the way to the hospital.

Even in my barely conscious state, I felt the doctor's concern. I learned later that he told my parents he must operate immediately to see what damage had been done and to determine whether there was anything he could do. Dad knew he needed to trust the doctor. Mama simply trusted Dad. They waited, hoped, and continued to pray.

It was very late when Dr. Fremstead reported to my weary parents what he had learned. The words of my diagnosis could not have been easy for him, even after years of practice: "His liver has been crushed beyond repair." His next words barely penetrated my father's consciousness: "I'm sorry, but your son can't live."

Dad's shoulders were bent as he put a heavy arm around Mama. "We want to be with him now."

Mama's eyes were dry, her face grim. "Can he stay here until he gets better?"

The doctor wondered if she had misunderstood. Maybe she hadn't heard him at all. He led my parents to the room where I lay, never expecting me to come out of my drugged sleep.

My parents prayed fervently for my life, never leaving my side as the night wore on. With the rays of the sun coming through the window, they continued to pray. Finally I stirred, opening my eyes briefly. Dad leaned over me. "Bert, do you want the elders to give you a blessing?"

The Mormon Church taught that men who were ordained to the office of elder in the Melchizedek Priesthood could use their priesthood to confer blessings of healing. I knew those blessings depended in part on the recipient's faith in that priesthood and that blessing. I wasn't sure how I felt about any of that, so I answered thickly, "Naw, that won't help."

Later I opened my eyes again and Dad once more asked, "Son, do you want a priesthood blessing?"

"No—I'm fine," I insisted. I just wanted to be left alone.

It grew dark. Mama's worried face looked down at me as I regained consciousness again. "I wish they'd quit flashin' the lights off'n on," I said.

Mama's quiet voice whispered, "Those are your lights going off, Son."

Later still, Dad leaned over me and said, "This is the last time I'm going to ask you, Bert. Do you want the elders to give you a blessing?"

Mama's face looked so tired. How long had I been here?

"Okay," I responded weakly. "I guess it can't hurt."

Dad quickly called a group of men who had been ordained elders, and they came. Uncle Edmund, Myron Barlow, and a small man I didn't know. Uncle Edmund was voice for the blessing. After they administered to me, I slept peacefully for eight hours—the first good sleep I'd had since I was hurt Sunday night. Dad went home to take care of things, but Mama stayed by my bed. When I awoke, a nurse was standing near the bed.

"Where are my clothes?" It was such a relief to feel better, and I was ready to go home.

The nurse laughed. "You've got a lot to learn."

She tucked the blankets around me; checked my pulse, my eyes, and my blood pressure; and gave me a drink. I still hurt badly, but I felt alive.

Only twenty-four hours after I received the priesthood blessing, a pain in my shoulder became unbearable. Dr. Fremstead said that nerves from the liver were laced through the shoulders—and that all he could do was give me a painkiller. Even with the painkiller, the pain soon became so intense that I again asked for the elders. The small man who had come earlier returned, giving me another blessing in which he asked the Lord to "rebuke the pain from this injury."

The pain stopped immediately. I knew then that the priesthood was real and that it was powerful.

I remained in Fremstead Hospital—actually the large home of Dr. Fremstead—and watched the leaves fall off the trees. I watched the snow drifting from the skies. I saw the new light green leaves grow back on the trees. And though I was very weak, I never felt pain. Almost a year after Win jumped on me, I had gained enough strength to go home. The doctor could not believe that I was alive, telling Mama that I was a miracle.

"Yes, Doctor, our prayers were answered," she smiled.

The doctor somberly gave me instructions as I left the hospital. "Albert, you must eat right. Your liver cannot tolerate greasy or rich foods. And having a glass of red wine in the evening would be good for your liver."

I learned quickly that when I ate the right things, I felt good. When I ate things that were bad for me, I became weak and depressed, unable to cope with the smallest problems. However, I never felt even the slightest pain from this injury after the priesthood blessing.

1922

Albert was raised in The Church of Jesus Christ of Latter-day Saints, also known as the LDS Church or the Mormon Church. Before Utah became a state there were a few Mormons who practiced plural marriage. It was eventually outlawed by the federal government and, as a result, the federal government would not allow Utah to become a state and threatened to confiscate all Church property. In response, in 1889, the president of the LDS Church told the members to stop taking plural wives. However, it took a number of years for the people to adhere to that counsel. Polygamy was considered a 'saving' principle and those who were living that way had a number of adjustments to make. The Church finally began excommunicating members who continued to take plural wives.

Albert knew his grandparents had lived polygamy but he also knew it was not acceptable any more. After he left home at seventeen, his parents had joined a fringe group of Mormons who had begun living polygamy secretly outside the Church. Albert was furious when he heard that his father had taken another wife. He went home with a plan to confront his father but saw his mother first. She helped him to understand that it had been a joint decision between both parents. She convinced him to attend the "cottage meetings" and learn from the group with whom they were associating. At that time, cottage meetings were a common way for members of the LDS faith to meet in small scripture study groups. These cottage meetings were usually held on Sunday evenings. This group had started out studying plural marriage and eventually decided they were supposed to live that principle in spite of the fact that it was against the law and The LDS Church may excommunicate them.

The following is Albert's perspective on what happened.

One Friday when I was visiting Mama in the hospital, where she was being treated for hemorrhaging, she asked Father, "How long have I been here?"

"Eleven weeks," he said quietly.

"I want you to have our friends fast for me. On Sunday have the Brethren come here and give me a blessing. I know I'll be healed. I've got to get well so I can live The Principle."

While all male adult members of the LDS Church were called brethren, I knew the Brethren Mama was referring to were those men living polygamy underground and The Principle meant plural marriage. The people from the cottage meetings fasted and prayed for Mama, and on Sunday the brethren gave her a blessing. She stopped hemorrhaging immediately, and by Thursday she was home doing all her work. I was convinced these men had the priesthood, which gave them the healing power of God.

A few weeks after she left the hospital, Mother told me something that helped me understand what drove the dedication of my parents—and many others—to the principle of plural marriage. "Before I got sick your father and I were lying in bed talking about living The Principle and he felt that it just wasn't possible right now because of our finances," she said. "We both felt an urgency to do so anyway. So we decided to pray and ask for confirmation.

"As we arose from our knees a shaft of light entered the room and it grew lighter until it was like daylight. Your father began to prophesy many wonderful things. I heard beautiful music and saw what I believe was the celestial kingdom. We were overcome with joy. We knew we were supposed to sacrifice whatever was necessary now for the blessings of someday living in the celestial kingdom."

Tears streamed down her cheeks as she related their experience to me, and I knew she was telling me the truth.

That Sunday we were fasting for Mother, I was passing sandwiches around to everyone at the cottage meeting so they could break their fast; I handed some of the sandwiches to a beautiful dark-haired girl with hazel eyes who I later found out was sixteen-year-old Katie Kilgrow. Her parents had just started attending the cottage meetings. After handing her those sandwiches, I took every possible chance to be where I knew she would be.

Many of the people who attended the cottage meetings continued to be active in the Mormon Church, and there were plenty of activities where the young could socialize, so I had many opportunities to see and spend time with Katie.

I courted her from my parents' tiny four-room home in Millcreek, riding the red cable cars and the yellow, steel-wheeled, electric street cars to her parents' home in West Jordan. At sixteen, she looked and acted twenty. At the dances I put her name on the dance card as much as I could. The girls lined up on one side of the dance hall and the guys on the other, and we would find the girl whose name was on our card. I loved to dance, and Katie was a perfect partner. Her thick black hair was always neatly in place, her eyes changed colors with her moods, and she smelled like violets. What a flirt she was! Every man at the dances wanted to hold her.

I had been studying the scriptures, praying, and listening to Father and the other men at the cottage meetings. As a result, I became convinced that plural marriage was a commandment of God and that I must live it if I wanted to achieve the highest degree in heaven in the next life.

Katie called me Albert, and I liked that. When we talked of marriage once, she said, "I won't marry you unless you intend to live the law of plural marriage."

"Why?" I asked. I was secretly delighted—I wanted to do exactly that but hadn't wanted to say anything to her about it.

"I want my husband to know I'm the best of the bunch," she quipped, teasing me. Then her eyes turned serious and she said, "I feel like I must live 'The Principle.' It's a law of God."

I was deeply impressed. I knew it took an unselfish woman to live that way and I wanted her for my wife. We were both active in the LDS Church, as were our families. Many of the people at the cottage meetings had not separated themselves from the Church. They believed, as I did, that it was Christ's Church and nothing could change that. But we also felt plural marriage was a correct principle and must be lived.

Katie was a beautiful, feisty, social woman who stood about five feet four inches tall. Born in Canada, she rode in a wagon with her family when they immigrated to Utah. At the age of thirteen she was cooking for several ranch hands and became an amazing cook, able to make a feast with little or nothing in the cupboards. As her relationship with Albert blossomed, her mother insisted they wait to get married until Katie was eighteen. Instead, they waited until she was just past seventeen and Albert was nineteen.

Albert and Katie had a very passionate relationship. She had a wonderful sense of humor and the ability to smooth Albert's ruffled feathers most of the time. With unbridled compassion, she always found ways to cheer up anyone who was down.

They were married in the Salt Lake Temple in 1922 and continued to be active in the LDS Church, until they were excommunicated after they started living polygamy.

1934

Katie and I continued to pray fervently that we would find a girl who would agree to enter our family. Finally, approaching the Lord while fasting, I told Him I would die fasting if I could not find a woman who was willing to enter my family.

Two days later we met Vio Frazer, she was about 5'3" and quite thin, with dark blond hair and a face somewhat scared from acne. She was very humble, a childlike woman of twenty-one. I had seen her once, a year earlier, but this time I received a distinct impression that I should ask her to be my wife. I nudged Katie and told her to ask Vio to dinner Sunday. Vio agreed to come.

After that dinner, I hired Vio to help Katie around the house for fifty cents a day. After a few months, I was taking her home one evening when I decided to drive up to "passion flats" above the State Capitol building. As we looked out on the city lights, I asked her if she would consider coming into our family.

"Yes, I will," she replied.

I was stunned, "When?" I asked her.

"I don't care," she answered, shrugging her shoulders.

That was it. We settled on the next Thursday. I had never been a man to waste any time—whenever I made a decision, I liked to act on it immediately—and this one was no different.

On February 14, 1935, Katie put Vio's hand in mine as the "Brethren" sealed us in marriage. She moved into our home right away.

Vio's arrival in our home was hard for Katie, who already had eight children under the age of thirteen. Since she had to teach Vio everything, Katie regarded Vio almost as another child. Katie didn't have much patience and at times was quite rude to her. I'm sorry to say I was also quite impatient. But Vio had the sweet honesty of a child and never complained. In fact, she apologized constantly for everything she did or didn't do.

Vio Frazer (pronounced "Vi") was very shy and content with little or no attention given her. She was grateful for anything—kind words, a touch, even a smile.

She was born in Canada and came to Utah as a toddler. Her mother, a much-in-demand midwife, was never home, so Vio was raised in the LDS

Church by an older sister. With a mother who was absent so much and a father who emotionally drifted in and out of her life, she received very little attention or affection. Vio is remembered as childlike and humble, a forgiving soul . She tried so hard to please, and as a result was often treated with cruelty and indifference. She was quite passive but sometimes took her anger out on her own children because she so desperately wanted them to be accepted by Albert. She adored him, and when he became his worst self she was sad that he would show that side of himself and receive the criticism that followed.

1935

On the way home from work one day, I felt prompted to again ask Maurine Owen to marry me. She was short, maybe 5'2" and had thick auburn hair and dark brown eyes. When she smiled it showed her high cheekbones and the light in her eyes. She spoke very little with her mouth but her eyes spoke volumes.

She had been attending all the cottage meetings so Kate and I had a chance to get to know her and we both felt strongly that the Lord intended her to be part of our family. Following my prompting that afternoon, I stopped at Maurine's apartment and declared, "I know you are to be my wife."

It was the third time I had discussed marriage with her.

She was quite nice this time, but said, "Well, I don't know, and until I do, I can't marry you."

I was sitting next to her on the couch. I gently held her shoulders in my hands and pulled her to me. I kissed her three times on the mouth and felt her give herself to me. That's when I knew she would be mine.

She didn't know, however. She was twenty-one years old and had never been kissed—and it scared her. She had watched many romantic movies and had read many novels about love, but the warmth of a real kiss was new to her.

"We shouldn't do this," she said. Her fine, high cheekbones were colored a deep pink.

"Will you pray about it?" I asked as I stood to leave.

Her eyes were riveted on the floor. "Yes."

I talked to Katie about it when I got home. "I'm sure she's supposed to be in our family," I said, "but she's a proud woman and I'm not sure she'll listen to the Spirit."

Katie said, "Don't worry about it. I had a dream the other day and saw her come past the window with a small satchel in her hand. She went around to the back door and said, as she walked in, 'Well, here I am.' I believe she'll come around."

"Bless your heart, dear," I said. "This can't be easy for you. I love you." As I held her I knew I was a fortunate man, and I said, "The Law is a spiritual law, and I am determined to be guided by the Spirit in bringing Maurine into the family. I have refused to allow myself to think of her physically."

"Don't say that for my benefit," Katie mumbled as she ran her hands over my chest. "And don't ever stop thinking of me physically." That was something that would never happen. The years had only made Kate more beautiful to me.

Several months passed. One day at a Sunday meeting, Charles Owen came up to me and said, "I have a young lady that wants to see you."

I felt quite cocky because Maurine had hurt my pride, so I wasn't exactly gentle in my response to her father. I gruffly asked, "What does she want to see me about?"

"Go see her and find out." Charles didn't like me, and wasted no effort letting me know that I wasn't good enough for his daughter. It seems that those kinds of feelings are normal for many fathers, but in my case I felt there was more to it—it seemed much more personal. I didn't even get the impression that his reluctance came from the fact that Maurine wouldn't be the first wife. He simply didn't like me.

A few days later, I stopped to see Maurine on my way home from work. When she answered the door, I stated without emotion, "Your father said you wanted to see me."

"Yes. Come in." She sat with me on the couch. "Dad and I fasted and prayed separately about who I should marry. We both had your name come to mind. I'm not real excited to be married but I know I should, and I do feel you are the right man for me."

She was as pure and honest as anyone I had ever known. I felt very humbled, but my pride would never let on. "When do you want to be married?" I asked.

"It's up to you."

"Then we'll do it today."

"I have to work tonight." She worked at the telephone company as a long distance operator.

"When is your next day off?" I asked.

"Next week."

"We'll get sealed now, then next week I'll bring you home with your belongings." It was important to me to establish the fact that we were being sealed. For members of the LDS Church, a sealing is much more than a simple marriage. A sealing is considered an eternal covenant between a man, a woman, and God—a covenant that transcends the period of our lives on earth and extends throughout all eternity.

"I'd like to wear something nicer than this old brown dress," she said, looking down.

"You look fine," I told her. I was afraid that if she took the time to find clothing that was more suitable to her, she might change her mind.

I took her, Katie, and Vio to see one of the brethren who had the proper priesthood authority to perform the sacred sealing covenant. As Katie put Maurine's hand in mine, I knew I had never loved my first wife more than I did at that moment.

Maurine was sealed to me on December 20, 1935. After the sealing, the four of us climbed back into the truck, and I drove to Maurine's apartment. Walking her to the front gate, I shook her hand and said, "Good night."

She wanted me to kiss her, but I couldn't. If the neighbors saw me kissing her, they would report us to the authorities. There were always people looking for polygamists to report.

One week later, on December 27, Maurine climbed out of my truck, grabbed her small satchel of clothes, and walked around to the back door as Katie watched out the window. She came into the house, saying to Katie in a matter-of-fact manner, "Well, here I am."

Maurine Owen was born into an active LDS family. Both her parents were very soft-spoken and maintained a peaceful atmosphere in their home. Both had been school teachers and emphasized learning in their home; as a result, she skipped a couple of grades, graduating from The LDS Academy (a high school) when she was only sixteen. Her father had become a farmer and made very little money, so after she graduated she was hired at the telephone company as a long-distance operator and could help her parents out financially.

Maurine's parents began going to "cottage meetings" where the principle of plural marriage was taught, and her father took another wife. Maurine had a deep respect for her father and accepted his choice to take another wife. She had moved into an apartment downtown to be closer to her job and, not a very social person, she loved having her own space in her small apartment where she spent all her spare time going to movies and reading novels.

Maurine's mother died giving birth. Shortly before she died, she strongly confirmed to Maurine her belief in plural marriage. This strengthened Maurine's belief that plural marriage was a correct principle and she intended to live it.

For a young woman who was not terribly social, Maurine lacked nothing in the proposal department: She received constant offers of marriage as a plural wife. The first time Albert Barlow proposed, Maurine blew him off even though he was very good looking. He asked again several months later, and Maurine still wasn't interested. Not only did Maurine consider Albert to be obnoxious, but also her father didn't like him. Her father had actually worked for Albert as a bookkeeper a year earlier, and the two had experienced a falling out.

The disagreement between Maurine's father and Albert made it difficult for Albert to follow the established tradition among polygamists. A man usually spoke to a woman's father if he wanted to approach her about coming into his family; after that, the man's wife would invite the woman to dinner or some other event where she could interact with the entire family. But because Albert was reluctant to talk to Maurine's father, he went directly to Maurine.

Bert and his three wives.

Frances Chloe

~

CHAPTER 2

1928

I WAS BORN JANUARY 5, 1928, to Albert Edmund Barlow and Amanda Kate Kilgrow. I was my mother's fourth child, all girls. My father was just over six feet tall and well built. He had dark hair and usually wore a mustache and I considered him very handsome. Mother was about 5'5" and had thick black hair. She always looked lovely when she went out, but I never saw her without an apron on at home. She was always cracking jokes.

We had a dear neighbor, Dr. Louise Ogden, who had rose bushes lining both sides of the walk leading up to her front door. One lovely spring day, when I was about two and a half, and the flowers were so pretty. I said to my sister, "Marie, help me pick some of these pretty roses."

We slowly walked along the bushes plucking petal by petal, chanting, "He loves me, he loves me not. He loves me, he loves me not," until every flower was gone. The walk was covered with petals and we were happy to run and tell Mama about our lovely fun.

Mama was surprised and scolded us, explaining that Mrs. Ogden would be very unhappy about what we had done. We felt pretty bad—not because of the scolding, but because we loved our neighbor; in fact, she was the doctor who delivered Momma's babies.

However, we didn't get off with a simple scolding; when Daddy came home, he took both of us down to the basement and whipped us. I felt terribly guilty and sorry about picking all those roses.

Our home was run with a mixture of strict discipline and an abundance of love. Mama was very fussy about the house being clean. On Saturday, our cleaning day, we went all out—mopping floors, changing linens, ironing, dusting furniture, and so on. Once the house was spotless, Mama sent a couple of us to the bakery to buy donuts as a treat for all the work we girls did. On Sundays we went to church together. We were members of the LDS Church.

Shortly after I turned seven my parents began living plural marriage, bringing Aunt Vio (pronounced "Vi") into the family. She wasn't related to us but in plural marriage a woman's children call her sister-wives aunt, even though they are no relation to the children. We were also raised to understand that all adults were called by their last name preceded by Sister, Brother, Aunt, Uncle, Mr., Mrs., or Miss. It was never appropriate for us to call adults by their first name only.

Aunt Vio was very thin with fine dishwater blond hair and maybe 5'4" tall. She was childlike, and Mama had to teach her everything—including personal hygiene, housecleaning, cooking, and other basic skills. She was very sweet and tried hard to please Mama.

Then just before I turned eight, Aunt Maurine came to live with us. She was about 5'2" and had very thick dark brown hair and dark brown eyes, high cheekbones and a quiet smile. She was so pretty and she acted like a queen; she was extremely orderly, and as she organized her things she let me try on some of her jewelry. She treated me like I was special, and I sometimes wished that she was my mother.

I was obedient, compliant; accepting everything my parents did without questioning them. Some of Mother's children didn't accept these two women though. One day I came into the kitchen and Aunt Maurine was on her hands and knees scrubbing the floor. Marie, who was about nine, was sitting on the kitchen counter eating cherries. She began spitting the pits at Aunt Maurine. I was shocked, "Marie, why are you doing that?"

"Oh.....," she had just noticed me. "It was an accident," she said. I felt so bad for Aunt Maurine.

About that time Daddy was called by our bishop, who was the head of our local LDS ward (similar to a parish), and asked him to come in for a "court;" a disciplinary counsel where a few local church leaders would ask him about the rumors that he had taken a plural wife. Daddy refused to go to the court, so my parents and Aunt Vio were excommunicated from the LDS Church; meaning that they lost their church membership. By then, Mother had nine children.

Some of the kids continued to attend church, but it was very hard on Mother; the excommunication embarrassed her. It became hard for us kids as well, because we started being harassed by the neighbor kids. Some of the them would stand in front of our house, arms hooked, chanting, "Look at Bert Barlow, he thinks he's Jean Harlow with wives Kate, Vio, and Maurine," a spoof on sex symbol Jean Harlow.

We were soon evicted from the house on Green Street because it was going to be demolished, and we moved briefly to a house on 2700 South. Then Dad heard that his uncle was starting a small polygamist community on the Utah/Arizona border, and Dad's father had moved down south along with others. Dad wanted to be closer to them, so we then moved to southern Utah. He first moved Aunt Maurine and Aunt Vio to Kanab where they lived in a tent. Mother came later with all her children, settling in a tiny house in Hurricane, just outside St. George.

We lived a fairly rustic existence. Ours was an old house with no running water. A few light bulbs hung from the ceiling and there was an outhouse. We fetched water from a nearby well for cooking and bathing. The whole country was dealing with the effects of The Depression and the drought, so our poverty wasn't a lot worse than that of others, but we had a lot more children, so many more mouths to feed.

When we weren't working, we played in the fields and bathed in the creek. But being off from work was a rare treat. All of us kids who were old enough went with Dad to the fields, where we picked peas and did whatever other jobs he could find for us.

Being the oldest child in the family, my sister Arlene was put in charge when Dad wasn't there. She was a strict taskmaster, keeping us in line and making sure we did what we were supposed to. I often picked the peas without really looking at them; instead, I gazed up at the sky, daydreaming and pretending I was somewhere else—or maybe I was even a princess.

One time we were in the field and we noticed that one of the landlord's cows had gotten out through a broken fence. Arlene was able to steer the cow back into the enclosure and fix the fence well enough that no more cows could escape until the landlord was able to fix the fence. When we got home, Arlene told Mother about the cow escapade. Mother told Dad. Dad then told the landlord so he could do a solid, permanent fix on the fence.

The landlord was so grateful he let Dad take us all to the theater in town, which he owned. We'd never seen a movie before, and we were so excited! We watched the movie—Snow White—four times that afternoon.

Things got so financially bad in southern Utah that Dad became desperate. By then he had thirteen children for whom he was responsible. The older kids were hard workers and the mothers were doing whatever they could to help, but between The Depression and the drought, times were hard for everyone. When he learned about a polygamist group in the Bountiful area—just north of Salt Lake City—who were practicing "communal living," he decided to join that group.

Our family stayed with the Bountiful group for about a year. Things weren't as rosy as our parents had hoped. Dad was expected to put in very long hours and often kept the older children out of school to work with him. In the Mormon Church, members are expected to fast (go without food and drink) once a month and give money to the poor. But the leaders of the group we belonged to asked us to fast quite often just to prove our faithfulness, and even when we did eat, there wasn't much food. When Dad's health started to fail because of the long hours and the stress of the situation, our Grandpa Barlow talked Dad into leaving the group in Bountiful and move to Salt Lake City. It wasn't a surprise when we moved; I think Dad would have done anything to get his father's approval.

It was about that time when the older kids started spending some time at Grandpa Barlow's house. (I always had a strong attachment to Grandpa Barlow. When I was little, he often set me on his knee and hummed to me.) While most grandparents in conventional situations are "empty nesters," with all their adult children having started their own families, Grandpa Barlow actually had children our age from his plural wives. I became good friends with some of his children, as well as with Dad's sister, Clara, and her children. We weren't welcome at Grandpa's house for long because several of Dad's older children were so rambunctious and got into so much trouble, that Grandpa finally told Dad, "The only one of your children who is welcome here is Frances. She can come any time she wants." I don't know why, but he favored me, and his wives always warmly welcomed me into their home.

Leaving Bountiful, we moved into a small home near 2700 South and 900 East. One day I saw through the large glass window in the front door that we had a visitor: the son of the Bountiful group's leader. He wasn't married, and had been pursuing me at church functions and other gatherings before we left Bountiful. I didn't like him—and besides that, I was only twelve and he was looking for a wife. I ran to Mother in terror, "Johnny's ringing the door bell. I don't like him! He won't leave me alone."

She calmly said, "Go to your room; I'll take care of him."

I never saw him again.

Sadly, the pursuit of very young teens was not all that unusual in the polygamous culture. My sisters and I were pretty mature for our age, and it seemed like some guys preferred young girls they could mold into obedient wives. Thankfully, our father didn't want us to marry young; he wanted us to be certain of what we were doing, as well as of our proposed husband, before we committed to marriage.

When the landlord found out how large our family was, he gave us notice of eviction. We prayed morning and night for the Lord to help us through our struggles, and this time was no different. As we were losing our home on 900 East, a friend of Dad's helped him get into an old home on 400 East and about 1500 South. With its nineteen rooms, that big, old house was perfect for our family. In fact, it was the largest home in which we had ever lived, and we were delighted to have so much space. The house had not been lived in for quite some time and needed a lot of work, but we were up for the challenge. We immediately started working together to clean and repair every corner.

The main floor was all living area. The parlor had a fireplace and cornice all around the ceiling, two pocket doors leading into adjoining rooms and a huge bay window, which looked out onto the front porch. Wide stairs led up to the porch, which ran nearly the width of the house front with double columns topping the porch rail. The adjoining living room had big wooden beams in the ceiling and built-in cabinets with leaded-glass doors near the window. A library off the living room had pillars on each side of the entrance and built-in bookcases featuring leaded-glass doors. There were also several beautiful leaded-glass windows throughout the main floor.

The Old House.

Everything in the house wasn't perfect, there was only one bathroom, and it was upstairs where five of the bedrooms were located. Aunt Maurine had three of the upstairs bedrooms; Aunt Vio had the other two, across the hall. In the basement there were three bedrooms, a great room, a laundry room with two huge rinse tubs, a furnace room, and a small fruit/storage room. Most of Mother's children slept in the basement. I was often my responsibility to tend all her little kids and help her in the kitchen.

In March 1944, soon after my sixteenth birthday, eighteen men were arrested for practicing polygamy—including my father. Our family all believed people in the LDS Church instigated the arrests because our lifestyle was now a black eye on their church. Of course, polygamy was against the law, and the Mormons weren't the only ones who had a problem with it—it was a repulsive lifestyle to society at large. I believe that the culture of the time played a big role in these arrests as well. The movies of the day portrayed married people sleeping only in twin beds.

The entire arrest was very traumatic. Police came banging on our door at 5 am. Arlene, who was pregnant with her first child, had stayed at our home that night and was asleep on the couch. The police assumed she was one of Dad's wives. Making a clean sweep of the house, the police eventually came downstairs and started banging on my bedroom door. The door was locked. As I struggled to get my robe on I asked, "Who is it?"

A gruff male voice responded, "Open up now!"

I heard Arlene's voice through the door, saying, "Open the door, Fran, it's the police."

I was completely confused as I opened the door. The policemen were so rude, assuming I was also one of Dad's wives. (Some polygamists do have very young wives, but not our dad.) They pushed me up the stairs, and the first thing I saw was Dad and his three wives in handcuffs. I could hear the babies crying upstairs. I was horrified. As they were about to slap the handcuffs on me, I said, "You've got to let me go comfort those babies. You can't just leave them up there alone, crying. You've got their mothers here, and someone has to take care of them." It worked; I was spared.

Our family was in shock. The episode was splashed all over the local newspaper, and I was so embarrassed I no longer wanted to go to school. (I was attending South High School on State Street and 1500 South at the time.) I wanted to stay home and help with the babies, but Mother insisted that I return to school so I reluctantly went back.

(My refusing to attend school could have added fuel to an already roaring fire, since I could have been arrested for truancy as a result.)

I was expecting to be shunned and ridiculed by the students, but a wonderful group of them actually defended me. My best friend continued to walk to school with me and talk to me between classes. Much to my

Jail house life.

Courthouse battle.

surprise, when I entered the school building my first day back, several guys from the football team surrounded me and walked me to class. One of them said, "If anyone says so much as one unkind word to you, let us know, and we'll beat the shit out of them."

My apprehension vanished. I was no longer embarrassed.

Things weren't quite so easy for my younger brothers, who were selling newspapers on the downtown street corners. As they did every day, they were barking the headlines to passersby, only this time it was about their own family. And it wasn't just my dad. Included in the group of men who were arrested were my father, my grandfather, two of Dad's uncles, and Marie's husband. They were bailed out until they could be brought to trial.

The story went nationwide, and soon we had photographers from Life Magazine at our home taking pictures of our family. Dad was very proud of his family, and I think he enjoyed the limelight—but the reality of prison was still looming in the future as the lawyers argued their case.

My three older sisters married soon after we moved into the big house, and about that time my brother Al and I became very close. That fall he also started going to South High. He was a tall, good-looking, blond sophomore, and he was so good to me. He often walked to school with my friend, and me and acted as my protector, advising me about which guys were nice and which to avoid.

The school was preparing for its annual Sadie Hawkins dance, and I spent some time teaching Al to dance. When we approached Dad for permission to go to the dance, he was absolutely against the whole idea. Because Dad didn't approve of the men two of my older sisters had married, he became very protective of me. He didn't trust men in general, and I guess he expected I would do as my sisters had done and wouldn't pick a good man either. As it turned out, Al intervened on my behalf: He went to Dad later and promised that we wouldn't hang out with anyone else and that he would stick by my side the whole time. Dad finally gave his permission, but only on the condition that we were home by 10 pm.

As soon as we got to the dance, Al paired off with a girl from his class. I joined some of my friends, who agreed to take me home. Al and I planned to meet under a large tree near our house so we could walk into the house together as if we'd never parted ways. It all sounded great, but when it was time for me to leave, my group piled into the car—and instead of going home, we ended up at the Salt Lake City Cemetery. Everyone was running around laughing and acting silly except for me. I became frantic, "Please," I begged the driver of the car, "If I don't get home on time I'll be in so much trouble."

Suddenly, two police cars pulled up. The police started rounding us all up, threatening to take us to the police station and call our parents. By then I was crying, "Please just let me go home, my dad will kill me if I'm late getting home."

One of the policemen finally softened, exacting a promise from the boy that he would take me straight home. He did. I stood at our designated meeting place—under the tree on Kensington Avenue and Fourth East—waiting anxiously for Al. When I heard footsteps, I turned. Mother was walking quickly up to me. "You are in deep trouble," she announced. "Your dad is furious."

As we entered the large dining room, Dad slapped me so hard I was thrown headfirst into the wall; he slapped me again in the face, and my nose began to bleed. He pulled off his belt and began to beat me as I hung onto the pillars outside the library. I lost count of the number of times he hit me. As I was about to faint, Mother touched his arm and convinced him to stop, telling him quietly, "That's enough."

I was in so much pain I didn't sleep at all that night. Despite my effort to hide what had happened and to act normal, my best friend couldn't help but notice that something was wrong as we walked to school. "You look terrible," she said. "Are you okay?"

I mumbled something, avoiding her eyes. When we arrived we went directly to our first class, physical education. She quickly changed into her gym clothes, but I told her to go ahead and that I would be out in a minute.

A few minutes later when the teacher came to check on me she saw the welts on my back and asked "What happened to you?"

She took me to the principal's office. They both questioned me and were talking about reporting my father to the police; they even encouraged me to move out of my parents' home.

Mustering all the persuasion I could I said, "Please don't report him, he's never done anything like that before and I know he never will again. He has enough trouble without that."

That evening I asked Mother if I could go to a movie with a guy from my class, and she gave me permission. I was hoping to leave before Dad got there, but he arrived home early and wanted to know where I was going. This time I told the truth. He threatened me with his belt if I left. I turned to him, squared up my shoulders, and said, "If you ever touch me again, I'll report you to the police, and they'll put you in jail!"

He never threatened me again. In fact, he seemed to be nicer than ever to me as it grew closer to the time he would have to serve his prison sentence. My three older sisters had been rebels, and I was the "good one," so Dad had always favored me. Though he never apologized for the savage beating he gave me that night, he bent over backward for me the rest of his life.

It took many years for me to forgive my father. Up until that beating, my father could do no wrong in my eyes. I was quite close to Dad's sister, Aunt Clara, and one day I told her about the beating Dad had given me. Aunt Clara told me that Dad had been badly beaten many times by his father. That didn't justify my beating, but knowing about it helped me better understand my father and the reasons behind his violent reactions.

By the time Mother died, Dad and I had once more become close; he was very kind and loving, supporting me in all I did.

It took several months, but by May 1944 fifteen of the eighteen men who had been arrested for practicing polygamy were incarcerated in the old prison in Sugarhouse (at the site of the current Sugarhouse Park). Without Dad's income, Mother needed all the help she could get to support the family. She asked Al and I to quit school and get jobs; it was hard for me to do, but I felt I had no choice. With that, I turned my back on South High School and entered the workforce.

With Dad in prison, things changed dramatically at home. Our regular family home evenings vanished, as Al and I worked most evenings. Mother took in extra children to earn money. Aunt Vio and Aunt Maurine also did whatever they could to contribute. Relying on the state for help was out of the question; the three mothers were afraid that if they applied for welfare, the state would take all the children out of our home, and they feared our family would be separated for good. It was an especially difficult time, but Mother maintained an amazing attitude of cheer, trying to keep our spirits up. Al and I were both able to eventually take some classes and earn our high school degrees.

Dad, along with the other men arrested, was released after signing an agreement with the state.

I didn't worry much about Dad enforcing the rules after he came out of prison. He wasn't in our home very often because he was dividing his time between his three wives who lived in three different homes. At first he split his time with each wife into days of the week—three days with Mother, three days with Aunt Maurine, and one day with Aunt Vio each week. His livelihood also took him out of the home quite a bit; he was driving truck or working construction. He was a hard worker and made pretty good money, but wasn't home enough to level frequent discipline against me and the men I dated.

Most of the guys I dated were very nice. I had been dating Jim, when my relationship with him started to get serious, I had mixed emotions. He was nice, tall, good-looking, and a great dancer; I also thought he was a good member of the LDS Church. But the more serious our relationship became, the more he pushed for sex. He finally asked me to marry him, and I really thought he was "the one."

Dad tried to talk me out of marrying Jim, as did a family friend. Apparently they could see through him and feared for my happiness. If not for the beating Dad had given me, I may have been more willing to listen to him—but I was still angry with him, and his arguments fell on deaf ears. I believed I was in love, and that's all I needed. We were married in my parents' home on August 16, 1946. It wasn't the most joyous occasion: Maggie, my new mother-in-law, sobbed throughout the entire evening—a precursor of her doggedly evil efforts to get rid of me.

I got pregnant right away but by the time my adorable little Duke was born, things were not going well at all. Jim was staying out late and had become quite distant. I was close to my sister Marie—just eighteen months older than I and already married with three children—and I confided my concerns to her.

"Have you noticed any change in his behavior?" she asked.

I confirmed that I had. She told me one of the worst things I could have heard at that moment: she suspected Jim was having an affair with one of my sisters.

I was shocked and appalled, but suddenly all sorts of things made sense. The next day I left Duke at Mother's and went to see an attorney so I could file for a divorce. In the forties divorce was frowned on by all of society, not just by the leaders of our church, but I felt I had no other option.

Once I arrived at his office, the attorney asked if I was feeling okay.

"I'm a little stressed; why?"

"Fran, you don't look good," he noted. "I'd like you to see your doctor then come back here in a couple of weeks."

That doctor's visit revealed that I was pregnant with my son Dan. I stayed married to Jim until the baby was born but had as little to do with him as possible. After I gave birth, I filed for divorce and began looking for work.

My parents were a great help and support to me. By then, Dad owned a fourplex close to town and offered to let me move into one of the apartments. Mother took care of my boys while I worked. I had an old car that was paid for, and even with my modest income I was able to pay Mother for babysitting and Dad for rent.

Unlike my parents, Jim gave me no support. In fact, he was a threat. He gave me nothing and wanted nothing to do with his two boys, but that was okay with me—I wanted nothing to do with him. And though he said he didn't want anything to do with us, he couldn't seem to leave me alone.

He tried breaking into my apartment several times. He finally succeeded twice, and both times he beat me up.

A good friend who had moved to San Francisco eventually called to see how I was doing. When I told her what had happened, she suggested I move to California where Jim couldn't find me. She offered whatever help she could provide.

When I talked it over with my parents, they agreed that it was a good solution. Again they provided support, helping me with train fare and agreeing to keep my boys until I could get settled. When I arrived in San Francisco, I stayed with a couple of friends from high school in a tiny apartment on 25th Avenue and Geary Boulevard. I found a job quickly because my boss in Salt Lake had given me a great reference.

I was a "girl Friday," and I worked my way up to office manager quite quickly. My boss, an elderly gentleman, called me into his office one day and said, "When you do the payroll, bring your check in to me. I'd like to see how much you make, because you should make as much as the salesmen here."

I was thrilled. I had barely been making ends meet, and I immediately thanked God for this great blessing. I also have to give my wonderful mother credit for teaching me to "act like a lady," because I believe that was a huge factor for the successes in my life at that time. For some reason my mother's other daughters didn't get that same message from her. However, I think I was a natural "people pleaser," and both Dad and Mother responded much better to that personality, giving me an advantage in many situations with my parents.

When I first arrived in San Francisco, I had applied for work at many places. Before long, a young man who had seen me at one of those companies began calling and asking me to go out with him for a drink. He admitted he had found my number on one of the applications I had filled out—and begged me not to tell anyone, as it could be grounds for him losing his job.

I was mildly flattered and thought his antics were kind of funny, but told him I didn't have the time to go out with anyone—and, besides, I didn't drink alcohol. Except for one small glass of wine in the evening by Dad, for his health, our parents didn't drink alcohol at the time. However, some of my brothers and sisters had started drinking.

That same young man kept calling me, and I finally told him I would meet him at the corner drugstore for a Coke.

At the drugstore, things didn't go quite as I had expected. He told me about his dentist, who was apparently the "most eligible bachelor" in San Francisco. I convinced him I wasn't interested and thought I'd heard the last of it. But the next day I received a phone call from the dentist—Dr. Connie Lindner—saying his patient insisted he meet me. After several more calls, I finally agreed to meet him at a bar, emphasizing that I didn't drink alcohol.

I didn't yet have my car, so my girlfriends dropped me off where I was supposed to meet the dentist—and he promised to take me home. He was tall, very good-looking, charming, and impeccably dressed, but I was stunned when he ordered a drink for me. I pushed it away, wondering why he would do that after I had made it clear that I didn't drink alcohol. After only a few minutes, I told him I needed to go.

He was agreeable—but instead of taking me to my apartment, we ended up on the beach—where the charming doctor came on like an octopus. I pushed him away, got out of the car, and stomped across the damp sand, ruining my new suede shoes. He convinced me to get back into the car, promising he would behave. But as soon as we pulled up in front of my apartment, he began to get aggressive again. As I pushed him away and got out of the car, I firmly said, "You need to grow up. Do not call me again!"

Connie would not take no for an answer and we dated almost four years before we got married. We were eventually blessed with two precious daughters, and Connie adopted my two sons. We built a large home in Los Gatos, California, but instead of a swimming pool we had an eighteen-hole putting green. We entertained often over the years, and our guests loved playing on it. My polygamist background was never a topic of conversion among Connie's family or our friends. Even though Mother and Dad came to stay with us for short visits on many occasions, we just never discussed polygamy. I had become quite comfortable in my life and among my friends, and I didn't want to expose myself to the curious questions and judgments of people who had little or no understanding of my family's lifestyle.

I stayed very busy between my children and the great social life we had. Connie was a giving person, but very intense, and was the only child in his family. He was good to Dad, Mother, and Mother's children, but wanted nothing to do with the rest of the family. He never came to Salt Lake. Once, just before Connie died, Dad came for a visit and Connie asked him how many children he had.

"Thirty-four," Dad answered.

"You are quite a man," Connie responded.

Connie passed away at the age of sixty—far too young. During his illness and after his death, I was truly blessed with longtime friends who were always there to help me with my family.

I had no desire to get involved with another man. However, several years later some friends and I were in Maui, Hawaii, and they set me up on a surprise blind date with Tom Heininger. He was a widower, and a mutual friend had nothing but good to say about him.

Tom was always a gentleman, very kind to my family and me. After a year, he asked me to marry him—and of course I said, "Yes." We've had a lovely life together. Tom has a home in San Juan Capistrano; we have a condo in Kihei, Maui; and I still have my home in Los Gatos. We enjoy staying in each of those homes around the year. Tom accepted my extended family from the start. He travels to Salt Lake every year with me and enjoys all of my family. A very laid-back man, he has the gift of taking people and life as they come.

As I look back on my experiences and my choices, I realize that my mother, who was the guiding light in my life, shaped many of them. She always had a way of taking the high road. She taught by word and example that if we faced something difficult, the final outcome would be worth the effort to overcome. She also taught us to be honest, true to ourselves, and treat others with kindness, among other things. She was sweet and fun to be around. I recall that she always had a smile on her face. Dad depended on her to keep the house running smoothly, and she never failed to do exactly that.

While my mother was my guiding light, I can't say the same about my father. I loved my father, and especially appreciated his emphasis on honesty and respect of others, but he did not inspire in me a desire to live plural marriage. His presence was so large in our home, but despite his position of "power" I always felt he was very insecure—something that may have resulted from mistreatment (including the whippings) he endured as a child.

I genuinely loved my father's other two wives. They were always kind to me, and I feel very blessed to have had so much love from so many people in my home the entire time I was living there.

Even though I was blessed by love from my mother's sister-wives, after observing my mother's relationship with my father and with her sister-wives I concluded that I did not want to live plural marriage in my own life. I wanted to be the wife of a man who was kind, intelligent, and true to his word. As for myself, I was determined to be exceptional in my way of living, to be someone of whom my parents could be proud, regardless of the lifestyle I was living. I chose a monogamous marriage, and it was definitely the right choice for me.

As with any relationship between a husband and wife, things haven't always been easy, but my marriage has been well worth the effort. I'm eighty-six years old and Tom turns eighty-eight soon. He is still the kindest, sweetest man I know.

My family has brought me such joy, though there has definitely been heartache, as with any family. I lost my oldest son, Duke, in an auto accident; he left no children. Dan has three delightful daughters, the youngest of which has given me an adorable great-granddaughter. My oldest daughter, Diana Marie, has two sons still living at home. And my youngest child, Catherine Frances, has a son and a daughter who live with her. Cathy's husband passed away very recently, and we are still struggling to deal with that loss.

While my choice of lifestyle was different from that of my parents and many of my siblings, I was able to maintain a solid relationship with all of them. I have always felt a high level of respect from my family members—especially from my sisters. If any of them have a problem with the fact that I did not practice polygamy, I am certainly unaware of it. I enjoy a warm, loving relationship with all of them, and when we have the opportunity to get together, we talk, laugh, and truly love each other. The support of my family and friends is such a blessing in my life

Bert's (and all of Kate's) family in 1952 to Doris, Maurine's baby.

Ruth Naomi

CHAPTER 3

1934–October 2014

AFTER GIVING BIRTH to four girls, my mother, Kate, had three sons. Then in 1934, she gave birth to me—her fifth daughter.

My earliest memories are of living in an old house in Parowan, Utah, where Daddy was working on a dam. At the time, Mama was in Kanab with the babies. My memories from that period are disjointed and random, but they string together to form my recollection in vivid bits and pieces, like bright specks of color in an otherwise bland tapestry.

Those memories bring with them raw emotion even to this day. Daddy brought home the rattle from a rattlesnake, and giving it to me said, "This is for Foofie, my little Daddy's girl." I was enchanted.

One summer night, staying with Aunt Maurine's family with my brother Lee, it was so hot Lee wanted to sleep outside. He took a blanket out onto the dry dusty ground. Sometime in the stifling darkness of that night, Lee's tapping on the window awakened me. I crept to the window and let him in. The next morning, we saw the tracks of a mountain lion circling the makeshift bed where Lee had been sleeping. I was terrified and grateful all at once.

One time Daddy took me with him while he hitchhiked to Hurricane; when I grew exhausted from walking, he carried me. I thought he had chosen me to go with him because I was special. Later I learned that I was his ticket—he figured people would give him a ride because he had a little girl with him.

Among those random pieces of memory is the conviction that many of the things we did when I was little seemed to be adventures. Like the time

Daddy loaded us all up in a truck; I was riding in the back with my older sister Fran. It seems as clear today as the day it happened. We stopped in a tunnel as we drove through Zion's Canyon, seeking a shady spot in which to eat. I can still almost taste the acrid flavor on my tongue. The beans were sour. But we were hungry—there was always so little food. Mama, seeing the expressions of want on our faces, conjured up her genius with food and promptly stirred some soda into the beans. We gobbled them up.

Throughout it all, we were together, and I took great comfort from the people I knew as family. I had the certain sense that we were never alone. We had been taught to pray, and we prayed a lot. As I reflect on those memories, I still recognize the comfort I felt then that God was watching out for us.

Things didn't work well for us in southern Utah; Dad wasn't able to make enough of a living to keep even a minimal amount of food on the table, let alone consider the occasional luxury. It was 1939, and we were starving. I was five, and the details are hazy—but I knew we were going to a place where Daddy and Mama hoped things would be better for us. Better sounded good; besides, a five-year-old has no choice but to go along.

Our caravan with eighteen people finally came to a stop in Bountiful. I don't know how Daddy came up with the old cars Arlene and Aunt Maurine were driving full of kids and he drove an old truck that was stacked high with all we owned tied down in it. Dad and our mothers joined a polygamist group there. It was a group that practiced two principles in which Dad strongly believed. Plural marriage and the United Order, a form of communal living in which all earnings and property are combined, then distributed on the basis of need. If there was anyone in need, it was we.

As young as I was, I could see the hope in Mama's eyes; maybe this would be the break for which they had been praying. They all went right to work, digging in and contributing to the group as best they could. Dad worked extremely hard to do whatever the group leaders asked of him.

For whatever reason, Dad's efforts were never enough for the leaders of the group. We were still starving; we were just starving in a new location. I remember sometimes taking Dad's lunch to him as he worked tirelessly on one project or another. On the way, I always peeked into the square of cloth to see what Mother had wrapped up. Most of the time it was nothing but a slice or two of bread with whatever she could scrounge up to create a sandwich.

We all knew that Dad had suffered a crushed liver as a young man, and it was essential that he take care of himself. I was too young to connect all the dots at the time, but Dad's health was gradually but steadily failing—

he was never able to get enough rest and never had enough healthy food to eat, despite the promise of communal living. I've often thought about how discouraged my parents must have been to learn that the things they had so desired and hoped would solve their problems did nothing but create new ones.

In 1941, when I was seven, it was clear things were never going to improve in Bountiful. Dad left the group, found a job at an auto company in Salt Lake, and was able to rent a small house. When he and the landlord shook hands on the deal, the landlord assumed the home was for Dad, Aunt Maurine, and her three kids—Vilate, Hazel, and Ginny. Instead, we all moved into it—in addition to Aunt Maurine and her three, we had Mother and her eleven children and Aunt Vio and her daughter, Ramona. When the landlord found out how many people were tucked into the corners of that house, he was furious. We were evicted and faced the very real specter of homelessness.

Once again our frantic prayers ascended to heaven, and God took care of us in the form of Dad's friend, Charles Zitting, who helped us find and secure a nineteen-room home on Fourth East. Nineteen rooms! It was old and needed a lot of fix-up, but Dad knew how to do the necessary repairs and was willing to work on the house. Even though there was only one bathroom for the twenty or so of us to share, we were thrilled. Little did I know at the age of seven that Dad was barely able to make the house payment of $45 a month. Our problems had not disappeared, but at least we had a place to live.

One of my most vivid memories of my childhood occurred on our first Christmas morning in that house. Racing upstairs to see what was tucked beneath the tree, my heart dropped: Vilate, Hazel, and Ramona—the three little girls who were just younger than I—all got dolls for Christmas. But search as I might, I could find no doll for me. In fact, there was nothing for me.

The tears threatened to spill as I quietly approached Mother and took her hand. "Why did Santa forget me?" I whispered.

Mother looked at the three little girls with their dolls. Her lips in a thin line, she looked at Aunt Maurine then put her hand gently on my shoulder and said, "Go ask your father."

I didn't know what Dad had to do with Santa, but did as I was told. I felt a few tears dribble onto my cheek as I gingerly approached him and asked, "Dad, why did Santa forget me? Have I been bad?"

Without saying a word to me, Dad leapt out of his chair, stood right in front of Aunt Maurine, and through a tightly clenched jaw, he ordered her, "Maurine, you go to your cedar chest right now and get a doll for Ruth."

The look in his eyes said all that needed to be said, and Aunt Maurine wasted no time fetching one of her treasured dolls and thrusting it at me. I felt awful for causing trouble, especially on a day that was supposed to be filled with such joy. I loved the doll, but something ate a hole in my chest as I realized that it was really Aunt Maurine's doll.

Dad was furious with Aunt Maurine for the rest of the day, and wasted no effort in trying to hide it. At the age of seven, I believed it was all my fault, though I couldn't put my finger on the reason. I later learned that Aunt Maurine had been working at Cummings candy factory and had secretly stashed away a few pennies here and a few dimes there until she had enough to buy Christmas gifts for her and Aunt Vio's children. It hadn't occurred to her to buy gifts for us—in her eyes, Mother was responsible for that.

Despite all the hardship that seemed to dominate our lives, our family had some good times. I remember rolling Easter eggs through the grass on Capitol Hill, cooking hot dogs over campfires in the nearby canyon on holidays, and playing checkers around the big kitchen table. I remember the warmth of singing together at family home evening. It seemed like Dad made everything a game when I was young, and I thought he was the best father in the world. Later I realized that my age had much to do with that perception; the little kids were always Dad's greatest joy.

As I got a little older, I occasionally attended LDS Church meetings on Sundays, taking my two younger sisters, Rebecca and Alhona, with me when they were old enough. I loved having them tag along; they were my real, live dolls and I did everything I could for them. It was an enchanted time, and my memories of it still bring joy to this day.

All that changed in 1946, when I turned twelve. I was born right in the middle of Mother's six boys, and she expected nothing out of them while I felt like her slave. The things of childhood—our dreams and games—were gone, and I was working right along with Mother.

I also started to see the error in some of the things Dad did. He was often angry, using his thick leather belt to beat the older kids. Lee, who was just older than I, seemed to get the brunt of it. Lee was unusually sweet and kind, yet Dad beat him for no reason that was apparent to any of us, including Lee. One day Dad finally beat me. I was startled when he turned on me, but I harnessed all my resolve and simply stared at him, refusing to cry. He said I had a "rebellious spirit."

By then, I was convinced that he had an evil spirit when he was angry.

Perhaps it was the rebellion Dad accused me of, or maybe it was nothing more than trying to escape a miserable situation, but I began to sneak out of the house at night. In 1950, I ran away and married Marv —something I figured was a surefire way to get out of that house. After all, between being Mother's slave and Dad's rebellious daughter, I couldn't get out of there fast enough. I was barely sixteen.

In Marv's mother I found a loving, patient soul that I had missed during my adolescence at home. She taught me to sew, she understood me, and she gave me badly needed confidence. I loved her so—but I didn't really love Marv. When he enlisted in the military, we moved to California. I got a job on the PX, where I met trouble in the form of Dave Johnson.

Dave knew my older brothers and sisters, and used that as an excuse to constantly flirt with me. It was a period of my life marked by restlessness, a time when I never quite planted my feet firmly in any one pursuit. When Marv went overseas, Dave continued to flirt with me—but then he left too. I quickly forgot about Dave, but almost as quickly forgot about Marv. I filed for divorce and went back to school at night to earn my high school diploma, and then got some college under my belt. I worked at many jobs but refused to stay at a job I didn't like—and if someone wasn't treating me the way I wanted, I didn't like the job. I left a lot of jobs in those chaotic days. Looking back, I have some idea of what was going on in my head, I think going without all my life made me intolerant of anything or anyone I perceived as taking something away from me.

While I was in the San Francisco area I sometimes connected with Fran, it was nice to have that connection but I didn't always feel comfortable with her friends. Dad brought Doug and Ed to California once and it was great showing them around, I enjoyed that a lot.

Jobs weren't the only thing I had difficulty sticking with. I married two more times before eventually coming back to Utah and marrying Dave Johnson, who had continued to pursue me throughout the years. I loved Dave but we locked horns a lot—even after we married---and I began to have children. I often wonder if he was the father I never really understood. I left him several times, but we always managed to get back together with renewed energy and commitment.

Over the years I worked at many jobs and held several management positions, but my children were always my first priority. All my life I had adored children, beginning with my younger brothers and sisters for whom I cared. Though I desperately wanted to have children, I didn't have that chance until I married Dave. Over the years I had many prospects for living a pampered life, but all I really wanted was to be a mother. Throughout their lives I've given my children all the love I could from the very depths of my soul, never hitting them in anger. Now I am doing the same with each of my adored grandchildren.

In 1968 I heard that my younger sister, Shauna, was planning a wedding and contacted her to offer any help I could give her. She expressed a great desire for a traditional wedding but worried about the expense. I got so excited and began to offer many suggestions including using the back yard of the home Dave and I were living in at the time. It was the perfect place for a wedding.

I had always wanted a traditional wedding and I adored my little sisters. It was an honor to give this to her. I worked so hard getting flowers as cheap as possible (she wanted daisies and it was September). I found many ways to decorate my yard and even my home in case it rained. She was stunning as she floated down the stairs leading into my back yard holding Dad's elbow. Her husband was dashing; over six feet, great build, thick brown hair and his eyes adored her. At the end of the evening I was exhausted but happy about the way it all turned out.

My brother, Al, was supposed to take pictures of it all and he did but I never saw them and I have nothing to remind me of this lovely day. I think he lost the film. I never heard from Shauna after the wedding. I often wondered why. At first I assumed she was just adjusting to marriage but eventually when I saw her at family functions and she seemed so distant I wondered if somehow I had offended her. I didn't do the wedding for her thanks but it would have been nice to know if she was happy about the way it turned out.

I spent almost two years taking care of Dave's mother before she died; it was a privilege for me to love her and make sure her needs were met. Then I took care of Dave, who was sick for about two years before he finally left me on Mother's Day 2013. The day he drew in his last ragged breath, he was still angry, just as he'd been nearly every day before. I never could figure out what made him so infuriated all the time. In retrospect, I wonder if he was waging a silent war against the dark demon of depression all those years.

I became "born again" through Jesus Christ in the eighties, and know He is my Savior. That knowledge gives me a deep and quenching peace—the only peace I have.

Note: Ruthie passed away in October 2014, and we still miss her so. We find great peace knowing that she was able to fulfill her greatest desire, that of being a mother, and that her children and grandchildren brought her such joy.

Ramona Kate

CHAPTER 4

1937

I WAS BORN AUGUST 15, 1937, to Albert Barlow and his second wife, Vio Fraser. I was Mother's second child and Father's twelfth. Living plural marriage was against the law, so out of fear of prosecution my parents refused to call a doctor when my mother went into labor; my father and oldest sister, Arlene—who was only fourteen—delivered me.

Mother's first child died when he was five months old. He cried constantly from the time he was born and steadily lost weight until Dad got some goat's milk and told Mother to stop nursing the baby. But the goat's milk provided only a temporary remedy, and both Dad and Aunt Kate were baffled about what to do next.

Finally Dad and Aunt Kate took the baby to the hospital, leaving Mother at home. They told the doctors that Aunt Kate was his mother. He was so small when he was admitted that they classified him as a premature baby. When asked the baby's name, Dad gave the same name as one of Kate's other children—Ianthus Worth (I.W., as we all called him). Aunt Kate stayed with Tommy until he died at the hospital. Mother was heartbroken; she never saw her baby alive after Dad and Aunt Kate tucked the tiny boy into the car and drove off to the hospital. He was buried in the Salt Lake City cemetery but his grave was washed away during a flood several years later. Mother was on her own to "get over it."

When Mama was pregnant with me, Aunt Kate worried constantly. "What if this one is sick, too?" She often asked. Fueled partly by Aunt Kate's concern and by her own nagging worry, Mama prayed almost constantly until I was born. At birth, I weighed only five pounds. "Why, look." Aunt Kate said. "Her little face is no bigger than a teacup."

Vio's family in 1944.

Mama said once, "I cried with joy every day as I nursed you because I could see you growing day by day. I know all that praying I did when I was carrying you must have worked. Not only were you healthy, you were very smart. Why you were potty trained before you were two."

She was very proud of how smart I was. Even Aunt Kate once said to her, "Ramona is sharp as a whip."

My earliest memories are of living in the big house on 400 East, where I was responsible for my younger sisters, Susan, Laura, and Faye. Mama was Aunt Kate's helper most of the time, and it was my job to make sure nothing happened to the three little girls while Mama was busy. Some of the other siblings weren't very nice to me, but my brother Lee always treated me with kindness. One of my fondest memories was when Dad took us to the rodeo and bought us a root beer—that was a really big deal for us, since we seldom received such luxuries on Dad's income.

I've heard stories from my siblings about Dad's violent temper, but he hit me only once while I was growing up. I was about ten and was sassing my mother. In my case, the regular physical abuse came from another source: Mother flew off the handle quite easily and hit me fairly often.

When I was thirteen, I was forced to go work for Aunt Kate. I remember feeling like a slave, because she made me do things that she didn't make her own kids do. However, I found ways to get away. Mother's family lived on Capitol Hill, and I spent a lot of time with my siblings roaming the Capitol Building and Memory Grove, something I dearly loved.

Working alongside Aunt Kate was simple compared to what happened next: In 1951, Dad bought a farm in Mountain Home. It was my job to get out of bed before the sun even started to show so I could milk the cows—sometimes only one, sometimes as many as six—before I got ready for school. Then I had to do it all again in the evening. I was fifteen.

Carl Zitting, a young man not much older than I, and the son of a good friend of Dad, sometimes came to the farm to work for Dad. One day as Carl was going out to chop wood, he asked if I wanted to go with him. Because it was so cold, he joked, "Will you warm up my hands?" No boy had ever paid attention to me before and, not quite sixteen, I was thrilled.

The next time Carl came to the farm, he asked me if I'd like to go with him to a movie. We went into town to see the movie, and afterward went to the only restaurant in Mountain Home. I really liked Carl and had the support of my mother, who commented on how polite he was—not to mention that he was always neat and clean.

In February 1954, the family moved back to Salt Lake and I began dating Carl on a steady basis. On my seventeenth birthday, Carl and I drove to Aunt Maurine's and he asked Dad for my hand in marriage. I knew Dad approved of Carl because Carl's father, Charles, was also a polygamist. He had served time in prison with Dad in 1944. However, I was young so after some preaching Dad said to me, "Are you sure this is what you want?"

We both assured him it was. He then said, "Well, I'd like you to wait six months and if you still want to get married I'll give you my blessing."

Grabbing me by the hand, Carl pulled me out to the car, where we set our wedding date for exactly six months later. To seal the deal, Carl gave me my first kiss.

Marriage was bliss for me. We moved in with Carl's mother, and before I knew it, I had three little boys—Don, Jeff, and Dennis. That's when I experienced my first real scare as a parent. Late one night Dennis became very sick. I was so worried by his condition that I took him to the emergency room at the nearest hospital. My thoughts were on the tales of my brother Tommy, who had died at the hospital as Aunt Kate watched. I couldn't bear to think of the same thing happening to my sweet baby. The doctor diagnosed him with pneumonia and said, "If you had waited until morning to bring your baby to the hospital, he would have died."

Soon after Dennis fully recovered, I went to visit Grandpa Barlow and his two wives, Aunt Cleo and Aunt Violet. Grandpa was very sick at the time, and I recognized some of the same symptoms, which Dennis had suffered. Pulling Aunt Violet aside, I told her about Dennis and said that Grandpa seemed to have the same thing—pneumonia. My difficult experience with Dennis paid off: A few days later, Aunt Violet called Mother and asked that she thank me. Once they treated Grandpa for pneumonia with a handful of home remedies, he regained his health.

Our family always relied on faith and home remedies. We went to the doctor only when all else failed. Part of that was because there just wasn't enough money for doctors—but another important reason was that doctors could report our lifestyle to authorities, creating a lot of potential problems for our family.

Carl and I shared a love for our children and established a number of fun traditions that bound our family together. On summer Sundays we loaded everyone into the car and went for a drive in the canyon, sometimes stopping to fish or cook hot dogs. On some weekends we also went camping.

During those happy years I gave birth to two more boys, Jim and Randy. When Randy was two, I was pregnant again and had just started to feel the baby move. We were thrilled with the prospect of adding another little one to our family. Suddenly I started bleeding heavily, and I lost the baby. My heartache turned into gratitude when the unexpected happened. Five-year-old Dennis darted out into the street one balmy afternoon and was hit by a car. Had I been dealing with a newborn infant, it would have been very difficult for me to nurse Dennis back to health.

It was a long and difficult road bringing Dennis back. After a four-and-a-half-hour surgery, the doctor emerged and said, "I've done all I can. I'm sorry but your boy is likely to be nothing more than a vegetable for the rest of his life."

I wasn't going to accept that outcome, and neither was Carl. We immediately went into action. We worked so hard with Dennis that after only three months he could say, "Momma." I was thrilled.

After another six months and he could get out of his wheelchair. That determined little boy worked so hard to gain strength in his limbs that eventually he was able to walk, though with a limp, and use his left hand and arm. Sadly, he was blind in his left eye. (Dennis has not let these handicaps hold him back; he has always held down a job and supported a family. He's fine to this day, and has the sweetest disposition of anyone I know.)

After five boys I was given the miraculous gift of a baby girl, Karla, followed by another boy, Lynn, and then three more girls—Angela, Jinna, and Vianna. But our blessings weren't yet complete: My last two children, Carl and Carlena, came as a pair. Through it all, Carl was a good and loving father and grandfather; he was a real blessing to me, taking care of all our expenses and doing all the driving.

Carl's health began to decline and he was so ill he wasn't able to work for about five years before he died. Even though he could no longer work, he always watched the kids and fixed dinner while I worked outside the home to help us get by. During one hospitalization, Carl died for four minutes, during which time he had an out-of-body experience. As a result, he felt strongly that he needed to stay on earth long enough to adequately prepare his family for the time when he'd be gone. He started having me take care of the bills and do most of the driving so I would be independent.

About a year before Carl died, the girls were cleaning the family room and decided to put the end table between the two chairs Carl and I sat in. Carl quietly asked, "Will you take the table away, I'd like to be closer to you."

That is a great comfort to me still. Carl passed away in 1984. Our twins were only seven years old. Not too long after he died, I loaded the kids up and drove to southern Utah, where we stayed in a motel. As we pulled into the driveway at home, it felt so good to be able to say that I had done it myself. I knew then Carl's efforts to help me be independent had paid off.

Five days before Carl died he told my brother, Ron, and one of our boys that he had put diamond rings on layaway for me. Because he had insured the rings, they were paid for when he died. On our wedding anniversary, just a few weeks after Carl's death, my family gave me a huge party and presented me with the diamonds Carl had bought me. It was such a precious surprise. Those rings always bring a smile to my face. He had said many times over the years, "Someday I'm going to get you real diamonds."

No one could have loved me more than Carl did. We had a lot of good times and some hard times, but those hard times are the ones that make you grow. Together we created a wonderful family and now have twelve children, thirty-three grandchildren, and fourteen great-grandchildren.

I've had some difficult times since I lost Carl, but I know I'll be with him again. Through it all, God has guided me, protected me, and given me the courage to go on. I've had several different jobs that were good for me and some that were even good to me. Best of all, the Lord gave me wonderful children and grandchildren who are very good to me.

Reflecting on my experiences in my childhood home, I've had a lot of time to think about the impact of my parents—especially my father. Though he did not always treat my mother as I thought he should, I felt that my father was basically a good man who was doing what he genuinely felt was right. In fact, I adored my father and loved time spent with him; he often took us for rides in the canyon and to square dances in Murray Park. I especially cherish the time he took me on a brief trip and treated me with such kindness. He often told me I was a special girl, and I believed him. I am convinced that my father did the best he could with his large family.

As I was growing up, I usually just assumed I would choose plural marriage for myself—I never felt that the way we were living was wrong. The only time I even questioned that came when I attended LDS seminary in the tenth grade. Our seminary teacher was very critical of polygamists and spoke derisively of them. It was the first time I ever thought that what we were doing might be "wrong," and it was difficult at first to reconcile my teacher's criticism with what I knew of our family.

That's not to say our family was without its challenges. It was interesting and sometimes disconcerting for me to observe the relationship between my parents and the other wives. Mom and Aunt Maurine were so good together, and I felt such love between them. That wasn't the case with Aunt Kate. I always got the impression that she loved only her own children and my father.

The situation got more complex when my father was included in the equation. I was certain he didn't love my mother—and I wasn't even sure she loved him. I didn't like the way my father treated my mother, and told my husband that I never wanted to be treated like that. It was only during the last few years of his life that Father began to demonstrate love for Mother and to treat her in a kind, loving way.

I can't say that those dynamics really impacted my choice regarding my own marriage; I loved Dad and I loved Aunt Maurine, and the situation was more one from which I learned a great deal through observing. I also can't say that I set out to live one lifestyle over another; Carl and I talked off and on about living plural marriage, but it just never happened. I think a main reason for that was not some devotion to one principle or another, but rather Carl's shyness; he was terrified of rejection.

My choice to marry Carl was absolutely the best choice for me, and I loved our life together. I didn't see my choice to live monogamy as one of going against my family, just as I would not have seen a choice of plural marriage to be going against society. I made my marriage decision the same way I made every important decision in my life: with a lot a prayer, a steadfast belief in God, and a perspective from the things my parents taught me. As a result, I'm very happy and comfortable with my own place in the world; it has been created through a lot of prayer.

My parents instilled in me a great faith in a Father in Heaven who guides us and gives us courage; that faith has been the defining influence on me throughout my life. My lifestyle ended up being different from what many of my family members chose, but I've always had a good relationship with my family and continue to do so.

I'm so grateful for the sisters I have who have become my best friends. My sisters and I are closer than ever, and I have never felt any kind of strain from them as a result of not choosing a polygamous lifestyle. I'm grateful that our love for each other goes far beyond the bounds of how any one of us might choose to live.

Hazel Earline

CHAPTER 5

1938

I WAS BORN FEBRUARY 4, 1938, in Kanab, Utah, to Albert Barlow and his third wife, Maurine. I was her second child. The first place I can recall living was in the large nineteen-room home in which Dad had all three families living together in 1941. Aunt Kate and her children were on the main floor and in the basement. Aunt Vio, Mother, and their children were in the five rooms upstairs.

There was only one bathroom upstairs and a sink on the main floor (until Dad later put a toilet and shower under the stairs in the basement). With four adults and more than twenty children sharing that one bathroom, there were many times that it was already occupied when I needed to use the bathroom. Standing or squatting in the hallway for what seemed like forever and hoping whoever was inside would soon open the door was a common occurrence.

In 1944 when the police raided the homes of many of the families that were living polygamy, I noticed Momma standing at the window crying. Mama didn't ever cry. I walked over to see what was going on outside the window. Daddy was out there with a cop on each side, being pushed into a police car. Daddy hadn't done anything bad. He worked hard to take care of his family, and he loved us all. I couldn't understand and I began to cry too.

Forty-five men and women were arrested on March 27, 1944. Of those, only fifteen men ended up going to prison on May 26, 1945, with a sentence of up to five years. About seven months after they had been incarcerated, all but five of the men signed an agreement that if they were released they would continue to support all of their children but would not live with their plural wives or have more children with those plural wives.

Maurine's family in 1944.

As part of the agreement, the men couldn't go home until they had moved all of their plural families out of their homes.

Daddy and Dave Darger, a family friend who had also been arrested, knew they had to comply with the requirements of the release. So in an effort to appease the law, they exchanged the living arrangements of their two plural families. They both hoped the shuffle would make it much more difficult for the neighbors and the schools to keep track of their lifestyle. Their parole officer actually told them he personally didn't care what they did, but warned that they couldn't offend their neighbors with their lifestyle.

We moved into the Darger home, and his plural wives and kids moved into ours. As far as the condition of the homes was concerned, the Dargers definitely got the best of the deal. The Darger home was not finished and there was no running water. The only heat was provided by a coal stove in the kitchen and a fireplace in the front room. But the physical structure was only part of what needed to be considered. I look back at those inconveniences with fondness, and I wasn't the only one. The situation definitely made more work for Mama, but she was happy being in her own place. All of us kids loved it because we were out of the city and had a lot of room to run.

We never again had all three families living in one place. As a result, we saw much less of Dad. Mom had more control over what happened to her children. Some of Aunt Kate's older boys were hard for her to trust, they had already molested Vilate and me.

A year and half later, in 1947, Dad bought a duplex on Vine Street; it was perched on the steep hillside just below the Utah State Capitol Building. Mom's family was situated on the ground floor on the downside; Aunt Vio and her family had the ground floor in front.

I have a flood of memories from living in that duplex. One day my little brother, three-year-old Haven, fell asleep in the closet. We looked for him everywhere and were frantic that something had happened to him. Our level of desperation was apparent when Mom finally called the police—doing so was extremely risky because alerting them brought with it the risk of another arrest for our dad. About the time the police arrived, Haven woke up and stumbled out of the closet, yawning and rubbing his eyes. Mom was embarrassed but happy to "find" him.

We had a lot of fun while living in the duplex, roaming all over the Capitol Building, its grounds, and nearby Memory Grove, Aunt Kate's kids who were our age often joined us. We imagined that we lived in one of the beautiful mansions in the neighborhood. We also spent time roaming around Temple Square. In those days, young children were allowed to explore by themselves, Mom was pretty laid back and gave us a lot of freedom.

Or it could be she was just too busy to keep up with us—by then she was taking in extra children to tend for needed money.

Our parents encouraged us to attend Sunday school and Primary in the LDS Church, and we went whenever we could. We also attended the Church's monthly "ward show"—a free movie with a price we could afford.

In 1949, Dad bought a fourplex on Blair Street, at about 400 East and 400 South. Mom, pregnant with her eighth child, rented out three of the apartments and squeezed the rest of us into a tiny one-bedroom apartment. Dad put up a blanket to separate the living room from the dining room and that became Mom's bedroom. We were still close to town, just at the south end.

With Dad's time split between three homes, he decided to spend a week at each home, and he called each evening to see how things were going in the two homes in which he was not staying. The only change in that schedule occurred if one of his wives or children got seriously ill. Dad had a very tender heart when it came to sickness, and he immediately changed plans and stayed wherever he was needed to help with an ill family member.

Soon after we moved to Blair Street, I went to stay at Aunt Vio's house on Vine Street for a few days. That night when Dad called for his nightly check-up, I asked to speak to him. Tears choking my voice, "Daddy, can I come home?"

"Would you feel better if I come up there to stay with you?" he said.

My plaintive yes must have touched his heart. Not having a car at the time, he walked at least half an hour from 400 South to the duplex on Vine Street. Aunt Vio severely scolded me for making Dad feel he had to come all that way, especially that late at night. "You should not ask your dad to do that!" she said. "He worked all day, and now he has to walk all the way here for you when he needs his rest!"

I did feel bad for Dad, but I felt a warm, secure sort of pleasure knowing that he would do such a thing for me. The next morning he had to get up early and walk back to work, which was very close to Mother's place. He woke me up, and we walked home together.

In 1950, Mom went to work for the summer. She left Vilate, who was 13, in charge of the kids, and me in charge of the meals and house. I was twelve. I talked Dad into letting me sell donuts to pay for a bike, and as soon as I fixed breakfast and did the dishes, I jumped on my bike and rode. I liked to ride at Liberty Park with my brother Johnny, who was also 12, one of Aunt Kate's kids. Sometimes I called him, but often he slept over at our house after selling newspapers downtown until late in the evening. It was great fun to ride with him.

I had a teacher at Oquirrh Elementary whom I liked very much—and she must have liked Vilate and me because she took us to her mother's place for a weekend. She also submitted our family's name in the annual Sub-for-Santa. Not long before Christmas, West High School put on a play, and our family received tickets to it. We learned later they wanted to check out our family without us suspecting anything—two classrooms at West High School had taken our family's name for Sub-for-Santa.

We had the best Christmas ever. We all received everything we asked for plus huge boxes of food. It was more food than we had at Thanksgiving, including a big turkey with all the trimmings. Mom was so happy.

By the time I was fourteen, in 1952, Mom was living in the big house on 400 East. Dad had sold the duplex and the fourplex and had bought the two ranches in Uintah County. Mom and her girls took over the boarding house Aunt Kate had established in the big house.

Before the ranches, Dad had started taking his older kids, and often his wives, to the polygamist dances that were held every other Friday in Murray Park. We loved those dances. Dad took turns dancing with us, teaching us to waltz and fox trot. He was a very social person and enjoyed showing us a good time. Sometimes on the way home from the dance he would stop at the A&W Root Beer stand and get each of us a nickel root beer.

Because he was gone a lot, Dad started letting me and Vilate go on our own to the various activities sponsored by the different polygamist groups, including dances, skating parties, canyon parties, and Sunday evening meetings. He trusted the boys from polygamist families—and besides, he hoped we would choose to marry one of those men.

There were many different polygamist groups, all of which had different leaders (a situation that continues to this day). As I was growing up, most polygamists in the area knew each other and even associated, regardless of the group to which they belonged.

There were (and are) also "independents," polygamists who do not support a leader but who believe they are responsible to teach only their own family. My father was one of the independents—he didn't belong to any of the polygamist groups because he didn't believe any of them had the right to lead those outside their families. Nevertheless, he respected them—and, after all, polygamy was the issue. To Dad, it didn't really matter which group his children associated with. He simply wanted us to live polygamy.

At about the same time we started going to all the activities, Dad taught us we had made covenants—sacred two-way promises—before we were born. He emphasized that we needed to pray and ask the Lord to help us find the person we had promised to marry. From that day, I started praying for the man with whom I had made covenants.

About a year later it occurred to me that I had been praying for a long time, yet God still hadn't shown me the man I was supposed to marry. I figured I just hadn't prayed hard enough. Not one to give up, I explained to the Lord that it didn't matter to me if I was the first or the hundredth wife—as long as my husband was the one with whom I had made covenants. I patiently kept praying. I was fifteen.

I wanted to quit high school, it seemed like a waste of time to me. The school counselor suggested I enroll in a program at the Utah Technical College where I could get a high school degree and college credits at the same time. I did that, and also got a job as a carhop. I guess I was pretty mature for my age. My brother Dave was going to the college as well to be a mechanic and sometimes gave me a ride home from school.

In 1954, Vilate and I were still attending the social activities available in the polygamist culture and then she became a plural wife. She seemed happy, but I missed her and having the close association with her as my sister. Once a woman was married, she gave her life to her husband and his family.

Just before I turned sixteen, I was extremely busy between school, work, and my social life—but Dad decided to allow me to date boys whose parents practiced or believed in plural marriage, as long as the boys asked his permission. Dad had learned a lot from his experience with Aunt Kate's daughters, and he was trying a different approach with his younger girls. Mother was quietly obedient to him and expected us to be as well.

I was still looking and watching for the "right" man, and all my dating was done with that goal in mind, to find the man with whom I had made covenants. Whenever a relationship started to get serious, I suddenly found myself not liking the man. I was baffled by it at the time, but now I know the Lord was helping me find the right person---I prayed and tried to live in harmony with my prayers.

About this time some friends and I went to a young couple's home to see their new baby, Joel. Surrounded by them and feeling the love they exuded, I suddenly realized how at home I felt—a feeling I had never experienced before. I had admired both of them from a distance—especially how clean the husband, Allen, was—and now I knew Allen Zitting was meant for me.

I had found the man with whom I believed I belonged, but what could I do about it? I couldn't just walk up to a married man and tell him I wanted to be his wife. So I did what I had been doing all along, I kept praying. One day I felt that I needed to talk with my Grandfather Barlow, so I took the bus over to his house. Allen's wife, Laura Jean, was also Grandpa Barlow's daughter from his fourth wife. He listened quietly as I expressed my feelings, putting my mind at rest with his patient counsel.

I went on with my life, praying and expecting that I would hear from Allen. I quit dating because I knew who I "belonged" to. But being used to a busy social life, I soon got restless and irritable. After what seemed like an eternity—but in reality were only a few months—I went back to Grandpa's house.

"Why hasn't Allen come to see me?" I cried to Grandpa. "What am I supposed to do?" (Remember I was only sixteen).

Among other things, Grandpa said, "Your life is like a scroll. Be patient and take things as they come."

I was comforted by his words and went home renewed, determined to wait and let my life take its course. That doesn't mean the wait was easy—I had plenty of offers to go out and have fun.

Later I learned that Allen was waiting for the go-ahead from the "priesthood counsel," the men whom he believed had the authority to lead him. It seemed like forever to me, but just six months later Allen called Dad, wanting a word with him. Dad approved the match but said we were both too young. He wanted us to wait for a year so I could make sure I still wanted to go through with it. At the time, Allen was twenty-one and I had just turned seventeen. I'm sure my father's counsel was colored by his own experience; Dad had eight children before he took a second wife.

Allen worked nights and so did I. Occasionally he picked me up from work and took me home, where we would sit in the front room and talk until daylight. He also took me to meet his family. A few weeks later, he went to Dad and said, "I don't believe in procrastination."

We were married the evening before Easter, April 9, 1955. I quit school and work, settling into the home Allen was providing for his family. There were some difficult adjustments. It was hard for him and Laura Jean to bring another woman into the family. And as time went on, I began to realize that Allen and I might not be able to have children together, something that was very difficult for me.

Laura Jean was so good to me, sharing with me her children and her pregnancies. I looked at her often as she was working around the house, cooking and cleaning, and felt if anyone was a saint, she was. I grew to love her very much and we were able to talk things out. It took me awhile because of my stubbornness, but I learned to clean and handle things to her liking, realizing her ways were actually best.

My relationship with Allen was a little different. I loved him but never quite felt at ease. I was so afraid of doing or saying the wrong thing.

During this period there were still scares about polygamist raids. In 1953, authorities in Arizona had raided a polygamist community on the Utah/Arizona border, even taking one woman's children from her. Less than a year after I married Allen in October 1955, Dad was arrested. The legal wrangling took the state almost four years, but finally Dad was convicted and was incarcerated in the Utah State Prison for almost four years.

The home where I lived with Allen and Laura Jean was in a Murray neighborhood south of Salt Lake City. I couldn't be seen living there without raising suspicion and risking Allen's arrest and possible incarceration. I was very careful not to be seen outside during the day, and never went out the door except on moonless nights.

After dinner on my birthday, Allen took me for a ride after dark. He took me up to Zitting's hay field (which is now a big subdivision) and let me run as much as I wanted. I missed being active so much that all I wanted to do was run to my heart's content under the big, bright moon. It felt so good.

I became very unhappy for a variety of reasons after that evening on my birthday. I was just so weary of having to hide all the time. One morning I was outside hanging clothes before daybreak so the neighbors wouldn't see me and as I was getting all the laundry pinned to the line, I seriously considered leaving Allen. Then the thought practically hit me between the eyes: You can't win a fight by giving up. Those words came to me with such force that they stayed with me forever. I never again considered leaving Allen.

Tired of being trapped in the house most of the time, I finally asked Allen if I could get a job in the spring of 1957. At first he wouldn't hear of it. Then, realizing how much I needed it, he agreed but he did not want it to be a "dead-end" job. To help me prepare, he bought a typewriter. I practiced on it all day for a month. He went with me, posing as my brother, to find a place to live. We found a basement apartment where I would be comfortable, and I was able to find a good part-time job.

In July, Allen was hospitalized following a serious haying accident. The news upset me so, I hardly slept all night. The only way I could visit Allen was with my Dad and Mom, posing as a friend. It was awkward and unsatisfying. I wanted so badly to give him a hug or hold his hand—anything to give a little comfort.

That evening I answered the door to find my sister, Vilate, and her little girls, who had come to stay for a week. Very few people knew I was married at the time, but Vilate's husband Clayne knew—and when he realized I was living alone, he brought Vilate and her girls to keep me company. They came to meet me at the bus every night. She really empathized with my situation. Like me, she couldn't be seen with Clayne, in his yard, or his house. It was such a welcome week of freedom for her to be able to stay with me.

Allen was soon out of the hospital and home again.

Before his accident, Allen had asked Laura Jean and me if we would like to have Roy Johnson, the leader of our group, give us a patriarchal blessing. After the blessing as we sat and visited, Brother Johnson turned to me and Laura Jean and said, "You girls need to prepare yourselves—this man is going to be called on a mission."

We talked it over later and assumed the group was going to start sending missionaries out. But that is also a term used to indicate someone has died and is doing the Lord's Work on the Other Side. I didn't connect it until later.

I found a good full-time job with a finance company and was able to start helping the family financially. As soon as the days grew short enough in the fall, Allen moved me back home. He took me to the bus stop before daylight and picked me up there after it got dark at night.

About this time I dreamed in detail about Allen's funeral and the activities surrounding the funeral. I felt uncertain how Allen would want me to act—whether he would want me to be acknowledged as his wife. The feelings I experienced in the dream were so vivid that the same depressed, uncertain feelings lingered after I woke up. I tried to ignore the dream, thinking that Allen couldn't possibly die. After all, we were too young—he was barely twenty-four and I was only nineteen.

About two months later, I had the exact same dream. I woke filled with consternation and feeling foolish but said nothing to Allen. I did mention the dream to Laura Jean then promptly forgot about it and went about my usual business.

The Lord didn't try to warn me again.

One evening when Allen was gone, Laura Jean said, "Hazel, I don't think we're going to have Allen around very much longer." She couldn't explain her feelings, nor could I. The next day I was at work, suddenly at about ten, I felt like crying. Though that sudden gloom dissipated a little, I was shrouded with depression all day, something I couldn't understand. As I was riding the bus home I kept thinking, "As soon as I see Allen everything will be all right." No matter what was bothering me, I always felt better as soon as I laid eyes on him.

When the bus pulled up to my stop I was greatly disappointed to see not Allen, but Laura Jean and Allen's brother, Lorin, waiting for me. They broke the news that Allen was dead.

I couldn't believe it.

Allen had been working with some of his brothers in an excavation company. He had been digging a trench and jumped down to check it. As he did, the walls caved in, killing him instantly.

Lorin and Laura Jean had waited for me so the three of us could go together to the county hospital to identify him. When I saw him lying there, all dirty and cold, it simply wrung my heart. Laura Jean started sobbing, so Lorin led her out and helped her with the paperwork. I knelt by Allen, holding his hand, dumbfounded. I just couldn't come to terms with the fact that he was gone. It was too sudden. He was too young. I reflected on the incredible kindness of the Lord, who had tried three times to prepare us.

Allen had kept his secrets so well that not all of the Priesthood Council even knew who I was to Allen. Several of them had become aware that there was someone else while Allen was in the hospital six months earlier, but most had no idea it was me. The feelings I had felt in my dream—Should I make myself known? What would Allen's wishes be?—went unanswered.

For the most part I stayed hidden throughout the funeral and the associated activities. I didn't go to the viewing the night before. I went to the funeral with Carl and Ramona—she was my sister and Carl was Allen's brother. Because I was with them, I could sit in the family section.

The funeral director finally closed the doors to separate the family from the congregation, allowing us to look at him once more before the casket was closed, I was trying to see Allen over everyone's head when Brother Musser, another leader in our group, made eye contact with me. He immediately cleared a path between the casket and me so I could stand beside Allen just before the lid was shut. Throughout the entire procedure Laura Jean was very considerate of me, leaving the decisions about what I should do to me. I never felt left out.

Just before they lowered the casket into the grave, Brother Musser again was so thoughtful. He plucked two roses out of the casket wreath, handing one to me and one to Laura Jean. Allen was buried on December 15, 1957, leaving us with Laura Jean's four children. The oldest turned four the day before the funeral, and the youngest was six months old.

From the moment I had learned that Allen was dead, my heart had been so heavy. But as soon as Allen was taken care of properly I felt lighter; I felt happy, and the sun was even shining for the first time in days.

Laura Jean and I got along really well at first. I had a full-time job, and she was able to get Social Security benefits. We had outgrown our little house, and with Allen's life insurance policy, our house was paid off. We found a new home that we enjoyed very much, but eventually things started to change. I was getting very restless and yearning for male companionship.

While I was growing up, my father was often very critical of the men who had taken on the leadership of the different polygamist groups. He believed there were a few men who had the authority to perform a "sealing" or marriages but they didn't have the right to collect tithing, fast offerings or "counsel" anyone outside of their own family. The experience he had with the small group he joined in Bountiful in the early forties taught him to distrust anyone who took upon himself authority that didn't belong to him. I heard and internalized that criticism.

So when I married Allen, I did not believe the Priesthood Council Allen believed in was inspired to lead us. Right after Allen and I got married, I made one or two snide remarks about the Priesthood Council. Allen corrected me instantly but with kindness. I never said anything critical about the Council again. Without any pressure he just taught me their principles and made sure I got to church meetings as much as possible. It wasn't until Allen's death that I experienced strong feelings that the members of the Priesthood Council were inspired to lead us. As I reflect on that, I feel that Allen was helping me understand from his position in the next life, things he couldn't teach me when he was alive.

Laura Jean and I had been going to Brother Musser once a month to pay tithing and visit. He had given me good counsel during those visits, and those experiences combined with others expanded and increased my testimony. Armed with that firm testimony, I went to Brother Musser and explained my feelings about desiring male companionship. I wanted to know what Allen wanted me to do—and if he did not want me to get married, I needed help to overcome the feelings that were building up in me. We talked, but he left the decision up to me. I had a lot to think about.

A few months later, I called Brother Musser to ask him if I could go south for the Labor Day weekend, a time when they had "work weekends" in Hilldale, a small polygamist community. Everyone who could go went to help on the large projects that were being done. Brother Musser said, "Yes, that would be a good idea, as all the people will be together then."

I knew by his answer that I would be told whom I was to marry. I had been praying continually that whomever they told me to marry would be right for me. I caught a ride to Hilldale with some friends and had an enjoyable weekend, but by Sunday nothing had been said about it.

As we were shaking hands after the Sunday meeting, Brother Johnson asked me to stay behind—and he and Brother Musser took me into a separate room to talk. Brother Johnson said he felt Lorin Zitting, Allen's brother, was the person I should marry. He advised me to talk it over with my father.

"I don't need to do that," I responded. "I feel good about it." Lorin had been a good friend since I was a teenager.

As we left Hilldale, I went home with some friends who had a private plane—the first time I had ever had the opportunity to fly. Lorin called the following Tuesday. Neither of us wanted to go forward with this counsel unless both of us felt it was the right thing to do. The phone call established that we did. That evening Lorin and his wife, Sylvia, picked me up. We drove to Brother Musser's, and he performed the marriage that night. It had been five years since I lost Allen.

Lorin and I found a trailer house for sale in Taylorsville, I lived there a little more than a year. Amazingly, I got pregnant right away. That first year he often came to see me to take me out. We had some good times getting acquainted, which I believe is key to a good, sound, lasting marriage. I've never regretted those times. Allen and I had never gone anywhere overnight together until a few weeks before he died. I can't help feeling it negatively affected our relationship.

When I agreed to marry Lorin, I made him promise he would never make me live with Sylvia. I have always enjoyed Sylvia's company, but housekeeping was way down her priority list. As time went on, however, I could see that my demand was very selfish. Lorin was having a hard time keeping two homes. I had quit work when my first child was born, so I was no longer making a financial contribution. As for Syl, she was restless and wanted to work now that her baby was a year old. She found a night job as a waitress, and Lorin helped his oldest child, Gayle, with the kids when he was there.

"Lorin, someone needs to be with Syl's kids, I need to move in and help with them," I said one day.

Lorin was sweet. I think he was relieved, but his response was, "I promised you I'd never ask you to do that and I won't break that promise."

With my persuasion he agreed.

We had been trying to live quiet lives and continued to do so. My baby and I moved into the basement rooms and the back yard was enclosed by a six-foot privacy fence. When I moved in, Lorin asked if I could teach the children to be clean. Until then, the kids were afraid to sleep in the basement—it hadn't been used much and was overrun with mice.

Syl's five kids were different than other children I'd been around. Lorin usually playfully gave me a hug and a swat on the butt as he left the house. I, of course, laughed and gave him a hug back. One day Syl's four-year-old son, Tom, gave me a swat on the butt. I turned on him in shocked surprise, ready to really lay him low. He was so scared when he realized I was angry, and he said with a trembling voice, "You always laugh when Daddy does that."

Needless to say, Lorin and I had a good laugh about it, and there was no swatting on the butt in front of the kids after that. My life with Lorin has had many ups and downs. The best part of it has been having my spouse as my friend and my lover. The other best part has been the fifteen wonderful children with whom we have been blessed including a set of twins at the end. Our children work together to help Lorin and me with whatever we need. Recently they bought me a car, and each takes a turn making the car payment once a year.

As for me, I went back to school after I turned fifty, maintaining a GPA of 3.75. I worked in a finance company until 2000. Since then, I've been a full-time assistant librarian, which I still enjoy at the ripe old age of seventy-six. I'm quite proud to be the second child of Dad's who has a B.S. degree.

My choice to be part of a plural marriage resulted from the fact that I felt it was right—which can largely be traced to the teachings of my parents. Those teachings were not only spoken, but also lived. My father tried his very best to live the gospel as he saw it, and he tried to pass that on to his children. He always tried to show us children a good time, taking us on Sunday drives and on trips to the canyon, where we sometimes camped out.

Maurine's family in 1953 to Shauna.

I followed the teachings and example of my parents instead of the norms of the world by living plural marriage. I am at peace over that decision because I know that God led me to that choice. One of the choicest benefits for me is the opportunity for friends right in my own family as I grow in my relationships with not only my God-fearing husband but with my lovely sister-wives.

I maintain a good relationship with my siblings, even though some of them did not choose the same path I did. I have felt no strained relationships in my family because of my choices. That's much the same in my own family. Our children don't all live our lifestyle but they treat each other, us, and Lorin's other wives with great respect.

Following the path I believe God had for me has led me to a great sense of peace and happiness, for which I am extremely grateful.

Virginia May (Ginny)

CHAPTER 6

1940

I WAS BORN JUNE 23, 1940, Maurine Owen's third child and Albert Barlow's sixteenth—his middle child. I felt a great abundance of love all my growing-up years, especially from my four parents. My brother Doug, one of Aunt Katie's children, and I were inseparable. Daddy used to put one of us on each knee, call us his "cubs," and sing a little ditty to us. Often he took only the two of us with him to see Grandpa Barlow or one of his friends. During those visits we sat very quietly on the couch next to Daddy for what seemed like a long time. I loved spending time with Daddy, but was always glad when he quit talking and we could go home.

I was almost four years old when some policemen burst into our home early one morning and arrested our father. I was in Mama's bed. It was dark outside, and a policeman stood at the bedroom door next to Mama. Why is he here? Why is he looking away? Where is Daddy? Something is wrong with Mama.

With a lump in my throat I wanted to cry, but instead I simply said, "My throat hurts, Mama."

Her quiet, sad voice said, "It's okay, Dear, go back to sleep."

I missed Daddy very much while he was in prison.

One of my most painful childhood experiences was also one that created a firmly knit bond between one of my mothers and me. As I came into the back yard one afternoon, I saw that Doug was burning trash. Seeing a rubber hose in the fire, I pulled it out, asking, "Why are you burning this?"

I heard him holler, "Dad told me to!" and at the same time I began screaming—the hot rubber had hit my legs. Aunt Kate instantly bolted out of the house, grabbed me and dragged me up the stairs to the dining room. Sitting me on the table, she expertly cleaned my wounds, bandaged my legs, comforted me, and gave me a piece of her bread and jam to eat outside on the back steps. All the while, Mama watched, a worried look on her face—but it was Aunt Kate who rescued me. I knew she loved me. I still have a large scar on the inside of both knees from that burn.

Mama and our family moved into our own place when I was only five, but I still spent a lot of time in the homes of my "other mothers"—they had children my age, and I missed all of them. I loved Aunt Kate and Aunt Vio and helped myself to food in their kitchens as if I was their child. Daddy got us together as often as he could and tried so hard to keep us as one family.

When I was six, all the mothers and any children who were able, were doing whatever they could to help with expenses. My mother made aprons, training panties, bibs, and other items for her children to sell door-to-door. She also tended other people's children to earn money. Though the times were very tough financially, we had family prayer most evenings and my parents petitioned the Lord for help. They often spoke of the answers they received to their prayers. These experiences gave me a foundation of faith in a Father in Heaven who I felt cared about us.

Daddy loved music—his mother had played the piano, his father the violin—and he managed to buy Mama a piano about a year after he got out of prison. She often played the piano in the evenings. She played hymns, and we kids stood around the piano and sang.

Daddy thought nothing of whipping his children whenever they disobeyed or were naughty. Once in 1944, when I was a preschooler, I watched as he took his belt off and whipped all the kids who were older than Doug and me. He beat them on their bare backs. Mama sat with her head in her hands, Aunt Vio paced, wringing her hands, and Aunt Kate stayed in the kitchen. All of us younger children were watching and I was confused. Why weren't Doug and I getting whipped? What did the kids do to be punished like that?

I never forgot that incident, and years later I found out what precipitated it. Imagine my guilt when I realized it was because of something I had shared with Mama. She had overheard me and Doug talking, and got me to admit to her that some of the boys—who were eleven and twelve—were molesting the six- and seven-year-old girls down in the basement. Mama took the information to Daddy, assuming that he would punish only the boys. But Daddy whipped them all.

Mom was not meek or timid. She was a strong woman but believed that a wife was supposed to submit to her husband. She tried very hard to do that, even in cases when she knew Dad was out of line. She was his third wife and she was a very peaceful person. I knew Dad adored my Mom, and she him. The only sign that she ever disagreed with him was the look in her eyes. She basically controlled us with a similar look. I learned very young how to please Dad, and I always felt very sorry for the kids who never seemed to be able to please him.

It was the summer of 1947 when I was seven that I talked Mama into letting me take the bus to Aunt Kate's house to play with Doug and Becky. We lived on Capitol Hill and Aunt Kate lived in the big house on 400 East. I was relentless when I wanted something. I just wouldn't give up.

"Please, please," I pleaded, "I've done it a hundred times with Vilate and Hazel. I'll go to the Darling Store and catch the bus like we always do. I can do it, please?"

Reluctantly she agreed. I walked the four city blocks to the bus stop and rode to Aunt Kate's. When it was time to go back home she said, "I have a jar of mayonnaise that your mother needs. Can you take it to her for me?"

Of course I could carry what was a one-gallon glass jar of mayonnaise home to Mama, I could do anything.

I climbed up the stairs of the bus with that heavy jar of mayonnaise and found a seat behind the bus driver. As we got close to town, the buildings all began to look alike. My stomach churned, I couldn't figure out where to get off. That's not all, I couldn't pull the cord if I wanted to get off because of the heavy jar. Finally, I just got off when the door opened.

I walked and walked and walked, soon my arms were aching as I carried the jar. I was so weary. I wanted to sit down, but the only place where I could sit was on the curb with my feet in the gutter, and I just couldn't do that. Finally, exhausted beyond my ability, I noticed a step. There was an open door behind the step, and it was dark inside with loud music playing. I didn't care. I just needed to sit down.

As I sat on the step with my arms tight around the jar and a lump in my throat, a couple eventually came out the door, stepping carefully around me. The woman turned around and, looking at me, asked, "Little girl, are you lost? Henry, I think she's lost. Go in and call the cops."

She pulled me up and tried to relieve me of the jar, to which I still clung tightly. I was not going to relinquish this necessary commodity that Mama needed. "Here," she said, "let me wrap my coat around you, you're shivering."

She pulled me in front of her, holding me close to her body. She wrapped her coat around me and my jar as her cigarette smoke curled around us. Soon a "paddy wagon" pulled up to the curb. The policeman sized me up and announced, "We can't take her in this. We'll be back."

The lump in my throat kept me from crying out, "No, please! Take me!" It was getting dark, and I was so scared. I kept silent.

Finally another police car came and I ended up in the front seat with my jar on my lap. It had grown very dark.

"Your daddy's worried about you—it's been on the radio that you are lost," the policeman said, glancing at me.

I clung to my jar in silence, staring straight ahead.

When Daddy opened the door and saw me he grabbed me up and held me tight for a long time as I clung to his neck. Then he carried me to bed. I don't know what happened to the jar—I assume Mama took care of that.

The tradition in our family was that when we turned ten, Mama planned our only birthday party. Hazel had hers just a few months before I turned eight. Hazel's party looked so fun that when I turned eight six months later I invited a couple of friends to come home with me for my "birthday party."

When I arrived home with my friends and told Mama that my friends had come for my birthday party, she gave me one of her "looks," and I knew I'd made a very bad mistake. But she never said anything that would embarrass my friends or me. Instead, she gave my friends some cake and Jell-O for a simple birthday treat.

Soon after I turned eight, Mama and I walked to the old library downtown so I could get my own library card. As I quietly tiptoed around in that dark, old, building with its rows and rows of books, I was awed. I came back often and became an avid reader like my mother.

Mom also taught me to be honest with myself. If I came to her with my woes, her response was always, "What did you do?" or, "I wonder how she/he felt when you did that?"

I began to understand at a relatively young age that things were not always as I saw them. Whenever I was feeling sorry for myself, she tried to help me understand the other person's feelings so I could forgive and forget. If I ever complained about something Dad did, she explained why he did it. As a result, I learned to make excuses for him.

When I was eight, Dad bought a fourplex on about 400 East and 400 South and moved Mom's family into it. It was on a dead-end street, and I had many friends—we all enjoyed playing on that quiet street. It was there that I received my first "whipping" with a switch. As young as I was, I had to find the switch and bring it to Dad to use on me. I was angry—but I wasn't angry with Dad for the switching, I was angry with Hazel for tattling on me, which had earned me the switch. Hazel was always bossing me around.

One night I woke to Dad spanking my little sister, Linda, who was nearly two years old. He kept screaming, "Shut up!" Of course the baby cried even harder as he spanked her; finally she was just making breathless little noises as she gasped for air, but Dad continued to spank her. I silently cried as I listened to him hurting my baby sister.

The next day I told Mom, "It makes me cry when Daddy spanks the baby."

"I know, Dear, it does me too," she said quietly. "But after he does, they never give me any trouble."

Her comment didn't mean anything to me at the time; it was just her attempt to help me understand my father. Much later, when I was in my sixties, I was trying to figure where my anger came from. I realized then that my memory of Linda's beating meant that maybe he had done the same thing to me. And to avoid his wrath, I became a "Daddy pleaser." No wonder Mom could control us with a "look"—she had the "enforcer" to back her up.

When I turned ten, Mom was working at a clothing factory, so she had enough money to let me invite ten friends to my birthday party. Those parties included a treasure hunt with ten presents, and because she had more money, each of my ten friends also "found" a small gift as well. At that party, I got to have ice cream with my cake—a tenth-birthday first for all of us in the family.

In the spring of 1951, when I was almost eleven, Dad sold the fourplex and bought a farm in Weber County. Mom had to move back into the big house on 400 East, because all her daughters made her the ideal one to take over the boarding house/child care business Aunt Kate had established there. In all reality, though, she wasn't the ideal one. Mom hated that house, she was not social, she was a lousy cook (according to Dad), she had nine children with another due shortly, and she was not the world's best housekeeper. A boarding house complete with more children to tend was a nightmare for her in spite of the fact that her daughters were a big help to her.

Dad soon traded the place in Weber County for a ranch in Duchesne County, and he sold the duplex so he could buy another place to raise feed. Aunt Vio's family was put in that second place. Aunt Kate had boys, so they could work on both ranches. All of this uprooting occurred because Dad had always dreamed of being a rancher. He had watched movies of John Wayne as the big rancher. He had six grown boys, so why couldn't he make it work? Dad was a dreamer, and he worked hard to make those dreams come true. He just didn't manage money very well.

In order to survive in the boarding house/child care business, Mother kept my two older sisters home from school a lot. I had played with my baby sisters as if they were my dolls, so it was now my job to come home from school and play with all of the little kids. I was great with children, and now there were as many as ten extra kids. Some of them just plain lived with us; others lived upstairs with their mothers when their mothers got home from work; and some were just there for the day. I loved most of those kids as much as I did my little sisters. However, I learned to be an army sergeant in order to control them. On some days I was in charge of as many as seventeen young children. I'm not proud of some of my bullying tactics I used with those kids. There was probably heady "power" in some of my methods.

I adored my younger siblings. I remembered each of their births from Betsy on down because all but Doris was born at home. We called Doris the "Hard-luck Baby" because of the problems she had as an infant. We attributed those problems to her being born in the hospital. That was the first time mother didn't stay in bed for ten days following a birth. Instead, it was three days in the hospital bed and then home to all the kids.

"Grandma" Ogden, the doctor who delivered most of Dad's children at our home, had retired, which was why Mother ended up giving birth in the hospital. After Dr. Ogden delivered a baby she came every day to bathe the baby and mother for ten days. When Steven was born, she brought all of us kids a new toothbrush. She was a very gentle soul, and I loved her. Mother often quoted her wisdom on child rearing. From her obituary I learned that Dr. Ogden had birthed a large family of her own before going back to school to become an obstetrician.

Vilate, Hazel, and I loved all the babies Mother had. We taught them to walk, talk, and play games. However, when Bonnie was born, we had three little sisters in a row—and had really hoped for a baby brother this time. So when Dad came excitedly downstairs to tell Hazel and me that we had a new baby sister, our reaction wasn't what he expected. "ANOTHER GIRL?" one of us cried. "Who cares about another girl?"

Dad exploded. "YOUR MOTHER JUST WENT THROUGH HELL FOR THAT BABY" he screamed. "Don't you ever let her hear you talk like that! EVERY CHILD is a gift and don't you forget it. You get upstairs and be happy."

We did and we were. That exchange had a huge impact on me. It began to dawn on me how much each child meant to my father. His parenting skills were lacking, his self-esteem was small, and his ego was huge—but he had a loving heart and he would help anyone, especially his children.

The boarding house with all the extra kids was hard enough, but that wasn't the only source of stress for my mother. Dad would drain the checking account to fund the ranches, so Mother couldn't pay the utilities and buy the food she needed. Dad would drive down from Duschene County and arrive late at night with a five-gallon can of fresh milk. Mother would have to find jars to pour the milk into so it would fit in the fridge and then the two of them went right to bed. Dad used Mother to satisfy his needs, and in the morning he took whatever money she had before he drove back to the ranches.

Mother was drained emotionally and physically. Recovering from giving birth to Bonnie, she was done. I remember Aunt Katie coming to the house, making Mom an avocado sandwich, and the two of them talking quietly in Mother's bedroom for a long time. If anyone knew Dad, Aunt Kate did. She talked Mother into hanging on a little longer. Mother may have "hung on," but she shut Dad out, her way of punishing him. Of course her children were not aware of this shutting out, no words were spoken by her. Only Dad felt her cold disapproval.

In spite of all Dad's efforts, he lost the ranches. He moved Aunt Kate and Aunt Vio back to the Salt Lake area and Mother stopped renting out the upstairs rooms.

By then Mother's oldest child, Vilate, who was also Mother's closest friend, had become a plural wife. Dad had a reputation for being a blabber-mouth, and because Vilate's husband was concerned about being arrested, he didn't want Vilate to see our family. So Dad agreed to let Mother see Vilate secretly and not tell him if Vilate was pregnant. Before long he couldn't stand to be left out. As a result, he and Mother started having heated arguments about the whole situation.

That's when I first started hearing my parents argue. Instead of just giving Dad a "look" followed by the silent treatment, as had always been her practice, Mother actually began to argue with him. It was awful. As a result, Mother agreed to quit seeing Vilate and her first grandchild. Mother added that grievance to the list of things she held against Dad. She was basically shut down emotionally, going through the motions but not really there for any of us.

Once I woke to my parents arguing one more time and this time I heard Dad say, "Okay, I'm leaving and I won't be back. Is that what you want?"

No answer from Mom and then, "I said I'm leaving, is that what you want?"

I heard a quiet, "I don't care."

I prayed, he didn't leave and the fighting went on for months.

By early 1955, both Vilate and Hazel were plural wives and had gone into hiding. I missed them so much.

Vilate had been my "other mother," and Hazel had just begun to be nice to me after bossing me around for years, her way of teaching me to be responsible. I assumed I would be a plural wife as well. In my nightly prayers, I had prayed for as long as I could remember, that I would "marry the right man."

I began dating in the polygamist culture when I was fifteen and became good friends with the young man I dated—probably because we didn't do any necking, but simply held hands or occasionally hugged. We were each praying to know if we should get married, and eventually something happened that made me feel pretty sure he was not the "one" for me. We were on a drive one afternoon, and I explained why I didn't want to marry him. He was extremely quiet. When we reached my house, he said, "I was going to tell you today that I felt certain we were meant for each other, but I guess I was wrong." I was stunned. I ran into the house crying. I realized that if he had expressed his feelings to me before I expressed mine to him, I never would have said a thing—I would have simply gone along with him. I was never that certain about anything, and it was my nature to just "go along to get along" with my friends and older adults.

In October 1955, my father was arrested again for living polygamy. His picture was on the front page of the local newspaper, and I was so embarrassed that I changed high schools. I began to attend Granite High School because I had cousins and other polygamist friends who went to school there. While most polygamist men kept their lifestyle hidden as much as possible, Dad was one of the few who gave all his children his last name. He was very proud of his wives and children, often bragging about them. He was released on bail and spent the next three and a half years fighting for his right to live his religion.

When my baby sister Martha was born late one evening, I was just home from work and my sister Frances was also there. I didn't hear the baby cry, which I had learned from other births to anticipate. Dad finally came out of the bedroom, looking anxious, and said, "The baby's here but she isn't breathing."

Fran immediately went into the room to see if she could help, and I was close on her heels. By then the doctor pronounced that the baby was breathing, and he handed Dad the baby as he turned to take care of Mother.

Dad wrapped the baby up in a blanket and handed her to me, saying, "Hold this cotton in front of her nose to make sure she keeps breathing." Then he too turned to focus on Mother.

I held that precious package for a very long time. She looked so much like Barbara, who was only seventeen months old. As soon as they could, my parents took Martha to the hospital, she lived only four days. I was crushed. I adored my little sisters.

Our parents held a small service in the living room of our home and someone donated a tiny casket for our baby. As all of us sat grieving Dad carefully explained, "It's better that our baby died. She would not have been normal if she had lived."

I learned when I was pregnant with my second child that Martha Louise had Down Syndrome and she also had a hole in her lungs. Mother was almost 43 when she gave birth to her.

When any of the older children in the family found work they were expected to give their mothers most of the money they earned until they moved away from home. By the time I found a job at the Harmon's Café on 3900 South State Street, I was required to give Mother only half of what I earned. I was working with many teenagers outside the polygamist culture, and because I was very friendly—even a flirt—I was asked out often. I would always laugh and say, "You'll have to ask my father."

One young man finally did ask my father, and after a short interview, Dad agreed to let me date him. He was active in the LDS Church, and we often discussed religion. By then I had read the Book of Mormon with my family, with Dad preaching his doctrine every Sunday and whenever else he could get in a little sermon. I was sure the Book of Mormon was true and I believed Joseph Smith, the founder of the LDS Church, saw what he said he saw.

As I dated this young man, I defended plural marriage. It was normal to me, and I was aware of several benefits for the women who lived it. In response, he quoted scripture to me, showing me why polygamy wasn't supposed to be practiced anymore. One evening as we were discussing the subject, I thought to myself, *Why am I arguing with him about this? I know it's good, and it doesn't matter whether he does.*

What we live with growing up is normal for us. I intended to live plural marriage.

My friend and I became very close and we were necking a lot. I thought I was in love, and late in 1957 we went to see Dad to tell him we wanted to get married. Dad convinced us to stop seeing each other for two months and if we still wanted to get married after that, he promised he would give us his blessing. Two months later, I realized I was just in love with love, and I stopped seeing the young man. Dad assumed I had seen it his way, and he trusted me to continue to do so.

I began dating many young men outside of the polygamist culture without Dad's permission. He was out of town a lot selling stocks and bonds, earning a lot of money to pay attorney fees as he fought for his right to live his religion. He also spent a lot of time at the other wives' homes. Mother was the one at home, and she never questioned what I was doing or who I was with. If Dad happened to be home when a date was scheduled to pick me up, he would ask, "Do I know him?"

"You can meet him when he picks me up," was my flippant answer. I'd always be ready with my coat as the young man rang the doorbell. I would invite him in, introduce him, grab my coat, and usher him out before Dad could ask any questions. I was Dad's little "sweetheart" and could do no wrong.

During this time, a man and his wife began courting me to enter their family. The man did say he didn't know if I was meant for him, and asked that we both pray about it. He said, "You don't need to stop dating other guys. I'm not afraid of the competition."

The problem was, I was necking with the competition by then—and, of course, I wasn't necking with him. I was not attracted to him at all, but I did love his wife, who was a wonderful person.

In 1958, I graduated from high school—one of the few of Dad's children to do so. I got a job at the phone company as a long-distance operator. My sister Arlene co-signed with me so I could get a car, a 1952 red Pontiac convertible. I loved taking my younger siblings in my car to places like the Great Salt Lake beach, Saratoga Springs and Lagoon. I would take a couple of them with me to "drag State" in the evening sometimes.

I continued to see the married man and his wife about once a month but felt no pressure to "know" if I should marry him. I included him in my nightly prayers but only casually, until I'd been seeing him about six months. One day when his wife wasn't there, he said, "I still don't know if I should marry you but I do know I love you." (It was very inappropriate for him to even approach me if he didn't *know* I was supposed to enter his family.)

When he said he loved me, I felt pressure to know through a spiritual confirmation whether he was the right one for me. The following Saturday, I finally had a date to go dancing with him without his wife. I prayed earnestly at the beginning of the week to know, and I received no answer. Convinced that plural marriage was the right way to live, on Tuesday I prayed, telling Heavenly Father, "I'm going to tell him I'll marry him on Saturday. I don't love him, but he's very nice and I'm sure I can learn to love him. I love his wife very much, and I'm sure I can get along with her."

Wednesday evening I took Betsy and Steven for a ride in my red convertible. We were dragging State Street, and I saw some guys I knew. "Pull over," the driver in another car shouted to me.

I pulled over to talk, and after a short conversation, the cute one, whose name was Vince, said he'd meet me at my place. He took his friend home and came to my house. The two of us went for a drive. I was very attracted to him and had been for almost a year.

That evening I told him, as I did every guy with whom I went out, "I'm going to have fifteen children." I loved coming from a large family, and I wanted a lot of kids.

At that, Vince looked at me with a grin, shrugged, and said, "You gotta tend 'em."

On Thursday he took me bowling, and on Friday we went to dinner. The married man called me Saturday morning to tell me he couldn't make the date for that night and asked if we could do it another time. So I went with Vince again on Saturday and Sunday. Monday I moved into a studio apartment near downtown Salt Lake City with a friend, and Tuesday morning Vince showed up with a large sack of groceries. He was putting on the "full court press." He later told me he knew I was the girl he was supposed to marry long before we met on State Street. He was just waiting for me to stop dating his friend. In 1959, four and a half months after our first date, I was pregnant and married to Vince. He had not been the most stellar influence on me. I had never used alcohol until I dated Vince. I had also stopped praying for the first time in my life. Looking back, I think I was in a fog, letting life happen to me.

For a few years I believed I made a mistake. But one day I received a strong confirmation from God that He put Vince in my life because we needed each other. I ended up with the "right man" in the only way I could. My father could have talked me out of marrying Vince if I hadn't been pregnant, his only daughter to be in that situation. For that, I was the black sheep of all Mother's daughters. And Vince would never have married me, he was too indecisive to do that. However, he was keeping track of my periods and we were married within a week of when we knew I was pregnant.

About the time I married Vince, my father was sent to prison again. Sentenced to five years, he was released a year and one month early. He lost his fight to live his religion. It was so hard on our family.

I began praying for my unborn child, very excited to be having that experience. I was grateful for Vince's family. They were always kind to me.

Vince and I continued to drink together but I was not happy. I was ashamed of getting pregnant before I was married, and I had a very difficult time understanding Vince. He was either angry or horny—there was no in between for him. He also used swear words I'd never before heard—including using the name of God and Jesus Christ as profanity, which shocked me. And a vast philosophical difference separated us. I married him convinced I could talk him into accepting polygamy, and he married me believing he could convince me that polygamy was evil.

In reality, Vince couldn't stand Dad and thought polygamy was disgusting. He believed that any woman who would share a husband simply couldn't love him very much at all.

After my precious baby arrived, my life began to spiral out of control. I had once again quit praying. I really believed I was a "bad" person, and getting drunk became my goal when I drank. I did some very destructive things during that period.

I was baptized into the LDS Church—not because I believed it was true, but because I thought it would stop the constant harassment from Vince about polygamy. The baptism was somewhat of a sham. I had already been baptized in the Jordan River by my dad's uncle at the age of eight. We went to church one Sunday so I could be confirmed a member of the church, but we never went to church again except to get our babies blessed. Vince always wanted our babies to be blessed. His sister, Betty, was active in the LDS Church, and her husband always performed the blessings in their ward or parish.

When I got pregnant with my second child I began to pray again. I started out by wanting to pray for my baby, but I also realized by then that I must pray every night, or there would be no end to the destructive choices I would make. I continued to put one foot in front of the other for several years, sinking deeper and deeper into the abyss I had created for myself.

The only thing that kept me sane was the babies we conceived. Each time I had a new baby I felt that little bit of Heaven only a newborn can bring. However, I didn't know how to "control" them as they grew. I was using Dad's parenting style instead of Mother's, and I hated myself for it. I realized that I was taking my fear, anger, and frustration out on my children.

During those bleak years I received the great love and support of my family. My younger sisters tended for me often for little or nothing. Shauna especially would take over my kids as if they were her own. Steven and Bob helped us move many times.

Mother loved my kids as they were the first grandchildren she had been able to see and hold. She cherished her time with them. Whenever I had a new baby one of my younger sisters would come and stay with me for a few days to help me.

Since Mother tended for us often, my parents became aware of some of the problems we were having. Father never quit preaching to me, and several times he encouraged me to leave my husband. Mother, on the other hand, said only once, "If you're 50 percent of the trouble you're having, you need to take care of your 50 percent."

I prayed but felt my prayers were simply bouncing off the ceiling. Vince insisted I was "brainwashed" and that polygamists were "sick." I loved my family and defended them; I especially defended my father, who Vince seemed to hate more intensely with each passing day. Whenever he wanted to really insult me he would spit out, "You're just like your father!"

As a result of Vince's drinking we lived in abject poverty and the only time he was physically abusive was when he drank. I believed God was punishing me for being a bad person. I fell into a deep depression, contemplating suicide continually. Eventually I wondered if there really was a God, even though I continued to pray every night.

I dealt with eczema on my hands for many years, and as my life became more and more difficult, the eczema flared up so bad I couldn't use my hands because they were so intensely cracked and bleeding, with pus running down my arms. My sister Betsy came for a few days to help me because I couldn't change my baby's diaper or pull up the toddler's pants. I went to a new dermatologist and got a stronger steroid cream to treat the eczema. Although the new doctor helped me know what I needed to do to control it, I continued to suffer with it and I still have scars.

One Sunday in the autumn of 1965, Bishop Snyder, who was the leader the LDS congregation I belonged to, but never attended, knocked on our door. I invited him and his counselor in. They asked if I would teach Primary one afternoon a week. (This is a class for children under twelve.)

Vince, who happened to be home at the time, quipped, "She can't. She has to answer my phone." (I answered his business phone.)

"I could teach Mutual," I said, hopefully. Mutual is the meeting for teens held one evening a week, and I was desperate for something spiritual. I had been raised having family prayer in the evening, a blessing on the food, and listening to our parents talk about their spiritual experiences. I missed those things of the spirit so much, but didn't feel I could even ask for them in my own home—I was completely intimidated by Vince and felt too useless, unworthy, and stupid to stand up for anything I wanted. I was suicidal for about three years around this time.

As a child I had lived just up the street from Temple Square and we often played there in the summer. I remember standing, looking up at the beautiful temple, and thinking to myself, Someday I'm going to go in there. (Only active LDS Church members with a temple recommend from their bishop are allowed to enter a temple.) I had attended Primary with my friends from the LDS Church a few times, and as a teen I had several good friends who encouraged me to come to Mutual. I envied them the fun activities they attended in their church.

I really didn't give religion much thought. If something was right for my dad, it was right for me. Despite his significant flaws, I adored my father. Mother always pointed out the reasons behind his behavior, so I accepted that as an excuse for the terrible things he did.

So with that simple comment, "I could teach Mutual," my situation started to change.

Turning to his counselor, the bishop said, "I think we do need someone in the Mutual, don't we?"

"Yes, I think we do."

That short exchange began my difficult climb out of the hell into which I had sunk. I still didn't know if the LDS Church was true, but I wanted my children to have what my friends in junior high had, the many wonderful activities. I gave birth to my fifth child, and my relationship with Vince had never been worse. My anger when he was sober, and his when he was drunk finally came to a head, my baby was six weeks old when he came banging on the door one evening (he never would carry a key). I jumped out of bed and rushed to the door as he banged again. When it started out that way, I knew it was going to be bad.

Sure enough, he began screaming the minute he walked in and he started slapping me as I backed up I fell to the couch as he proceeded to continue slapping me on the left side of my face over and over screaming at me. It went on for about a half hour. I had learned long before not to say anything when he was drunk. His anger finally wound down and he went to bed. I went into the children's bedroom to check on them. My three little girls were huddled together in the closet. My toddler was lying in his crib staring up at the ceiling. As I sobbed, inside I thought, I deserve this but my children do not.

The next morning I took my five little kids and went to Mom's. She gave us the very back room in the basement and I checked my two oldest children into school. I got a job as a hostess in a restaurant I had worked at many years before, working nights so my sisters could help Mom tend my children and put them to bed. I went to Legal Aide and filed for a divorce. My father had counseled me more than once to leave Vince and he was glad to have me home. Seeing my bruised face and black eyes he was very angry.

Vince came every day, begging me to give him another chance. I prayed earnestly every evening that God would help me do what was best for my children. Five weeks later I woke late after working and was sitting at the table, watching Mom move around the kitchen. She looked very tired. *What am I doing to my mother? She doesn't need to care for my children.*

Dad walked into the kitchen, "Well, Sis, Vince came to me last night and pleaded with me to help him get his family back. I think you should give him another chance."

I knew my prayers were answered. Vince had stayed sober for the whole five weeks, which was a miracle in itself. He hated my father and never would talk to him. My father didn't like Vince either, and would never counsel me to take him back. I gathered up my children and went home. Bishop Snyder welcomed me back, giving me the same class to teach, and I began to turn to him for counsel instead of my father. I knew he loved Vince as much as he loved me. I knew he would be objective in his counsel.

Vince didn't hit me like that again for many years. He still drank, screamed and threatened but he was a little more controlled. I never lost my fear. I still had to beg for money to buy food for my children.

I slowly began to get direction in my life. About nine months later I was desperately praying for help with my horrible lack of parenting skills. I was parenting like my father and hated myself for it. (Vince accused me of being an army sergeant with the kids.) As I pleaded with God to help me change, a voice in my head said, "You could quit drinking." It had never occurred to me to stop drinking. I simply didn't see anything wrong with it. Everyone Vince and I associated with drank. My father had a glass of wine most evenings, and most of our family gatherings included alcohol. I knew Vince's drinking was a problem, but it never occurred to me that my own drinking was getting out of control. However, I immediately made a covenant with God—not only that I would never drink again, but that I would do whatever He wanted me to do if He would just help me change—help me be a better mother.

I had no idea how hard it would be to stop drinking. It took four years for me to stop wanting to have a drink, because the only time I felt good was when I was drinking. Changing the way I parented took a lot longer than that. In fact, my last three children were the only ones who were never hit in anger. They knew a different mother than my older children. If I had not been raised in a polygamist family (who believed in procreation), I may have stopped after having had six children, because having and raising those children was so much harder than I had thought it would be. But the fear that I might be punished somehow for using birth control kept those precious babies coming.

In the summer of 1967, seven months after I quit drinking, I was introduced to the Al-anon program, a twelve-step self-improvement program for people who have a loved one with a drinking problem. It is a spiritual program, and it was what I needed at that time to help me understand the mess my life was in. Between my activity in the LDS Church and my weekly Al-anon meetings, I gradually climbed out of the hole I had stumbled into.

I began to find happiness and I slowly began to gain a testimony of my truth. I voraciously read my scriptures and every self-help book I could get my hands on. I was finding so much peace that I wanted to share it with the world, especially my sisters, many of who were dealing with alcoholism and/or abuse. I no longer limited my prayers to nighttime. I prayed morning, all day, and every evening before going to bed. I had learned how to "listen to my heart," and it was amazing how my prayers were answered. I stopped asking God whether Dad was right or the Church was right, and had started asking, "What do you want me to do with my life?"

It was about this time I decided to prove to myself that I was not "brainwashed." In the process, I became more and more convinced that the LDS Church was where the truth was for me. The feedback from my parents was, "At least she's in the Church." It was their way of saying that I was less than those obedient children who were living plural marriage.

(Many parents have a certain standard for their children, and anything different is just not good enough. Maybe my own children who are not active in the LDS Church today feel like I'm that way. I hope not.)

Because the physical and emotional abuse continued when Vince was drunk, I eventually knew I had to get a divorce. Through the Al-anon program I learned to understand him and love him like I never thought I could. I hoped divorce would push him to quit drinking. It didn't. Divorcing Vince was the hardest thing I had ever done. I felt so sorry for him and somehow felt responsible for his misery.

I pleaded with the Lord to protect me from myself. I was so scared to be single, and vulnerable to the loneliness that comes with it. The year I divorced Vince the eczema on the bottoms of my feet became so bad that there was blood in my shoes. The eczema never afflicted my feet again after that year. I've wondered if it was a sign that I just didn't want to move forward.

Vince had never abused the children, he loved them very much. After I divorced him he was very good to me, he helped any time I asked him.

By the time my divorce was final in early 1979, I had a strong belief that the LDS Church was led by a prophet of God. That was a huge step for me. Polygamists do not believe the Church is led by a prophet, which is their major issue with the Church.

I was finally able to go into the Salt Lake Temple. I could hardly believe I was inside that beautiful building. As I watched the serene sisters who worked there, I thought, I want to be one of those women. (Today I am an ordinance worker in the Salt Lake Temple.)

During the eight years that I was single, I had many wonderful miracles happen that helped me with the huge responsibility of being a single mom of eleven children. Partly as a result of those miracles, I finally knew that the Lord knew who I was, knew my name, knew every desire of my heart, and loved me more than I ever had supposed. He knew I needed the temple, a place of refuge, to help me keep my perspective and maintain my standards.

Also at this time my sister Linda, who lived near Park City, made me feel very welcome in bringing my children to her home on weekends as a getaway. Her generosity was a Godsend for me. During that time I was also able to attend Salt Lake Community College and earn an associate degree. Shauna had begun taking parenting classes and encouraged my daughters and I to go with her because by then they had children too.

Then in 1986, after eight years of being single, God provided me with a good man, Lynn Webb, who was able to help me sift through the baggage I had carried for so many years and learn to trust again. He is not an angry person, never uses foul language, and has knocked himself out to earn the love of my children and they do love him. He has four children, so I now have the fifteen children I wanted as a young woman. He dealt gently with my anger for many years as I continued getting the help I needed to get to the bottom of the volcano inside of me.

I have served three missions for the LDS Church with Lynn. Several months after we came home from Australia in 2007, I was watching the news and saw authorities in Texas taking children away from their parents because of a pedophile who had used polygamy to gain access to many children. Day after day I watched this horrible scene of children being herded away from their parents, and I cried so hard.

One day Lynn came in and said, "Why do you watch this if it makes you cry?"

"I don't know," I blubbered, continuing to watch.

I finally found help and was able to get rid of the last of my anger. It's been more than six years now, and though I can get a little tense at times, there is no remaining anger at all inside of me. All of us have baggage, and getting to the bottom of it is hard but necessary for peace and forgiveness. The last fifteen years have been the most content years of my life. Since marrying Lynn, I have never had eczema on my hands. I guess I feel like I now have all the help I need.

The experience of growing up in my family is inextricably connected to my father, for better or for worse. Most of my best memories include my father; teaching me to swim, going to Saratoga Springs, going to Lagoon, cooking hot dogs in the canyon, Sunday drives, rolling Easter eggs on Capitol Hill, Christmas caroling, etc.

I have a deep respect for him because he never gave up and because he served time in prison in defense of his beliefs. As I have matured, I have found that I don't accept some of those beliefs. For example, Dad taught us that God is a punishing God (a form of pressure exerted to convince us to live plural marriage). I believe God blesses us for doing what's right and strengthens us when we have to deal with adversity, that he loves us perfectly no matter what our choices.

Reflecting on the principle of plural marriage, I don't think I set out with a clear course in mind, regardless of what I told everyone (including myself). I straddled the fence between two worlds—polygamy and monogamy—as I dated, believing that plural marriage was the right thing to do but enjoying the fun of dating many "worldly" boys. I tried to convince myself, and the boys I dated, that plural marriage was the "way." However, when I found myself pregnant, I married my baby's father, still convinced on the surface that I wanted to live plural marriage. When it came right down to it, I didn't really want to *live* plural marriage—I just wanted my husband to agree with me. He didn't. I never really took a stand either way. I simply let life happen to me, a course that required no courage at all on my part.

My father's influence created great conflict in my heart. I was supposed to be obedient to my husband but Dad never quit preaching plural marriage, which my husband hated. My husband was so angry I could never please him, and, was his abuse to me worse than Dad's with Aunt Vio, or than Dad brutally beating children who wouldn't obey him? It was really hard to know what I deserved in my own marriage and to know what was truly unacceptable.

The courage for which I always yearned finally came when I realized I was responsible to my children and I had to make a choice. That choice was a process of letting go—of learning to stand my ground with, first my father, and then my husband, even though I knew it would fuel his abuse against me. I knew I had to quit trying to please my father and/or my husband and just focus on how to please God.

I believe that God guided me to the life I currently have outside the polygamist culture. For years, I felt "unworthy" because I wasn't living plural marriage. Today, I feel worthy and extremely happy with the life I have and grateful for the hinges God provided for me to break from polygamy. I believe that God has helped me to be my best self and that I'm doing what He wants me to do. I know that I have made the best choice for me and for my children.

In my first marriage, I tried to be obedient to my husband. In my current marriage, I focus on being obedient to God. My current husband is my partner. We are equals instead of him being my "master." That dynamic demonstrates how much I have been able to distance myself from the atmosphere in the home of my childhood—my father believed he was the master of his wives and children, and strict obedience to him was the rule. In contrast, my husband and I both believe that agency is the rule and that obedience to God brings blessings.

I maintained a good relationship with family members because I'm a "people pleaser" and I knocked myself out to stay close to them despite our differences. I always knew Dad loved me. Mother not so much. I often felt like the "red-headed step child," never as good as the children who chose to live plural marriage. I gave birth to my mother's first grandchildren, and at first I received great attention for that—until other grand kids started multiplying by the dozens from my siblings who were doing "the right thing."

My sisters and I have maintained a good relationship. I respect their right to choose their own course, and all but one of my sisters always respected my choices. Even that one now respects my choices because some of her children have opted to leave the polygamist culture, and they are all very good to her.

Carol Susan

CHAPTER 7

1941

I WAS BORN ON MARCH 30, 1941, the third child of Vio Frazer and the seventeenth child of Albert Barlow.

When I was about eleven, Ramona taught me to ride a bicycle while we were living on the ranch in Duchesne County in 1952. Ramona was "the princess," and we were her subjects. She made everything so much fun for us that we didn't mind doing her jobs for her. I knew she cared about me—unlike Laura, who was bossy, and Faye, who was spoiled because Mother always worried about her.

After we moved back to the Salt Lake Valley we were able to go to the big house at Christmas and play games and have fun together, I love those memories. In the summer we would go up to the canyon and cook hot dogs and hamburgers. It seemed like Dad always got mad at Mom for forgetting something.

I was very shy and school was hard for me. One good thing about that time for me was the fact that I became good friends with Janet Cooper. We remained friends for many years. Because I hated school so much, Dad let me drop out when I was sixteen. School "wasn't important for girls" anyway, according to Dad.

Dad was out of town a lot selling. Once he came home on my birthday and he had bought me a "peg" skirt. I was so surprised because he had never bought me a gift before and he didn't like peg skirts. He thought they were too tight. It made me feel very good.

During my childhood Mother cried a lot because Dad wasn't very nice to her. Mother wasn't the best housekeeper, and I saw Dad throw things on the floor more than once because he didn't like "stuff piled on the furniture." I watched Dad treat my mother differently than he treated either Aunt Kate or Aunt Maurine. I often wondered why he was so unkind to her.

Once when I was a teen, I was taking a bath and Dad burst into the bathroom. I was very uncomfortable—and after standing there for a minute he left. We never locked any doors. If we did he would pound on them till we opened them. It was just easier to leave them unlocked. But this was the first time I was in the tub naked when it happened. He probably hesitated because he needed to use the toilet and had to decide whether to kick me out or use it in front of me. Thank goodness he did neither.

Dad never spanked me, but his strap was always hanging on the wall as a threat. Mom, on the other hand, used a switch on me whenever she was upset about something I had done. Actually her yelling at me was worse than the switch.

I don't remember too much about my siblings who belonged to the other mothers, except Becky. She was always nice to me and protected me and I felt close to her. I also looked up to Ginny.

One day Janet and I were walking down State Street when Gene Peterson and his friend came along and offered us a ride. Gene and I began dating, and when we asked my father if we could get married, he gave his approval because he knew Gene's father. It was 1959, and I was barely eighteen. Before I married Gene, Dad asked me if I was a virgin. When I admitted that I had experienced sex once, he said, "You must tell Gene before he marries you. A man has a right to know if his wife is a virgin."

I swallowed my pride and did as my father insisted. Reflecting on all the things that happened later, I regret it and think it was a big mistake. Telling Gene I wasn't a virgin gave him an excuse to abuse me, and his lack of respect for me was similar to Dad's lack of respect for Mother.

Gene worked for his uncle selling fruit, and at one point he decided to go to Seattle to work with his brother. Without much discussion about it, we packed up and moved to Seattle. Things were not going well in my marriage at all. Gene was always abusive to me, but I believed I deserved it—from my perspective, everything was always my fault. But when he began abusing my small son, David, I knew that wasn't my fault.

In Seattle at that time, Gene could not be arrested for abuse unless there was a witness to the abuse. Finally a neighbor saw him abusing me, and he was arrested. While Gene was behind bars my parents sent my sister Ginny to Seattle to help bring my four young children—Jerry, Kathy, David, and Kennedy—and me back to Salt Lake. I felt that Ginny had saved my life.

Once Gene was released from jail, he followed me to Salt Lake, wanting another chance. I took him back only because I yearned for male companionship and knew it would be wrong to go out with other men. Once I took Gene back, the abuse continued, which was no surprise to me.

I didn't know what to do. I had no money, nowhere to go, and four little kids for whom I was responsible. Again I was rescued by a sibling. One day my brother Ed showed up and started helping me pack my things so I could leave. The second Gene figured out what was going on, he confronted Ed and bellowed, "You are not taking them out of here!"

Ed was firm as he replied, "The hell I'm not! You're not going to beat on her and these kids anymore."

Ed was at least six feet tall, and Gene was not about to take him on in a physical fight. So we continued to pack, and I left Gene for good. I was able to stay with Mom for a while until Dad got me a place to live.

I hooked up with my friend Janet again, and she introduced me to a man named Charles Bogue. He was in the military, so I ended up in Maryland and gave birth to a son we named Andrew Charles. Soon we were shipped out to Germany, where I gave birth to Mary Ann. Because of back injuries Chuck had sustained in a helicopter accident in Vietnam, he received a medical discharge, and we came back to Salt Lake. When we arrived in Salt Lake we moved in with Laura for a few weeks, and Laura registered my daughter Kathy in a school program for children with special needs. Laura ended up keeping Kathy for the full school year since the school where I moved didn't have such a program.

Sadly, Chuck was even more abusive than Gene. He pointed a gun at me once and threatened to shoot me. Then one day Ramona called. My son Kennedy told Ramona's son that Chuck was shooting my boys with a BB gun when he took them fishing. I was horrified. When I told Mother, she told Dad.

Dad told me to leave Chuck. I did.

From the time Chuck qualified for disability, all of his disability checks were sent to his mother. And with Chuck's mother in charge of all the money he was receiving, I didn't get any of it.

One day Chuck came to see the kids and insisted on taking them with him. As he left with his two children—Chuck and Mary Ann—he said, "I'm going to give these kids to my cousin to raise and have you declared an unfit mother."

I called my mother in tears to let her know that Chuck was taking my two children away from me. I was terrified; I loved those children with all my heart, and my baby girl was only a year old.

Dad helped me find a lawyer then told me to pretend I wanted Chuck back. I had to be very sneaky about carrying out my plan, but I was able to do it with the help of a friend whose husband hated Chuck. He got Chuck very drunk one day, and I was able use that little window of time to get a court order. Chuck was legally ordered to move out of the house and leave our children to me.

Dad and Aunt Katie helped me buy a home in Rose Park, Utah, where I lived until I married Michael Buchanin. We asked Dad to buy the house from us so Mike could use the money to buy a trailer. We packed up all the kids and moved first to Colorado; then to Evanston, Wyoming; and finally to Boise, Idaho. Mike was a kind, generous man who took good care of my kids and me when he was sober. But he was also a mean drunk—and I finally divorced him when I got tired of his drinking.

Because my children were growing up away from my family, I would find a way every year, to take them to Salt Lake so they could spend time with my family. Mother's children all made me feel very welcome to invade their homes with my six kids. My children have great memories of these visits to Salt Lake City.

Soon after divorcing Mike, I met Frederick Rains. We were married only a few months when he went to prison. I faithfully visited him every week for ten years, but when he got out he was such a jerk that I divorced him too. That was enough for me—no more marriages.

In 2012, my son Chuck was working with a circus in Texas when he was found dead in his quarters. His wife had him cremated, so I was never able to see him and say good-bye. That was so hard for me.

I'm very grateful I went against my parents' beliefs and got my tubes tied. It took a lot of courage for me to do, but I never could have managed had I continued to have children. I'm grateful for the precious six that I was given, but I knew at the time I could not take care of any more. I'm now living in a good senior care facility in Boise Idaho and Jerry visits me every week, bringing David with him sometimes. Mary Ann has always been the stable one in my family, the most responsible one who seems to be able to smooth out all the wrinkles for me. I've started doing some artwork that I really enjoy.

I know I left a piece of myself in Salt Lake City and there are times when I wish I lived closer to my sisters. They're all very good to me. I'm aware that God was watching out for me many times in my life when I wouldn't have survived without His help. I know I'm supposed to be in the care facility I'm in because I help a lot of people here to adjust to this environment. I've mentioned a few times that I'd like to go live in Salt Lake and they always say, "You can't leave us, we'd miss you too much."

I know God helped me to be where I am.

Rebecca Ann

CHAPTER 8

1941

I WAS BORN in the old family home at 1538 South 400 East in Salt Lake City, Utah, on October 14, 1941, to Katie and Albert Barlow. I was Father's eighteenth child and the twelfth of Mother's thirteen children. I have many fond memories of the old home where all three families lived. Mother's bedroom was on the main floor in the "parlor," and Maurine and Vio, along with their children, had rooms upstairs. Most of Mother's children were in bedrooms in the basement. As children, we roamed wherever we wanted to go in that big house. I often pestered Aunt Vio with tons of questions until she said, "Why don't you go tell your mother she wants you."

"Okay," I'd say, and off I'd run to tell Mama exactly that.

At first I was always excited when Daddy came home, because he set me on his lap and read the Sunday funnies to me. Then one day I watched as he whipped all the big kids. I wasn't sure that he wouldn't whip me too, so after that I hid from him, extremely afraid of him. It wasn't long before he went to prison, and though I missed him, it was nice to be able to relax, unafraid of being beaten.

Because there were so many of us we children had great fun together. My older brothers built stilts and taught us to walk on them. We also played hopscotch, tag, hide-and-seek, and the other fun games kids played in those days. Once, Loni and I talked Doug into putting on some lipstick and a play dress. We were sure we could fool Mama into thinking he was someone else. Of course, she played along with us—and we were so thrilled that we had fooled her.

When Daddy was released from prison in 1946, he moved Aunt Vio and Aunt Maurine out of the big house so that he could avoid being arrested again for practicing plural marriage. I was sad that my other siblings—who were my best friends—were gone. I wasn't completely cut off from them. However, they rode the bus to our house as often as they could, that big house had a lot of room for hide-and-seek and other games.

I loved it when the boys and Ruthie came home from school. I adored them when I was small. Lee was an especially sweet brother. When he joined the Navy, I was able to go downtown and see him off on the train. He picked me up and took me on board with him, lifting me up so I could see out the window. I remember with great joy that some of the young men passed me over their heads to the door, where my smiling mother took me in her arms.

IW, John, and Doug sold newspapers on the street corner downtown, and I later learned that they gave most of what they earned to Mama. One year as Christmas was approaching. She asked what I most wanted for Christmas. I innocently told her that I wanted a doll with blonde hair and a pink dress. Christmas morning Loni and I both received dolls. I later learned that John had bought the dolls. A few years later I asked for a storybook doll, and John bought that for me too. He was always generous to us.

Ruthie was also kind to Loni and me, and I had a deep sense that she loved me. She took good care of us, putting our hair up in rags or metal curlers so we would look nice when she took us to LDS meetings on Sunday.

Because Mama had so many responsibilities weighing on her, Ruth was our "other mother." Once, Ruthie got Loni and me into a church play. We stood on one side of the stage in our brand-new pajamas and said a poem about why we were on stage. Ruth was so proud of us. She taught me how to clean, kept us in clean clothes, and shined our shoes. She even had me read to her every night, telling me that I'd be held back in school if I didn't learn to read better.

I suppose Loni and I were actually her "live dolls" from the time we were born. She was my best friend during my developing years, and I owe her a great deal for helping me with self-esteem when I reached a very low point in my life.

I loved going to the LDS Church Primary after school and to the Church's Sunday school on Sunday. I remember the first time I heard about Jesus. Holding up a picture of Him, the teacher told us that Jesus was the Son of our Father in Heaven and that He loved us very much. She told us that He made all the birds, flowers, trees, and everything. Her lesson penetrated my heart so deeply that I never forgot it.

Shortly after Halloween in 1951, we moved to a ranch in Weber County. At the ranch, Loni, Doug, and I were always together. Doug had an accordion that he could play by ear, so he could play any song we requested. The small room we played in most had two small windows through which Loni and I would watch the trains go by. One time the train stopped, and Mother let us take a warm loaf of bread and some jam out to the men in the caboose.

The snow that winter was six feet deep, and the boys made the most wonderful sledding track for us. John put me in front of him on the big sled and we careened down the track. In the spring I watched as John harnessed the two horses and, walking behind them, plowed the big fields so we could plant tomatoes and potatoes. One day Dad brought some of the other siblings out to the farm, and all the kids decided to race our three horses down the long dirt driveway. I decided to run over to where most of the kids were just as the horses were running by. One of the horses knocked me over and kicked me, breaking off my back teeth. I was fairly shaken up by the experience.

My brother David and his family lived in a trailer next to the house. One day Mom was in the city and Betty, Dave's wife, was watching us. I wouldn't get out of bed, so she sent David in to persuade me to get up. He resorted to what he figured would be a foolproof method: He put a blow snake on the bottom of my bed. I jumped up screaming as loudly as I could. The more I screamed, the more he laughed. When I finally stopped screaming, he apologized to me.

When we sat down to eat, I refused to eat what Dave's wife, Betty, had cooked. It was awful. When she threatened to whip me for not eating, I ran into the closet. I heard her voice through the closet door saying, "If you like it so much in there then you can stay in there." With that, she locked the door. Dave had already left for work.

I started to cry, and of course Loni felt worried. Betty turned to Loni and threatened, "You'll go in there too if you try to open the door." With that, Loni started crying too. I cried so hard for so long that my face was covered with tears and snot.

Loni finally went out to the field and got Johnnie. He took me out of the closet, gently cleaned up my face, and tenderly held me until I stopped crying. That experience affected me for the rest of my life. To this day, I spend as little time as possible in small rooms, even the bathroom. I don't even like sitting in a doctor's exam room unless there is someone with me. Just remembering the experience makes me cry.

Nine months later we moved to the town of Bluebell in Duchesne County. Each day when we got home from school we were expected to change clothes immediately, feed the animals, and do any other chores we were told to do. There was a lot of work to be done on the ranch: we had twenty-four cows, a big flock of chickens, lots of rabbits, two geese, three horses, and two pigs. Loni and I did whatever we were told, but because we were still quite young the brunt of the work fell to the others.

While we were on the ranch we had many visitors—nieces, nephews, and the siblings from the other two families. I'm sure those visits were hard on Mom, creating even more work for her, but I loved it.

One time the feed for the cows got so low Mom was begging God in her constant prayers to help her find a way to feed them. As she was praying one day, she felt prompted to go outside. She followed the prompting and saw a farm truck filled with a load of hay barreling down the road. As the truck pulled up to her, the driver leaned out of the window and said, "So—you are the person I'm supposed to deliver this hay to. The Spirit told me to load the truck with hay and drive down the road, where I would see a woman standing by the road. I was to unload the hay for her."

Mom was so stunned she was speechless. She pointed to the barn and followed the truck, watching as the man unloaded the hay. When we arrived home from school she eagerly shared the story of the amazing miracle with us. Our Father in Heaven had watched out for us again.

While some folks were kind to us, there were many in Bluebell who were not. I don't know if it was because of our lifestyle or because we were simply "outsiders." When I finally got the chance to go to 4-H camp, I was thrilled—but one other girl and I were treated so badly that I couldn't wait to get home. I was heartbroken and never went to camp again.

One day Mom was gone and IW was in charge. He began hollering at Loni and me to get the breakfast dishes done. Before we could do anything, he lost his temper and began to physically abuse me by smacking me on the head, shoving me across the room, and knocking me to the floor in the kitchen. Just then Lee pulled up with his wife and rescued us; he took us to his place in Vernal until Mom returned. About a year later, Lee died from a blood clot in his brain. I was devastated. He was the kindest soul, always playing with us, putting us on his shoulders, and buying us ice cream cones.

Despite the considerable efforts of Dad's whole family, we lost the ranches and moved back to Salt Lake. Dad bought a home in Murray for Mom's family and one in South Salt Lake for Aunt Vio and her children. Aunt Maurine stayed in the big house because by then she had the most kids at home. Mom and my brothers got jobs right away. Loni and I took whatever babysitting jobs we could get to help out. Doug, who had been so much fun, started drinking when we moved back to the city, which caused a lot of negative changes in him.

When I started junior high school I met my best friend, Patty Withers. She and Patty Rice watched out for me when Dad was arrested in 1955. Dad's picture was on the front page of the local paper, and there were some kids who wanted to beat me up because I was part of a polygamous family. Patty Withers, Patty Rice, and several other kids surrounded me, protecting me from the bullies.

It was a very difficult time for me. At about this same time, a man for whom I was babysitting molested me. When I came home I got in the shower and cried as the water washed over me but couldn't wash away the horror of what had just happened to me. As the hot water turned cold I knew the dirty feeling I had wasn't going to go away. I suffered a great loss of confidence as a result. I didn't talk to anyone about it for many years.

My sister Ginny helped me get my first real job at Painter's A&W as a car hop. I turned my paychecks over to Mother and used the tips to buy school books and clothes. It was about this time that Dad went to prison again, and I needed to live closer to my job. I moved in with Arlene for a while until her husband put the moves on me. Once that happened, I went to live at Aunt Maurine's house. She was always very nice to me.

During this time my brother Ed and I went to several dances together. We never told anyone we were related. We were so good that we were awarded a couple of albums as prizes in dance contests. I loved him for doing that with me. About that same time, Ruthie helped me get into a finishing school that helped restore some of my battered confidence. As a result, I met and dated quite a few decent guys.

In 1959, after Dad entered the Utah State Penitentiary, Mother's children helped her buy a home in Bountiful, just north of Salt Lake City, she asked me to move home again. By then I had a car, and I found a job at Hill Air Force Base working on a lunch truck out of Salt Lake City. It was a period during which I had so much fun dancing at the Rainbow, where I saw Nat King Cole, the Everly Brothers, and other popular performances.

I was having too much fun for Mother's liking, and one day she told me I needed to settle down and put the fun behind me. She and I prayed together that I would find the right man to marry. A few days later I was at work, taking money from the customers when the Spirit whispered, "This is the man you are to marry."

I looked up at the person from whom I had just taken money. I was a little shocked. His name was Rod Ringler. When I arrived home and told Mother what happened, she asked, "What are you going to do with this information?"

I shrugged. "I don't know," I said.

She suggested I invite him to dinner, and the rest is history. We planned to be married in November, but he got military orders to go to England and had to leave on August 23—so we obviously couldn't wait until November. We were married in Mother's home in Bountiful on July 21, 1960. We lived with Mother until Rod left for England, he was very kind to her.

In March 1961 I arrived in England to a small flat in the little town of Huntstanton in Norfolk County. Neither of us had ever had a place of our own, so setting up housekeeping was quite a foreign experience. I arrived on a Saturday, and all the shops in the village were closed. Rod took me to a fellow airman's place for dinner, and we spent the evening talking. I wanted to be held in that big lug's arms, and he would hardly touch me. That evening when I complained about his being so distant, he said, "The guys have been teasing me and told me not to get all lovey-dovey and mushy when you got here or it would embarrass them."

He definitely made up for it.

We managed to get by over the next few days. The landlady furnished us with a blanket and some sheets; we had pillows from the barracks, but no food. We were invited to lunch on Sunday. On Monday we were so slow getting out the door that all the shops were closed again—unbeknownst to both of us, the village shut down every day from 11 am. to 2 pm. I was getting very hungry, and Rod was not prepared—he was totally new at being the husband in charge, and he was embarrassed because of it. You might say we were living on love. We managed to borrow some groceries, and eventually we got into the swing of things. There were several wonderful couples that we became close to in England. Some became lifelong friends.

I had always wanted to be a member of the LDS Church, and one day I saw two LDS missionaries walking down the street toward town. I ran up behind them, linked my arms through theirs, and proclaimed, "I want to be baptized." They came to our home and gave us the discussions, and Rodney and I were baptized in the mission home in Petersboro while we were stationed at Sculthrope Air Base. I was seven months pregnant with my first child.

Mother wasn't there to help me understand the pregnancy, nor was she there when Ruthie was born on January 31, 1962. In fact, Rodney wasn't even there for her birth, he was on an alert pad on base. The whole thing was a little frightening for me, but I learned that we sure do grow up and learn fast under those kinds of circumstances.

When Rod got orders to go to France, we took the train to London and then took a cab to the airport. The cab driver drove us past Buckingham Palace. It was magnificent, and I've always been glad we had even that short glimpse. When we got to France, we flew over Paris. It was wonderful!

We were stationed at Phalsbourg, Moselle, France. It was on top of a mountain and was bitter cold in the winter. Getting there with an infant was quite an adventure. At one hotel I kept Ruthie's milk cold by running water in the bidet and letting the milk sit in the water, hoping she would drink it before it got sour. At that time I also realized I was starting another pregnancy.

While we were stationed in France we had a chance to rent a used Volkswagen so we could see some sights. We saw an old castle that had been blown apart during WWI, and we toured a concentration camp the Germans had built in that part of the mountains. It was extremely difficult for me to see the gas chambers and the ovens in the concentration camp. It's still hard to understand that humans can do such terrible things to each other.

Renate' was born in March 1963 at Tou laRoseier Air Base in France. Her birth happened too quickly for her father to witness it. I sometimes complained to Rodney that he was always gone, and he reminded me that the Air Force was his first wife. I was his second.

He was determined to have a retirement income for his family. Before we married, I told Rod I wanted to have fifteen children. He grinned and said, "That's fine, but you need to understand that you will have to raise them pretty much on your own. My orders from the government come first."

Ruthie loved her baby sister, she became my little confidant. We shared everything. Rodney was sent to Libya eight months after we arrived in France. I had very little money and found it extremely hard to scrape by. Rod came home one week before Christmas to find that for the previous three months our baby had been living on canned milk and Cream of Wheat and that I had been living on tuna, bread, and milk. He was furious until he found out there were other families who were in the same boat.

Our experience in Europe certainly wasn't all drudgery. Rod's brother, Harry, and his wife, Renate', were stationed just across the border in Germany at Ramstine Air Base. We were able to go see them twice while we were there. I was also able to go to the Oktoberfest once, which was such a fun experience.

When Rod's squadron received orders to go to New Mexico and Rod's name was not on the roster, we were so happy. We had been hoping to be released from the 366 Fighter Squadron because it was always being assigned to temporary duty. Everyone around us was packing up to go when the other shoe dropped—we found out we were going too. Our little family of four left the base right from the flight line. The good part was that they loaded us up, babies and all, so we didn't have to deal with any buses, trains, or commercial planes. It is so hard to travel in a foreign land with little children.

We bought a Volkswagen before we left France. It was brand-new and it was paid for. We found it waiting for us in New Jersey when we arrived at the air base there. In the short time we had before Rod had to report to his unit we decided to visit our parents and show off their new grand kids so we bought a roof rack for the car, a small cooler and found a cheap motel. The next morning we headed for South Fork, Pennsylvania, where Rod's folks lived. We had a wonderful reunion and our adorable babies were a big hit with their grandparents.

After only two days we headed for Utah. We were so poor we conserved every way possible. Rodney had been given only one week from the time he left France to report to the Holloman Air Base in New Mexico. It sometimes felt as if the military treated everyone the same instead of considering those men and women who needed to care for families.

At one point on our journey to Utah we stopped when we saw a picnic table on someone's front lawn. We started feeding our girls when a lady came out of the house and offered us some lemonade. It was so cold and sweet, I really appreciated that. We drove almost non-stop because we had so little time.

When I saw the beautiful Salt Lake Valley I cried, I was so glad to be home. It felt wonderful to hug and kiss my mother. I had not seen her in almost three years. I was excited to show her my two little girls and for them to see their grandmother. Two days later Rod left us there and drove to New Mexico to check in at the base.

Rod found us a little two-bedroom furnished house. After cleaning it up and painting it, he came to Salt Lake to get his little family. I had only spent two weeks with Mother, but I knew I wasn't that far away now and felt confident that I would see her again soon.

We were only in our "cute little house" for a week when we realized it was infested with bedbugs and roaches. I was horrified. We moved out the next day. We were at Holloman for only two and a half years and Rod was in Alaska for four months of that time. When Ralene was born in May 1964, Ruthie thought she was her own real, live doll.

My little girls were my best friends and playmates. I didn't have a phone, so I didn't talk much to anyone, but I received great letters from Rod while he was away. When he was home, he was the most loving and kind husband and father. I felt so blessed.

When Rod was sent to Vietnam for a year, my sister Ginny came and helped me drive the girls to Utah so I could be with Mother while Rod was gone. Even better, my sister Ruth lived close by and we had some great times with our children together. This was such a comfort to me, as I had such a fear that Rod would be killed. Some of our neighbors from New Mexico were killed. I cried much of the first month we were apart.

Little Rodney was born in May 1966 while Rod was away. After that we were sent to Goldsboro, North Carolina, where we became active in the LDS Church. Of all the places we had lived, the people in Goldsboro were the friendliest.

I gave birth to Rebecca in January 1968—and Rodney still hadn't witnessed any of the five children's births. Our life was great, even though Rodney spent half the time in Florida. When he was sent to a tech school in Texas, we decided to go to Utah so I could stay with my family while he was in school.

While we were in Utah, we went to the Salt Lake Temple on October 3, 1968, to receive our endowments and be sealed as a family. Our escorts in the temple were the bishop who married us in July 1961 and his wife. When they brought our children into the sealing room all dressed in white, I started to cry. The memory still makes me emotional. Rebecca wouldn't hold still, so we did a lot of chuckling.

Rodney got me and the kids settled in Arlene's home and then drove to Texas. I enjoyed my family for a while, but with five children I began to feel like I was a burden to Arlene and her new husband. I called Rod and told him I needed to come to Texas. He was more than happy to reunite our family, and he sent me enough money so the kids and I could take the bus to Texas.

Five little kids on a bus is not the best situation. As if that weren't a big enough challenge, three hundred miles into our journey we got a new driver. He looked at my tickets and said, "You don't have enough money for all of you to get to Texas."

I began to cry. I pleaded with him, saying, "I bought what they told me I needed. I don't have any more money. I have five kids here, and the baby is only ten months old."

He grunted and turned away. Then he called out over his shoulder, "If anyone complains about those kids, you are outta here."

I prayed all the way to Texas, and seeing Rodney was a huge relief. We lived in a very small trailer, but we were so happy to be together. It was our first Christmas together since he had returned from Vietnam.

Rodney got orders for the Philippines, so we left Texas and headed back to North Carolina so the packers could box up our things. The kids and I were off to Utah so I could be close to Mother while Rodney was gone. He barely had enough time to get us settled in a home in Utah before he left for the Philippines. Soon after he left I found out I was pregnant again—it was all those going-away and coming-home presents. And because we had been in Texas, we had done it up big. I was expecting twins.

By the end of my second trimester, I had to farm my kids out because I was too big to take care of them. At six months, I was already the size of a nine-month pregnancy. My doctor finally got hold of the base commander and had Rod sent home to help. And with that, he actually got to see his first babies born. Rachel came first at 8 pounds 15 ounces, and Robert was a very close second at 8 pounds 14 ounces. I almost bled to death, receiving twenty-two pints of blood and undergoing a hysterectomy. I was only twenty-seven years old. It was the end of my dream to have fifteen children, but that obviously was not the Lord's will. I'm just thankful it's all behind me.

Rod was home for only a month when he was sent back to the Philippines. I really tried to take care of our kids by myself, but it was hard. I had three babies in diapers and cribs. I couldn't quit crying.

I refused to impose my responsibilities onto little Ruthie and Renate', and finally Mother intervened. She called my doctor, and he called a psychiatrist. The psychiatrist had me committed to a psychiatric ward (where I stayed for three weeks) so the government would bring Rod home. He also enlisted the help of Utah Senator Frank Moss to get Rod home for one year. At the end of that year he got orders to leave again, but Senator Moss talked them into letting Rod stay for another year.

We had moved onto Hill Air Force Base, and it was a wonderful two years for our family. Rodney had become the crew chief for the base commander's airplane. So when he got orders to go to Thailand he took the orders straight to the base commander, meeting him as he landed on his return from Washington, DC. Rod was standing at the bottom of the ramp with the order in his hand. When the commander approached, Rod briefly explained our plight. The commander took the orders from Rod and said, "Ringler, you will never have to leave this base again."

We were thrilled—we had given up any thought of ever getting out of the 366 Fighter Squadron. We were now able to buy a new home in Layton, our income was so low that we qualified for a government 235 loan but we were ecstatic. We moved in May 1971. We raised all of our children to adulthood in that house and had two of their weddings in our back yard. We also held our twenty-fifth wedding anniversary party there.

Rodney was always so good for me. Once I was having a strong disagreement with him, and I turned from him in anger, saying, "Kiss my butt."

He came up behind me and kissed my butt. How could I not love that big lug? After the way some of my brothers treated me and the man who molested me, I wondered if I would ever feel worthwhile. Rod helped me heal from the hurt, anger, and low self-esteem I carried as I was growing up by giving me unconditional love. He was patient, gentle, and caring, which was a real gift to this feisty woman.

In May 1991 Rodney had a grand-male seizure just as a meeting he was in at work was concluding. Subsequent medical testing and surgery revealed that he had a gioblastoma, which is a malignant tumor. We fell back on our faith as he learned of his cancer diagnosis.

We always had family prayer, read our scriptures as a family in the morning, and had family home evening every week. Rod and I prayed together, especially as we struggled with different difficult times. My children often tell me they are so grateful they were raised in the LDS Church. I'm just as grateful I was able to raise them in The Church.

My sister-in-law is a cousin to LDS Church President Thomas S. Monson who was an apostle at this time. She asked him if he would give Rod a priesthood blessing. We went up to his office for the blessing. I was disappointed, because he didn't bless Rod to be well. As we got up to leave, President Monson said, "Wait a minute, young lady—you need a blessing more than he does."

I don't remember what he said, but I felt a great comfort, and I'm sure that's why I was able to get through that challenge in my life. My girls all came home to help me with their father. I couldn't have managed without them. These things are never easy, but with the Lord's help they are bearable.

A few of my siblings who came to see Rod before he left us.

I was numb. He had been my best friend ever, and he would continue to be that for all eternity. After he died on December 27, 1991 I couldn't function. I couldn't take the Christmas decorations down—and, in fact, I had a hard time finding a reason to live. Ginny came one day in January and helped me put all the Christmas paraphernalia away.

A neighbor who had lost her husband the same month Rod was diagnosed invited me to a Good Grief Group at Larkin Mortuary in Ogden. It helped me a lot to be with a group of people who were dealing with the same feelings I had. In fact, I even found it uplifting.

As I began to see light again, I was walking in the neighborhood and saw Grant Peterson, a friend and neighbor, raking his leaves. I asked about his wife, who was quite ill. Elsie died on Grant's birthday, February 19, 1992. I went to her viewing and told Grant to call me if he needed someone to talk to. About three weeks later he called, and I invited him to join our grief support group.

There were about six of us in the group, and we went to some dances, movies, and plays together. Grant took me to some family gatherings, one at the Red Flame in Bountiful. We danced and had a great time. When he took me home that night, I reached out to shake his hand, as was our custom. Instead, he grabbed me and gave me a kiss.

I was so shaken I ran into the house and started to cry. Soon I was sobbing. Had I betrayed Rod? Finally I knelt by my bed and cried to the Lord, sharing all my feelings. I heard Him whisper, "This is a good man."

I stopped crying and felt the comfort of the Holy Spirit. Grant and I became inseparable. We had a wonderful time getting to really know each other, comparing our past lives and the great love we had for our first partners. We have now been married for twenty-two years. Grant, who has cancer, is eighty-six, and I'm seventy-two. I feel so blessed to have been married to two very sweet men.

I'm grateful for the wonderful sisters with whom I've been blessed to share experiences and for the love that was extended to me by Aunt Vio and Aunt Maurine. I'm grateful to our father for all the brothers and sisters who came through him. And, of course, I'm grateful for Mother, who was always there for me.

I have a profound love for the Savior Jesus Christ—for His great love for me and for His infinite sacrifice for me. I know He loves us all and wants us to return to live with our Father in Heaven. I am also grateful for my membership in the LDS Church and for the guidance I have received through my church membership and my relationship with the Savior.

I knew my father loved Jesus Christ, and I have a great deal of respect for that. However, that's where my respect for my father ends. I had no relationship with him after I saw him beat my older brothers when I was only three. I strictly avoided him after that. Any ability he had to influence me ended with that brutal display of abuse.

When it came time for me to marry, my decision was not influenced one way or another by my father or by watching his relationship with his wives. It was based on an answer to prayer. Out of respect, I took Rodney to visit my father in prison before we married. After sizing Rodney up, Dad said, "You're going to marry him no matter what I say, aren't you?"

"Yes," I responded. "The Spirit told me he's the man I'm to marry, and I'm going to follow the Spirit."

To his credit, Dad told me that's exactly what I should do. Many years later, my father tried to talk Rod and me into living plural marriage. We respectfully declined.

For me, my choice to live a monogamous lifestyle was not what required courage. In my situation the courage came in following my husband to Europe and having my children there. I was so far from home and family. I missed my mother desperately, and we were so poor. But I am happy with my lifestyle and the experiences I have had, I would do it all over again.

Despite my father's initial reluctance over my decision to marry Rodney and to choose a monogamous marriage, my parents always seemed respectful of my husband and of my choice. In addition, I have enjoyed a good relationship with my siblings and value the friendship I have with my sisters.

Laura Smith

CHAPTER 9

1943

I WAS BORN FEBRUARY 7, 1943, to Albert and Vio Barlow—Vio's fourth child and third daughter. My name, Laura Smith, has great meaning to me: I was named after my paternal grandfather's second wife. Even though she died when I was only six years old, knowing her and hearing about her impacted my life tremendously.

My story is about the faith and prayers that brought me to where I am today.

In 1948, when I was about five years old, I was saying my nightly prayers with Mama when I asked, "Please let us have a new baby." I had asked for the same thing every night for some time. When I finished praying, Mama said, "Laura, you don't have to pray for a baby any more. The Lord has heard your prayers, I'm going to have a baby."

I jumped up and down with great excitement, crying, "Now I'm going to pray that it's a boy!"

Mama quickly said, "No, Honey, don't do that. Heavenly Father will give us whatever He has for us." Six months later, my prayers were answered when Bob was born. Perhaps because of my prayer experience, I always felt a close bond with Bob.

One day when I was very young, Mama said, "I count on you to watch out for Susan and Faye while I'm working for Aunt Kate. You're strong; I know you can do it."

The three of us were really quite close in age. Faye was a year and a half younger than I, but Susan was two years older. Looking back I understand what she meant by strong was that I was very strong-willed and had a lot of common sense for one so young.

Vio's family 1988. Left to right: Susan, Ramona, Ron, Bob, Evelyn, Faye; bottom, left to right: Mother Vio, Laura.

In 1952, when I was nine, we moved to Mountain Home, Utah, a small town in Duchesne County. There was always a lot of work to do, and we could play only after all our chores were done. I helped Ramona milk cows, chase pigs, and other chores. We didn't have television or any of the electronic entertainment so common today.

I was about ten when I was left in charge of Susan, Faye, Bob, and Evelyn while Mom went to Aunt Kate's for dinner. As she was leaving, she told me, "When all the chores are done, you can each have a gumball. Call me when you've finished your work, and I'll tell you where they are."

We were so excited—we seldom got candy, and even less often got gum! Because we shared a party line with ten different families, getting hold of Mom when the chores were done was not easy, but we finally got our gumballs and were blissfully sucking on them when suddenly two-and-a-half-year-old Evelyn grabbed her throat and started to choke. My mild concern—curiosity, really—turned into panic when I realized that Evelyn couldn't breathe.

I grabbed her and, screaming a prayer, began pounding on her back. Instead of sucking in the breath I hoped for, she became limp in my arms. As my panic was escalating almost out of control, I saw headlights coming down our lane. When my married brother Dave drove up to the house, I ran outside with Evelyn flopping in my arms, screaming at the top of my lungs, "HELP! SHE'S DYING! There's a gumball stuck in her throat!"

Dave grabbed Evelyn out of my arms, reached into her mouth, and flipped the gumball out. The color immediately returned to her cheeks, and she was fine. I knew Heavenly Father had come through for me again, this time saving my little sister's life. Dave told me he had a prompting to stop at our house on his way home.

We moved back to Salt Lake City, and Mom, with her family, lived in a small three-bedroom home in South Salt Lake. It was then that I began to attend "mutual," a program for teenagers in the LDS Church, with some school friends.

Once, when I was about fourteen, I was at Aunt Maurine's house waiting for Dad to take me home. Aunt Maurine wasn't home; the only ones there were some of her smaller kids. Suddenly Dad spilled something that quickly spread all over the floor. He yelled at me to get a rag. I didn't know where the rags were and said so. His already loud voice increasing in volume bellowed, "I SAID GET ME A RAG!"

I looked around for a few minutes but really didn't know where to look for a rag. I went back to him and said, "I don't know where any rags are, Dad."

He slapped my face so hard it almost knocked me down as he screamed, "DON'T TALK BACK TO ME."

I turned on my heel and quickly walked to the front door. He hollered, "Laura, where do you think you're going? YOU GET BACK HERE!"

I turned to face him saying, "Go to hell."

I walked out the door and I took the bus home. That simple act took a lot of courage, because it was the first time I had ever talked back to Dad. He arrived at Mom's shortly after I did and came in the house asking for me. For obvious reasons, I was terrified of him, but I slowly came into the living room. Dad looked at me and said, "I'm sorry, Laura. I was wrong."

I was totally shocked by his response and his demeanor. His apology helped me see him in a more human light. On the other hand, maybe he was mellower with me and reacted the way he did because he was still undergoing the legal fight to stay out of prison. Lashing out at me in an abusive way wouldn't have persuaded anyone to let him stay at home.

In 1961 I turned sixteen, and I began to date. I was never serious with any of the boys I dated. Dad had been sent to prison for living plural marriage, and one day his brothers and a brother-in-law, George Denos, went to visit him there. I didn't know George, but he had noticed me—and the reason he went to see Dad was to ask if he could begin taking me out. Dad told George that he had other daughters who were almost old enough to start dating but that "Laura is a rebel." George just smiled and said he'd like to see me anyway.

When George came to see me with his wife, Marion, they invited me to join their family. I told them I would pray about it, but the whole time I was thinking, There is no way I'll marry him.

Imagine how surprised I was when I did pray, and the whole room lit up with a light brighter than the noonday sun. That was enough of a sign for me. I knew right then that I was supposed to marry George.

I actually fell in love with George's wife Marion before I loved him. She became my mentor, friend, and sister. I still love her very much. George was extremely nice but definitely a pushover. But because of my powerful answer to prayer, I knew I was where I was supposed to be—so, in spite of some terrible circumstances, I stayed and managed to keep putting one foot in front of the other as I grew to love him.

I was living in a tiny two-bedroom apartment and pregnant with my seventh child—extremely difficult conditions in even the very best of situations. My brother Steve came to visit one day. He told me that he had a home in West Valley City—in Salt Lake County—and that he was going to quit-claim the home to me. He literally saved my sanity and likely saved my life along with it by allowing me to get out of the cramped quarters in which I had been living. We moved into the home, and the payment was only $75 a month—something we could handle.

Marion and I decided to send our children to the LDS Church because the polygamist teens were doing a lot of drinking, which neither of us liked. My Mormon neighbors enveloped me in love and kindness. We had been living in West Valley City for about fifteen years when six of my children chose to be baptized into the LDS Church. Later, two of my sons served missions for the Church, something of which I am very proud.

The year I was fifty-nine, things started going downhill. First I was diagnosed with breast cancer, and soon after I lost one of my grandchildren. Two years later my cancer seemed to be in remission when George was diagnosed with prostate cancer. As if that wasn't bad enough, the day he was diagnosed I suffered a heart attack.

Two days before George died just the two of us were together in his room. We had a very sweet talk that was a great comfort to me after he died. Since then he has come to me to let me know how much he loves me.

I was always a hard worker, and I worked a full-time job during most of the time I was having my sixteen children. It was extremely difficult to work full time and balance my responsibilities in our home, but my children were a huge help to me. The older children even paid me for room and board when they got jobs of their own.

Today I have fifty grand kids, and they are such a joy to me. Three of my children are active in the LDS Church. I have recently become a member of The Church, and feel very grateful for my membership in the Church.

As I look back over my life, making the decision to choose plural marriage was one of the most difficult decisions I've ever made. I knew all about plural marriage, including both the good and the bad aspects of it, because I watched it every day within the walls of my childhood home. Because of what I saw, I knew from a young age that I did not want to be part of a plural marriage. In fact, I always said I would not live plural marriage—undoubtedly something my father chalked up merely to my "rebellious" nature instead of to some very real aversion.

Much of my refusal to live plural marriage had to do directly with my father. I watched the way he treated my mother, and I knew I never wanted to be treated that way. If being part of a plural marriage opened the door to that type of mistreatment, I wanted nothing to do with it. It didn't occur to me that the problem was my father, not the institution of plural marriage.

For years I refused to entertain the possibility of plural marriage, and for years I publicly and loudly stated my opposition to it. You can only imagine the surprise of all those around me then, especially that of my family, when I announced that I would be joining a plural marriage. It was a move that required real courage and was possible only after a strong witness from God.

When my friends learned that I had decided to become a plural wife, they were distraught. Many of them cried. All of them tried to talk me out of it. The only thing that gave me the courage to pursue my course was my own stubborn determination fueled by my remarkable answer to prayer. As I became part of that family, I learned that George was nothing like my father. It took me a long time, but today I love and respect my father in spite of the way he treated his wives, children, and others. I realize he did the best he could with what he was given and with the experiences he had growing up.

Plural marriage was hard, but I was happy. I believe I was blessed for following the prompting of the Spirit and for obeying my answer to prayer—and I feel my choice was a good and appropriate one for me. Today I am happy for my membership in the LDS Church, something I had always wanted and something that has, of necessity, distanced me from the principle of plural marriage.

My family was shocked when I decided to marry George as a plural wife, but they always treated me with love and respect. I never felt any sort of strained relationship with my sisters over my choices, and my closeness to them is one of the joys of my life today. Regardless of where they are in relationship to plural marriage, I am one of them—I lived it and learned from it and loved my husband and his other wife, and now I am involved in a lifestyle that does not endorse plural marriage, giving me something in common with my sisters who have chosen monogamy.

In both stages of my life I have known great joy, and I try to respect and recognize the joy that my sisters feel in their various situations. We grew up under the same roof and lived a life there that moved from the chaotic to the sublime, and what makes us alike is much greater than what makes us different.

Alhona Rae (Loni)

CHAPTER 10

1943

I WAS BORN JULY 19, 1943, the last of Kate Kilgrow's thirteen children and the twenty-first of Albert Barlow's children. I had a very early exposure to The LDS Church. My sister Ruthie often took Rebecca and me to Sunday school in the LDS meetinghouse in our neighborhood. Rebecca and I also enjoyed going to Primary during the week. I still have the green felt bandelo and awards I earned at that time.

I was often sad as a child, crying a lot for no reason. As I reflect on that, it seems there were always a lot of people around—so many that it stressed me. Whenever my mother left to go somewhere, I clung to her legs and screamed because I was afraid she was not going to come back and Ruthie had to hold me and console me. I had such a terrible fear of losing Mama that I often stood under her apron and held onto her legs. On those times, Ruthie again had to come to the rescue, pulling me off and holding me so Mama could get dinner ready.

I remember sitting on the front porch reading the Sunday comics----who am I kidding? The pictures were great. I loved that sort of thing. Rebecca and I used to run down the street to meet the mailman as he walked up to deliver our mail.

Mama had several boarders she had to feed, and she also took care of their children while they were at work. It's easy to imagine, our food budget was stretched quite thin. At that time we also had a dog named Spike. One day when I was about seven, Mama sent me to the grocery store to get some bones for the dog. As I was leaving, she said, "Ask the butcher to leave a little meat on the bones for the dog."

What happened next is such a vivid memory. I can still see and smell the sawdust on the floor behind the meat counter. When I asked for some meat to be left on the bones, the butcher asked, "What do you do with all these bones?"

With a good measure of childlike innocence I replied, "We boil them first for soup, and then give them to our dog, Spike."

He smiled as he handed me a very large package. I walked home and came into the kitchen, very happy to have such a big package for Mama. She opened it, peered at its contents, and gasped, asking, "What on earth did you tell the butcher?"

When she heard my story she laughed and said, "Good hell, I can't ever go back to that butcher again." It was years before I understood what she meant.

When my brothers Al, David, and Lee joined the military and went off to war, I was devastated. I prayed every night they would return home safe. When they did return home safe, I knew that God answered prayers.

In 1952, I was about nine when Mom's family moved to Bluebell, Utah, a small town in Duchesne County. Dad had dreamed of being a rancher with his boys, and he was determined that it was time for that dream to happen. There were three brothers in my family who had been born between Ruthie and Rebecca. They were usually not very nice to me and were never nice to Rebecca. They were a lot harder on her because she fought them while I just quietly took their abuse.

Once I was sitting in the outhouse while my brothers hollered that they were going to tip it over. When they started to wiggle it, I started screaming and crying. I realized later that they were just having fun, but I was terrified at the time. It was so hard putting up with their behavior, and it made me feel small and of little consequence. Ruthie tried to help us feel better about ourselves, but she married very young, so she wasn't around much by the time we moved out to the ranch.

We worked hard at the ranch. I had to get up early with the boys and do a lot of the dirty work of feeding and cleaning up after the cows while the boys milked them. Rebecca and I fed the rabbits and chickens, gathered eggs, and brought in the wood that Johnny had chopped. It was really difficult work.

When Rebecca and I went to the LDS Church on Sundays, the members were often unkind to us. The adults often treated us with indifference, and the children our age would either ignore us or be rude to us. I couldn't understand why at the time, but I now realize that members of The Church always knew which families were practicing polygamy. And for some of them, our polygamist family was an embarrassment, and they wanted nothing to do with us. Even though our parents had been excommunicated from the LDS Church, we children had not, and we wanted to attend the church—especially because of all the activities the church had for young people.

I loved Christmas. Mom always let me set a beautiful table as she created a feast for her family. She was an amazing cook and enjoyed serving a large crowd. I acquired her gift for entertaining and her sense of humor. Because Rebecca was always there, doing everything I did, we were best friends and we still are. She has been a wonderful blessing in my life.

The ranching business didn't work out. Dad was never very good with money. We moved back to Salt Lake City to a small home in the Murray area. Then in 1955 on Halloween we had some friends in because Doug and Rebecca had planned a party. Dad slipped out the back door to go to Aunt Vio's. A short time later he came through the front door and without a word went directly to the kitchen where Mom was. That was unusual for him, he always acknowledged our friends.

Then a few minutes later there was a knock at the door and a policeman said, "Will you go get your father?"

The police had stopped Dad as he left our street and he asked them to let him bring his truck home and tell Mom where he was going. They did, but got impatient when he took too long in the house.

Dad was arrested for living polygamy. He had been imprisoned ten years earlier for the same thing, but this time the crime was considered a felony. He fought the charge legally by arguing that it was his right to live his religion. He lost his appeal. He finally entered prison in the spring of 1959 with a five-year sentence.

Dad's picture was splashed all over the front page of the newspaper, and the persecution I got at school was hard. As a result, I decided to live with Aunt Vio and go to school with her children. Her daughter Laura and I were about the same age and we became good friends. Laura was feisty—much like Rebecca—and I seemed to need feisty friends. I stayed at Aunt Vio's for about six weeks until the school year ended.

One day when I went to visit Dad in prison he said, "I am here because I believe the Principle [meaning plural marriage] must be lived—that's why it's called the Principle. I know the Lord is happy with my sacrifice in living this law of God, and I hope you will live it too. Because of your knowledge of this law you will be damned if you don't live it and your children will be counted as worthless."

I decided then and there that I would live plural marriage.

After dating several young men and feeling that they had no respect for me, I met Darwin Buehler. He was twenty-five years older than I, but I was attracted to him and agreed to be his second wife. I was just seventeen years old and had known him for only three months but Dad approved of him and *I trusted Dad.*

Darwin was good to me in many ways, and I loved him very much. I was so young and felt like the luckiest girl in the world. I was aware that his wife didn't know about me, but Darwin and Dad convinced me that she would be told "soon." I was naive enough to believe that was okay. My naiveté wasn't the only reason. I trusted Dad.

Darwin and I had a wonderful time together. He was a great lover. Drinking alcohol had always been our family's way of having a good time, and I soon began drinking with Darwin. Because he worked for the railroad, we took a few trips together on the train, but he always kept me a secret from his coworkers and his family. His mother never did acknowledge my children or me.

I lived at Mother's for a year and a half after Darwin and I got married, and it was while I was living with her that I gave birth to Amanda Kate. The birth was so difficult that I had a near-death experience before the baby was delivered. During that experience, I was in a beautiful meadow and felt no pain. It was the most happy, peaceful feeling I had ever had. As I stood in the meadow, I saw ten children and one white spirit in the field. I knew they were my children. Then I saw my brother Lee across a small stream. He called to me. I was so happy to see him, and I walked toward him as he held his hand out to me. (Lee had been deceased for several years.)

Suddenly as if through a haze I heard Mother calling, "Alhona! Alhona, come back. Don't leave me!"

I opened my eyes. "Oh, Mom," I told her, "I was in such a beautiful place. I saw all my children."

"You won't be having those children if you don't work with me here,." Mother said, "You have to push with all you've got."

As I pushed with all my strength, my precious daughter was born. I learned later that the delivery caused my uterus to tear, which subsequently caused some major problems.

Several months after Amanda was born, Darwin moved me to Pocatello, Idaho. I hated it there so before long, he moved me back to Salt Lake. My second child, Alan Wayne, became quite ill while he was still an infant. Since Darwin's wife Mary was a nurse, Darwin insisted on taking Alan to her so she could nurse him back to health. I didn't realize that was Darwin's way of bribing Mary to accept me as a plural wife. She adored my baby, and I didn't get Alan back for four years. It was a horrible time for me.

After giving birth to Stanley Neal, I started going to beauty school. When I gave birth to Beverly Alhona, I became so ill that I had to quit school for a year. At that point the tear in my uterus caused cervical cancer. The doctor wanted to remove my cervix, but I knew I had more children in Heaven waiting to come to me. When I told the doctor that, he said he'd do the best he could to save whatever he could.

After the surgery, the doctor told me he had taken part of my cervix and also part of my uterus—and said he doubted I could have more children. He put me on a hormone pill and told me not to get pregnant for at least eighteen months. Though I kind of blew him off, I didn't get pregnant, which was unusual for me.

One day when I was picking up a refill of the hormone pills I asked the pharmacist exactly what they were.

He gave me a funny look and answered, "They're birth control pills."

I hurried home and flushed the pills down the toilet. I found out that Darwin had known what they were and filled the prescription anyway. As soon as I stopped taking the pills, I got pregnant. At about five months I lost the baby—which was really more of a blob, because the baby wasn't even close to being formed. Despite my loss, I was thrilled. I knew I could still get pregnant.

I went back to school and got my license to be a beautician. At about the same time, I also woke up to the fact that Darwin was never going to let me have Alan back. I took my sister Ruthie with me for support, went to Mary's home, and got my son. It took all the courage I had, and facing Darwin's fury was the worst of it.

Four years after Beverly was born, I was finally able to give birth to Darlene Sophia. She was followed by Lynnette Rae and Sally Anne. By then I had a thriving salon business and I worked very hard to give my kids the fun things they wanted. Darwin paid the bills and I paid the thrills.

For years I tried to understand Darwin. Maybe because of our age difference he was very jealous. Maybe I said the wrong things, or maybe he just lost it. After a terrible blast of temper he would always give me wonderful "peace" offerings.

One day Darwin lost $3200 and he was understandably upset about it. Later the kids and I prayed that we would find it. A few months later I found the lost money and returned it to Darwin. Instead, he let me keep it and I happily accepted.

I next gave birth to Darwin Glen, Darwin Russell, and Daniel David. I was so happy. I had finally given birth to all the children I had seen in the meadow during my near-death experience. The white spirit must have been the baby I lost at five months.

After Daniel's birth I had a problem with bleeding, and the doctor told me I needed a hysterectomy or I wouldn't live to raise my kids. When

I called Dad for advice, he said, "Don't worry about it. If you let them take out your uterus, you won't have an eternal family."

When I told Darwin what Dad said, Darwin insisted I get the surgery. I'm so glad I did.

I never doubted that I was supposed to marry Darwin, and sometimes he was so kind to me. One time while we were at a gun show, I was looking at some travel brochures and I told him, "This is what I'd really like to do someday—go to Europe."

"Well," he said, "pick one of the trips out, and we'll go."

"How many days?" I asked, still not really believing him.

"Fourteen."

He was true to his word, and it was a wonderful trip—a dream fulfilled.

While Darwin could be so nice and so generous, without warning he would explode, so my life with him was in constant upheaval. I carried a lot of anger and began to understand that the peace offerings after the fights were nothing more than his way of getting me to forgive him. Those gifts became a sharp reminder of the physical and mental pain he caused me, I began to refuse them. It came to a point where I couldn't forgive him.

By the time Darwin got sick, I just didn't care anymore. I had given birth to ten children and tried to be a good wife and mother but I never seemed to be able to please him. He apologized to me for the pain he had caused me just before he died, but it didn't really mean anything to me. I was numb. Reflecting on his behavior during the years of our marriage, I now wonder if he had bipolar disorder. He certainly had many of the behavioral traits. It would be interesting to know.

Before Darwin died, he told me I needed to go to the LDS Church. That's exactly what I did, three of my children and I were baptized. Attending the LDS Church was one of the good memories from my childhood, and I wanted to be happy again. There was a significant issue standing between happiness and me, I had been numbing myself for many years with booze and I wasn't able to stop drinking.

I soon met Keith Bangarter, a very nice man, and married him. In fewer than ten years he left over money disagreements, but we remained friends. He helped me a lot with my self-doubts and encouraged me to believe in myself.

One day as I thought about my life and what I wanted, God helped me to see that I didn't need the booze or the tobacco I had used for years. I put them down that day, and today I do not use either of them. I became active in the LDS Church and have been blessed by the love that surrounds me in The Church and from my ten children, fifty-six grandchildren, and twenty-six great-grandchildren. I spent many years as a hairdresser working out of

my own home and enjoyed my work, but retirement was a relief. I had
so much trouble with my legs that standing on my feet all day was very
difficult.

Rebecca has been active in the LDS Church for many years, and she's
thrilled that I've become active and that I love it. I really enjoy going to the
temple. I feel so much love there. I love the fun sisters I have, and enjoy
getting together with them and getting to know them all over again.

Like Laura, I have been on both sides of the fence. I have been part of
a plural marriage, and I have been an active member of the LDS Church,
which does not endorse or tolerate plural marriage. At the time that I
entered plural marriage, it was the right thing for me to do. Today the right
thing for me is to be active in the LDS Church.

Looking back at the decision I made, I realize I chose plural marriage
because of my parents. They taught me that I would be damned if I didn't
live plural marriage, and I believed them. Even though I entered that
marriage without the first wife's knowledge, I trusted my father when he
said everything would be okay. I knew Dad loved me, so I believed him—
not only about the necessity for plural marriage, but also about the way in
which I was doing it. I realize now that while my decision was right for me,
the whole thing should have been done very differently.

My parents impacted my marriage even though I no longer lived
under their roof. I adored my father, but that didn't take away from the
fact that he was a difficult man. He often demonstrated great love, yet he
would frequently be abusive. His complexity made it hard for me to value
his advice. Late in his life he tried to counsel me not to hit my kids and not
to expect perfection. He was speaking from his experience and his regrets,
but I didn't listen. My mother contributed to my plural marriage because
I tried to emulate the way in which she treated her sister-wives with love
and fairness.

When I announced my intention to marry Darwin, my parents
were ecstatic but the siblings from my mother were furious. In fact, my
announcement was the cause of a huge fight that broke out on Mother's
birthday. She finally intervened and told my brothers and sisters that if
they didn't like what I was doing, they could leave. It wasn't long before
everyone calmed down.

Many of my siblings still tried to talk me into leaving Darwin, but
their actions spoke more loudly than their words. I had watched many of
them weather the storms of bad marriages, so I didn't think they had any
right to advise me on anything to do with marriage. They simply hadn't set
decent examples for me. It took a lot of courage to go against a band of
protesting brothers and sisters, but I truly believed it was the right thing

to do. I still think it was the right thing for me at the time, even though my marriage was very hard. As a result of that marriage, I have my ten wonderful children.

As the dust settled, my siblings became very supportive of me, and we all have a good relationship now. I feel there is a healthy level of respect among the sisters, and we enjoy a good, loving relationship. I am happy now as a single woman, and value the experiences that have brought me to the place I am in. When all is said and done, being happy with myself enables me to be accepting, loving, and happy for my sisters, no matter their individual choices.

Kate's daughters. Top row, left to right: Loni, Becky, Wanda, Ruthie, Marie. Bottom row, left to right: Fran, Mother Kate, Arlene.

Alice Faye

———————— ⌒ ————————

CHAPTER 11

1944

I WAS BORN ON AUGUST 27, 1944, in Salt Lake City, Utah. Dad and all of his family lived at 1538 South 400 East. The night I was born Dad was having a birthday party downstairs. I am Vio Fraser's fifth baby. The doctor, an elderly woman we called Grandma Ogden—and who delivered many babies of polygamist families—was downstairs at the party. She knew Mom was in labor, and when she went upstairs to check, Mom was so close to having me that Grandma Ogden said she didn't even have time to put on the little white cap she wore when she delivered babies.

I was born with a cyst on my left breast. When she removed it, Grandma Ogden said it was one-eighth of an inch away from my milk gland. I was blessed to be able to nurse all of my babies.

That wasn't the end of my health challenges. When I was eight months old, Aunt Maurine was taking care of me while Mom was working. When she handed me a toy, she noticed I would reach out for it only with my left hand. As she tried to get me to take it with my right hand, she realized I wasn't using my right hand at all. Mom took me to a chiropractor who said I must have had polio at some time. Later I found out that it was more likely a stroke that I had suffered while still in my mother's womb. It left me with a paralysis on my right side.

Because my right leg was shorter than my left walking was very difficult for me. A doctor convinced my parents that a surgery could be done to stretch the ligaments in my calf and behind my knee. Then they would put me in a brace, which would help me walk better.

So at five years old, from before Thanksgiving until after Christmas, I was at the Shriner's Hospital. My parents dropped me off during the week assuring me they would come and see me on the weekend. I was scared but reassured I would see them soon.

As it turned out Mama's sister died and they went to the funeral on Saturday instead of coming to see me. The visiting hours were very strict. I was sure they had left me because they didn't want me anymore.

I was a very picky eater and when food was brought in I only ate the dessert. A nurse came in, "Why didn't you eat?" she asked sternly.

"I don't like it."

She slapped my mouth saying, "You do not eat dessert unless you eat the rest of your food." Then she started forcing food into my mouth.

A few days later the friend of my sister-in-law, who worked in the hospital came in to see me. The food tray was sitting there with food untouched. "Why aren't you eating?" she asked.

"I don't like it."

"Well you could at least eat the dessert, you like it don't you?"

"Yes, but she'll slap me if I only eat the dessert," I said.

I never saw that mean nurse again.

One day I was jumping on the bed with a little plastic purse in my hand. It slipped out of my hand and ended up in the light fixture and it began to smoke from the heat of the light. The janitor soon came in and took care of that. After the surgery they put me in a crib and I screamed and screamed, "I'm not a baby, I don't sleep in cribs."

I woke up in a normal bed with side arms on it.

Mom and Dad came every weekend after the first one they missed. I was comforted by their visits. As a result of my stay in the hospital I started kindergarten a year late. The leg brace went from my knee to my ankle and I wore it for about six years. I still walk with a limp.

When I was eight years old, we moved to a farm in Mountain Home, Utah. On that farm we had one cow that was extremely aggressive and would not nurse her own calf. It was my job to open and shut the gate, letting the cow in and out of the barn so her calf could nurse. One day as I was tending to the gate I stumbled and fell. The cow pinned me against the ground and rammed my stomach over and over. Luckily I was so thin that her horns went into the dirt while her head repeatedly slammed against my stomach. Mom heard my screams, saw what was happening and hit the cow on her backside with an ax handle as she prayed aloud. When the cow lifted her head to see who was hitting her, Mom screamed, "RUN! RUN!"

I scrambled away just before the cow's horns came down again, preventing me from sustaining severe injury. We thanked Heavenly Father that a stomachache was my only discomfort from the incident. However, when Dad arrived home, Mom told him what had happened and said, "Keeping that cow is not worth putting the children in danger. I would rather see the calf starve to death."

Dad immediately butchered the cow, and we fed the calf with a baby bottle.

I was about ten years old when we moved back to Salt Lake City to a house at 50 Granite Avenue, just off 3300 South and State Street. We moved in on a Saturday. I was so excited when Mom said we were going to go to "Sunday school" the next day. I had never been to Sunday school that I could remember. I was disappointed when we arrived at Aunt Maurine's house and I found that "Sunday school" was there. My disappointment was short-lived as I was happy spending time with my sister Betsy.

Sunday school was held at Aunt Maurine's for many years. Aunt Maurine helped us learn songs from the hymn book. When Betsy and I learned one song perfectly, Aunt Maurine took us to a movie as a reward. My love for hymns brought me closer to my Father in Heaven.

In 1956, when I was about twelve years old, I was baptized. Dad wanted the kids that were old enough baptized before he went to prison. He was still fighting the legal system but felt like we needed baptism. When I was confirmed, the elders from the polygamist culture laid hands on my head and blessed me, saying I would "yet be a mother in Zion." According to my parents, this was a very special blessing and was not usually confirmed upon one so young. They had been concerned that because of my handicaps I may not be able to have children.

During the time we were living on Granite Avenue I was sick one night and wasn't sleeping well. I woke up to the smell of smoke. I hurried to Mother's room, woke her, and said, "I can smell something burning."

She walked through the house to investigate, and when she turned on the living room light she could see the wall by the furnace smoldering. There was a table next to the furnace that had a fringed cloth on it. The fringe had caught fire and burned a large hole in the wall. Had the Lord not blessed me to wake up, the whole house might have gone up in flames. We thanked God that there was no further damage to our home and that no one had been injured.

As a teen, I had my share of adventures. One night when I was in high school my girlfriend and I were walking home from a school baseball game. As we walked along State Street, a truck pulled up and the man inside asked, "Do you girls want a ride?"

"No thanks," we responded simultaneously.

When he threatened us, we took off running—and before we knew what happened, he used his truck to corner us in a parking lot. We prayed for the Lord's help and were prompted to run in separate directions. Thankfully the man simply left.

As a teenager, I prayed diligently to find out whom I should marry. One man was interested in me, but I didn't want to marry him. I found out God doesn't expect us to marry someone we don't want to. Another man asked me to marry him in plural marriage, but again I refused. I wanted nothing to do with that lifestyle.

While Dad was in prison I went to visit him just about every Sunday. One day while I was there, Dad said, "Louis Kelsch's son, Gary, is interested in coming to see you. He has one wife. How do you feel about that?"

"I don't know," I said. "I'll pray about it."

It was nine months before Gary's wife, Renee, called me and asked if she and Gary could come and see me. I agreed that I would meet with them the following night. I was a little nervous, because I planned to tell him that I was not interested in plural marriage. My nerves were somewhat calmed by the fact that it had been easy to tell the others no, and I assumed it would be easy to tell him no as well. However, when Gary and Renee arrived, a different spirit came over me. I married Gary eight days later.

Before we were married, Renee invited me to dinner at their house. When Gary drove me home, we agreed that we would be married the following Friday. As part of that discussion, I asked Gary if I could have as many children as I wanted, and if I could stay home with them and not have to work. He said yes to both. That was very important to me.

My sister Linda, one of Aunt Maurine's daughters, married Gary a short time later. Then in 1979 we moved to the Park City area. Health problems continued to be part of my life. My teenage daughter, Vi, loved children and enjoyed teaching the preschoolers. When she was fifteen years old, she became very ill. At first she complained of a backache, so we took her to a chiropractor.

After three months the chiropractor suggested we take her to a medical doctor, but it took three more months to determine that she had leukemia. She suffered for six more months with severe pain throughout her body. During one of her hospital stays she said, "Mom, if all this pain ends up helping someone—if somehow they learn something from my pain—it will be worth it."

As a result of her internal bleeding, Vi's breath smelled extremely bad. One day we watched in amazement as a miracle occurred. She raised her hand to her mouth as if she were drinking, although there was nothing in her hand. From that day on her breath smelled like sweet spices.

When the doctor told us Vi was dying, we chose not to tell her. Several days before she passed away, Vi began having spiritual visitations from family members on the other side. She was told of her passing by these visitors and was assured that she would be in no more pain.

One night as I sat by her bed, I said, "I'm going to miss you so much."

Vi said, "I know. I'll miss you too, but there are a lot of children in the spirit world who need to be taught."

Her passing was a bittersweet experience. Being a part of these beautiful miracles truly eased the sorrow of losing her.

While I was expecting Spencer, my twelve-year-old daughter Carrie was diagnosed with thyroid cancer. Because of some bad experiences in the hospital with Vi, we decided to try herbal medicine. However, her condition became more serious, and she underwent surgery to remove her thyroid, which saved her life.

When Spencer was born in 1987, the nurse could tell immediately that he was very sick. He was diagnosed with Strep-B and remained in the hospital for ten days. When he was released, the nurse said, "We recently lost a baby with this same illness. You are very lucky."

No, we were very blessed. I thanked Heavenly Father that Spencer's sickness was accurately diagnosed in time and that treatment was started immediately.

On February 13, 1990, I slipped on the ice and broke my right hip. The doctor told me I might not walk again. I prayed and rubbed consecrated oil on my hip every day. It was about a year before I was able to walk without assistance, but I feel that my ability to eventually walk was a blessing from heaven.

In October 1999, Gary went into the hospital with heart problems. It was very frightening for the whole family, because it was the first time he had ever been in the hospital. Then again in March 2006 he underwent open-heart surgery. During that surgery, doctors also installed a pacemaker to regulate his heartbeat. At one point his heart stopped beating, and he had to be resuscitated. After being in the hospital for ten days, he was released to go home.

In May Gary started having breathing problems. My daughter Betsy and I took him to the emergency room, where he was diagnosed with infection in his lungs. The infection eventually turned into pneumonia. His condition worsened until he was literally fighting for each breath he took. He was in an induced coma for three days, struggling to breathe. Ann Barlow, a sister-in-law, who was working as a nurse on the floor at that time, later told us she was really surprised that he pulled through.

Gary decided that the stress from work was causing his health problems, so he quit working at Fashion Cabinets, where he had been part owner for thirty-five years. His condition continued to improve and he enjoyed working out in the yard when it was good weather.

On July 4, 2010, Gary went to the emergency room again, where he was diagnosed with MRSA. The doctors wanted to replace the valve they had implanted with a tissue valve, and they told Gary that he had only a 50 percent chance of surviving. They strongly advised him to get his affairs in order. He went ahead with the surgery and was given strong antibiotics to clear up the infection and prevent pneumonia. He feels better now than he has in ten years. He continues to work around all three houses and yards, doing remodeling and whatever else needs to be done.

I've always been grateful for the good man I married and the thirteen children I've been privileged to bring to this earth, including a set of twins. My children and grandchildren are a great source of joy to me. With the children all raised, Gary and I have been able to have some wonderful trips together. Life is good.

Even though I chose plural marriage, that direction was not always completely clear to me. I prayed that Heavenly Father would guide me to the right person to marry. When I heard that Gary was interested in me I made it a matter of prayer. Again, I wanted to rely on God and knew He would never lead me astray. When Gary finally approached me about becoming his plural wife, I had received my answer to prayer. I felt very strongly that's where I belonged, and I chose to go into his family.

God is the one who influenced my decision and gave me the courage to choose plural marriage as a lifestyle. The factor in my choice had nothing to do with my relationship with my father, the relationship between my parents, or the relationship between my mother and her sister-wives. The only factor in my choice was the answer to prayer, and I feel that my choice was the right one for me.

I am very happy with my lifestyle, which has given me a beautiful family and a loving husband. My parents and siblings seemed to accept my choice, and I have been able to maintain a good relationship with most of them, including my sisters.

My father was loving and kind to me and always protected me. His memory still influences my life for good, and his example taught me to seek after the truth and gave me determination to be strong and steadfast in my beliefs.

Vio's & Maurine's children 1955 top row, left to right: Bob, Betsy, Faye, Steve; second row, left to right: Shauna, Doris, Evelyn, Ron; bottom row: Bonnie.

Betsy Maurine

CHAPTER 12

1945

OKAY, OKAY, I'LL DO IT! Ginny's always got us doing something. I guess it's good to have an instigator. If it were up to me, the family would never get together. I have pretty much done what I have to do to survive—I just go along, don't make waves. I love . . . well, I don't really know what love feels like. Don't get me wrong; I enjoy getting together with the family. Even though there has been a lot of conflict, it's safer in the family than out there.

I have always felt like I was in a tunnel, as dark and confining as a cave. Just as I started to see the smallest threads of light at the end of that tunnel, my daughter Cresta was killed in an accident. I immediately burrowed back down into the tunnel. I didn't know how to deal with all the feelings that boiled up when my daughter died. In the tunnel, I could get away from them. It was safer in there.

My childhood was frightening and chaotic, characterized by fear, anxiety, and hopelessness. At one point I became aware that something horrible had happened when I had been in my mother's womb for three months. I couldn't identify it on my own, so I asked Mom what it might be.

It corresponded exactly to the time Dad went to prison the first time. Mother had nowhere to turn for help. She and Dad's other two wives were afraid that if they got help from the state, the kids would be taken away. So they did whatever they could to support themselves and their children. Mother got a job at the telephone company where she had worked before marrying Dad. Aunt Vio got a job cleaning houses. Aunt Kate stayed home and took in boarders to make ends meet.

When she was pregnant with me, her situation was horrible—and Mom really didn't want to bring another child into the world. She was constantly worried about the five children she already had to leave with Vio, and couldn't imagine what she would do with another. All of her fear, anxiety, and hopelessness transferred to me—the child she was carrying in her womb.

Leafing through our photo albums, it's apparent that I had some real issues. I wasn't smiling in any of my childhood pictures. I remember hiding, wanting to fade into the shadows, not wanting anyone to see me. I was sure that whatever I said would be wrong or the topic of ridicule, so I said as little as possible. And I was just plain afraid of Dad—even more so after the first time he beat me.

I was four, and we were living in the fourplex. We had just sat down for dinner in that tiny kitchen, and Dad said, "Betty—say the blessing."

I was physically gripped by fear. *I didn't know how to say the blessing! Why was he asking me?* I had no idea what to say, so I just stayed very still and quiet, hoping he would simply ask someone else. It didn't work. "Betty, say the blessing!" He repeated, yelling this time.

I wanted to melt, dissolve into nonexistence. Everyone was looking at me, waiting for me to say something, do something. I had never paid attention during blessings on the food. I was four years old, and I simply didn't care. Nor had anyone ever taught me what to say during a blessing on the food. Even if I *had* paid attention to other blessings, I was so filled with fear at that moment that I couldn't even think.

Dad suddenly got out of his chair, grabbed a newspaper, folded it, and stormed around the table toward me. No one at the table moved or said a word—not even Mom.

I felt the sharp sting of the newspaper on my arm and leg. The pain threatened to release some of the feelings that had built up inside me, much as a volcano erupting. I trembled with the effort of keeping my feelings stuffed inside.

"Say the blessing!" Dad bellowed, smacking me again with the newspaper.

I looked up at Vilate, the one person who always took care of me. I knew how much she loved me when I saw the mortified look on her face. Her eyes held the pain of wanting to help me, to tell me what to say. The folded newspaper smacked against my tender skin again and again.

Dad was determined he would beat the words out of me. The steam was rising from the food, and I knew everyone was hungry. We always had the best dinners when Dad was there. As the family looked in silence, Dad defended himself by hollering, "She is just being rebellious!" Turning to me again, he screamed, "Say the blessing!" The newspaper slapped against me with his screams.

Thinking about that incident, the newspaper really hurt—but the most painful thing was that Dad thought I was a bad kid. Mom must have thought the same thing, because she never said a word. Everyone around the table wanted to eat, and all of them bit their tongues and sat in mute silence.

Dad finally gave up and stopped beating me. Someone else said the blessing, and everyone started eating like nothing had happened. That was the day I decided God didn't love me or even care about me. If I couldn't even say the blessing—talk to God—I must be really bad.

I've done a great deal of work toward healing, but merely writing about the beating still causes a knot of fear in my stomach as I write. *Who is going to be reading this? What will people say? Am I going to hurt someone? Is anyone going to believe me? Am I just being a pathetic victim? What in the hell am I doing?*

I never should have agreed to write my thoughts. I don't know how to write a story. This was such a stupid idea. Why am I doing this? Oh, yes—someone who should know said that when I deal with my past it will help my girls. *That* is my motive, and the only reason I am willingly writing this now.

In 1951, when I was six, I found out I was named after my maternal grandmother, who died before my parents met. But something wasn't right: Her name was Betsy, and I was called Betty. I decided then and there that I would no longer be called Betty. In fact, I refused to answer anyone who called me Betty. It took a while, but finally worked. I became Betsy.

Early on, I wanted to be one of the boys, because Dad seemed to like them better than he did me. Once, Dad lined all three boys up for a haircut and I insisted he cut my hair too. No matter how hard Vilate and Mom tried to talk me out of it, I persisted—and Dad cut my hair in the same style as the boys.

I was born in the middle of my three brothers, and I loved being with them. Ed was my hero, Haven was my friend, and Steve—my youngest brother—was my bud. I loved playing cops and robbers, cowboys and Indians, and marbles. We climbed trees, dug holes, and played football with the neighbor boys. I had the most fun with Steve. We were very close, and he is still very dear to my heart. All of us kids played a lot of hide-and-seek, and since there were so many of us, all the neighbor kids gathered at our house.

I was always physically active and good at sports. I'm sure this activity kept me from thinking about the painful things I saw and heard. But I

Maurine's three boys.

never liked school. It seemed like everyone else was better or smarter, and I constantly felt like an outcast, like I was stupid. I spent a lot of time just staring out the window.

I often felt empty and alone, so once when I got attention from an older neighbor man, it didn't take much coaxing to get me upstairs in his house. What he did to me reinforced the feeling that I was bad and that God would never love me. When I relived the experience later as part of professional therapy, I realized I left my body so I couldn't feel what he was doing to me. I blocked this traumatic experience out of my conscious mind until I was in my sixties.

Ginny is about six years older than me. What I remember of her is. I would say, a busy body of sorts. She seemed to be everywhere, knowing everything, and giving her opinion whether it was asked for or not. She was always sweet about it, and she thought it was her job to keep everything together, to be the Mom. She could see where Mom, and things were lacking and did her best to make it right. She was a very good manager, and Mom certainly could use an assistant since Dad was gone so much of the time. Sometimes Ginny's advice was good and sometimes not so good.

I always did what Ginny said to do. It must have started when I was very young. I don't remember ever even questioning her. She is the only one who asked me to do things. I looked up to her and respected her. She seemed to be the authority in the family. Mom was quite laid back and escaped into her novels so Ginny made it easier for Mom. Ginny had a big heart and wanted the best for everyone. She was not selfish in her actions or advice. She seemed to know what was best for everyone and how to make things work out but, like I said not always.

I was about thirteen and I had agreed to take some of the younger girls to town. We were going to ride the bus. I had done this many times by myself to meet Faye, Aunt Vio's daughter. Faye and I were pals; we did a lot together. We conspired on the phone what time and where we would meet, usually at Auerbach's, and we would go to a movie, go to the taffy shop, to Kresses to see her Aunt Zola, or whatever we wanted.

So, I planned with 3 or 4 of the little girls to ride the bus up town, play for a time and then come home. Well, Ginny got wind of the plan and decided I should take Barbara. I did not want to take Barbara. Barbara was young, possibly three, spunky, and hard for me to handle, especially away from home. There would be enough pressure without that. Ginny did what Ginny did best, she didn't want Barbara left out and talked me into it. I gave in, who says no to Ginny? Not me. Its not that she was mean or anything she just had a very sweet way of talking me into stuff.

Well, so we went on our little outing, everything went fine until it was time to come home. I let the girls know that I was ready and they were fine with it. Barbara was young enough that she probably was not paying attention to that conversation. When we started to get on the bus Barbara refused. She was not ready to leave, and no one was going to make her. I tried to talk to her and tug her to get on the bus before it left as all of the other people were on and I was done with the fun and games of it all. The stress of keeping track of everyone and keeping everyone happy was hard. I felt like I had done my part of being a good big sister and was ready to go home. The more I tugged and demanded, the louder Barbara screamed. Of course everyone was looking at me like I was killing her and it really embarrassed me.

So, consequently we missed the bus. It's a good thing the other girls did what I asked or it would have put me over the top. I was so mad at her but I held my cool, got her to get on the next bus, and got us home. I swore I would never take her anywhere again.

Growing up, I did what I was told and felt responsible for my five younger sisters, since Dad repeatedly told me, "You are the big sistah that takes care of the little sistahs."

I could never tell if he was teasing when he said it, but each time it penetrated more deeply into my soul. I didn't know exactly what I was supposed to do to "take care" of them, but I felt bad and guilty every time they fought or got hurt. I felt like a complete failure if I was unable to make them happy.

I felt quite rebellious as a teenager, but was too afraid to do anything very bad. Once I got so mouthy with Mom that she slapped my face. Mom, being who she was, apologized later even though I very much deserved it.

Mom and Dad had warned me never go out with anyone who drank alcohol. So I was not impressed with Quin or his friend Nate when I met them because they both drank. However, I saw Quin a few times, and he continued to pay attention to me. I was mildly attracted to him, and Dad thought it was great that I was seeing the son of one of his best friends—in spite of the fact that he drank.

When I met Quin in 1962, I was sixteen. On my seventeenth birthday, we started dating, and Quin put on the "full-court press," which was a little scary for me. When I expressed my concerns to Ginny she tried to intervene. She told me that Mom didn't want me to get married so young, and she suggested I tell Quin that I needed a week without seeing him so I could think. Just two days later he showed up with a card and a promise ring. Things progressed pretty quickly after that, and we soon married. I was only seventeen and a half and very naïve.

After we had been married only two weeks, I had supper on the table when Quin came home from work. He took one look at his plate, picked it up, and threw it across the room, saying, "I don't like peas."

I was scared to death. Where did this monster come from? I had never seen anything like it. Mom and Dad never had fights in front of us. Mom never said much. She had a "look" that let us know we were in trouble—and she even used it on Dad. He often criticized Mom, but never threw things or used bad language.

After that incident with Quin, I no longer wanted to be there with him. But I was crippled by substantial fears. *What will Dad think? No one just leaves. I'm already married; I can't get out now.* And finally, *everyone will think I'm bad.* In the end the fears won out. I did nothing, and soon I was pregnant. I did my best to adjust to my new life.

One time after I had a couple of kids, Ginny and I was at Mom's visiting. I think Ginny had about six kids by then. Mom had saved up her pennies for quite some time to buy curtains for the large bay window in the front room. She had to get the rod, the curtains and the drapes special made, so they were very expensive. The drapes were a deep and beautiful rose color, satiny material with a textured pattern.

Ginny and Mom were in the library talking and then Ginny came out of the library and said, "Why don't you take those curtains down, wash them and put them back up for Mom?"

I didn't really want to but.......? And not knowing the difference between curtains and drapes, I washed them all and shrunk Moms beautiful drapes. I didn't even notice when they came out of the dryer without a wrinkle and I hung them up. I was the tomboy of tomboys, not paying attention to that kind of thing. If drapes or curtains were even mentioned in our house of a million kids, barely getting by, did I hear it? Days later when I was at Mom's again with Ginny, she said, "Why did you wash the drapes?"

"You told me to."

"I told you to wash the curtains not the drapes."

I just looked at her like, what? "I thought they were all curtains," I said.

"No, just the light weight, white ones underneath," she said with a very heavy heart.

Mom never said a word but I'm sure she was devastated.

When I was very young, I remember hearing Dad say, "If you don't live polygamy, you will never see God." I reasoned that even if God didn't love me, I could still be with Him—still see Him. I sure didn't want to go to that other place; who knows what was down there?

I felt almost paralyzed by several of Dad's other teachings: "Women are no good without a man," and "The woman always does what the man says." I didn't realize how many of the things Dad taught us in Sunday school were stuck in my head until many years later.

Quin and I lived in a tiny apartment above my mother-in-law's home, and she was very sweet to me; she taught me many homemaking skills, which I really enjoyed. By the time I was pregnant with my third child, Quin decided to take another wife. We never talked about it; Quin just assumed, and I went along with it.

We were still living in the tiny apartment above Quin's mother. We didn't really believe in the principle of plural marriage. We just did what everyone else we associated with was doing. There were many important things we didn't do, however. We didn't pray together. We didn't say a blessing on the food. We didn't study the scriptures. And we didn't do any of the other fundamental things the others were doing. We were just a couple of kids doing what our parents had done without understanding why they did it. I realize now that I married my father. Quin wasn't there for me emotionally, he didn't know how to be.

I was scared to death of people who got angry, especially men. The worst of Quin's temper didn't manifest itself until he married my sister Doris. I realize now that Quin wanted me to stand up to him, but I didn't know how. Doris was able to stand up to him but she did it in a destructive way. As I learned later in Al-anon, we were the typical alcoholic family and we were stuck on a merry-go-round. At that point, I began to lose it.

I knew I had to leave or I would go nuts—and even the scary world out there had to be better than what I was living in. I became suicidal.

As I was sitting on the porch on one of those dark days, I thought, *there is no way I could leave my children for Doris to raise.* Something inside me clicked. I decided there had to be a better way.

A week later, Mom invited me to go with her to southern Utah to visit Hazel for the weekend. I thought, *sure, why not?* That Friday evening, a van arrived to pick up Mom and me; it was full of people I didn't know. I wasn't comfortable enough to sleep, even though it was late by the time we arrived at our destination and everyone other than the driver had fallen asleep. The driver noticed I was awake and spoke to me, even though I was in the very back of the van.

The next morning Hazel lined up her whole family to introduce them to me—including Tom, the driver of the van. He was very friendly and struck up a conversation with me. When I found out he was a diesel truck driver, I was very interested and asked lots of questions. He asked if I'd like to go outside and see the truck he had just built.

My interest in Tom grew, especially because of the amazing things he knew. Later Tom asked if I'd like to go with him on a run in the diesel to a nearby town—something that would only take a couple of hours. I jumped at the chance.

When we arrived at the business Tom needed to visit, it was closed until the next morning. Tom called his brother to come and get me, since he needed to stay overnight to get the load. I refused, saying I wanted to stay there with him. I had no concern about staying in a hotel with Tom. I knew he would continue to treat me with total respect, I fully trusted him.

His surprise registered clearly on his face. He was thirty-two and had never been married; he didn't even date. Now he was in a different town with a married woman who wanted to stay overnight with him.

As for me, I had been so deeply depressed for so long—even losing my desire to live—that I was thrilled to just get to a strange place with strange people who had strange ways. Little did I know that a cute young guy would spark my interest with these big powerful trucks in which I had always been fascinated. It was as if my head was full of fog, and I didn't much care about anything. I was like a little kid with a brand-new toy, and I wasn't about to let someone take it from me.

We arrived back the next day too late for me to ride back to Salt Lake with Mom. I had no idea why she and Hazel were so upset with me. Frankly, I didn't have enough energy to care. Tom said he needed to take the diesel to Salt Lake the next week, and he offered to take me home then. You can just imagine my delight at the thought of a whole week here with Tom in a funky little country town, free to do and say whatever I wanted.

Tom brought me back to life that next week. The poor guy knew what everyone was thinking, and he did his best to stay away from me—but I sought him out, and we spent a lot of time together. In every interaction he continued to be very respectful, friendly, interesting, and fun as he told me jokes and stories. I learned to laugh again. Tom even took me out on a never-used dirt road and let me drive the diesel. I could tell he was nervous and he cut it pretty short, but I loved it. It was so exciting.

I followed Tom around like a little puppy; I went wherever Tom went. I met his mom, Sylvia, and loved her too. I went with him to his brother's house, and as they talked I stayed close to the truck. As they visited, I thought about home for the first time since leaving. I had a dark and bleak impression and thought, *the devil is in that house.*

Tom and I had become friends, and I told him how I felt about the drinking and the abuse that went on at home. He suggested I go to Ala-non when I got home.

I enjoyed the five-hour drive home, listening to more of his stories and jokes. He was a happy-go-lucky, positive man with a live-and-let-live attitude. He never complained or said a bad word about anyone. I realized that this man never did so much as brush his finger against me, yet he paid more attention to me and treated me with more respect than did my own husband, who was supposed to love me.

Tom had instilled in me enough life to light the flame inside my heart that had slowly been snuffed out. It had been extinguished so slowly that I didn't even recognize that I was frightened and alone in the dark. I started going to Al-anon, where I got lots of support and the feedback I needed to keep that flame lit.

Quin could tell I was moving out from under his thumb, and it scared him. His response was to get meaner and meaner, until I found a way to leave. Grasping at straws to survive, I finally divorced Quin. My family did not believe in divorce and most of them turned their backs on me.

After I left I did whatever it took to survive, materially and emotionally; I even did some destructive things, hanging on to life by a mere thread. But I eventually learned to live in that big scary world out there and find happiness. The people in Al-anon gave me unconditional love, and at the Alano Club I met a guy who became a very good friend. As I grew to know and appreciate him, I found out that all people in the outside world were not bad, as I had been taught. My self-esteem improved enough that I found a lawyer and was able to get child support from Quin. I also went back to school and discovered I was not stupid; I graduated, got my nursing license, and found a good job.

I know I was shut down during most of the years of my marriage. With the help of my Higher Power, I found a group of people who put on an experiential workshop and started learning how to open up. That process continues. I'm still learning to open up and I'm still growing in ways I never thought possible. I have a great relationship with my eleven children and my grandchildren. I'm learning to love, to trust, and to be open with my feelings.

In the process, I learned to take care of myself, to take one day at a time, and to do what is best for me. As a result, I've been able to help my children avoid some of the mistakes I made. Due to the many traumatic circumstances that occurred during my divorce, my children bonded with each other and have continued to stick together. Today, they are all leading very productive lives in the world outside of polygamy.

I loved Quin as much as I was able to love at the time. He's a very insecure but sweet man when he's sober. He and Doris have stayed married and seem to be quite happy together. I'm glad it is working for them. I appreciate the way Doris has carried on the Sunday gatherings and holiday get-togethers. It has given my kids a place to come. All the kids, hers and mine, are close and love getting together.

I envy the relationship my children have and wish that my relationship with my own family of origin could be that loving and close. But when I left polygamy and the family turned their backs on me, there were many years of isolation, estrangement, and sorrow that hurt to this day. Years later I was able to come back to the family through the efforts of my mother, who was aware of Quin's abuse. I have since reconnected with most members of my family, but things will never be the same again.

There are still strained relationships between some of my sisters and me. When I left polygamy, I felt like—and was treated like—an outcast. While I have reconnected with some and enjoy a fairly good relationship with them, I have to accept the fact that I will never again be close to some of my sisters. I am learning that whenever I interact with them I have to follow my feelings instead of trying to figure out the "right" thing to do.

When I married my husband, I was deeply in love with him. We had a cute little family, a good marriage, and a very satisfying relationship—until he took another wife. At that point, everything turned to a living hell.

My "decision" to live plural marriage wasn't really a decision at all. When my husband began paying attention to my younger sister and decided to marry her, I didn't want him to—but I didn't dare speak up. I was trapped in the world my father had created. All I kept hearing were my father's words that were drilled into us during his Sunday school lessons. *The world outside is bad. Stick with family; you are safe here. We are the righteous ones. We are the ones God loves because we are doing what He wants us to.* And, worst of all, *If you don't live polygamy, you will never see God.* Those words have haunted me for years, and I still resent my father for preaching those lies.

From the moment my sister entered our marriage, my heart wanted out. I wasn't invested in the "tri-marriage" my husband created. I merely tolerated it. It was not plural marriage or polygamy; to me, it was disaster in the name of religion. I finally felt I was dying and had to escape plural marriage to survive and take care of my children.

My life was a downward spiral from the moment our marriage became a plural one. No matter which way I turned, I was going against someone or something. When I became a plural wife, I went against the norms of the world, but the "world" of my childhood was so overpowering that I couldn't see beyond it. Later, when I summoned the courage to go against the wishes of my family by leaving my marriage, my father didn't care why I had to get out. He never even *asked* why. He just knew I was wrong—because *the man is always right.* Despite his rejection, I'm glad I left when I did. Had I stayed, I never would have learned to love life as I do now. I'm not even sure I would have survived.

The rejection was real, and it was bitter. As long as I lived polygamy, my father thought I was wonderful, even though my situation was far from wonderful. The second I left my plural marriage, I was no longer wonderful—and that's putting it mildly. Years later, after doing a lot of healing, I realized I had endured that marriage to please my father. I had clumped God and Dad together into one person who loved me conditionally, as long as I was doing the "right" thing.

I hadn't had a very good example of the "right" thing. As I watched my father interact with his wives, what I saw was an overruling patriarchal authority. Even though my dad did not always make the best choices, he was the man, and what he said was law. Mom and her sister-wives got along on the surface, but I could easily sense the underlying disharmony and discontentment each of them felt. I was not around Aunt Kate very much, but I loved Aunt Vio, and she and Mom got along pretty well. Basically, though, Mom coped with the whole thing by simply avoiding it. Her novels and her chocolate saved her life.

After watching my mother, I knew my survival depended on simply getting out. So I did. Weaved through it all in my mind was the harsh voice of my father, criticizing and belittling me. To this day, he still impacts my life. Because of him, I am still afraid of men. In my heart I know he did the best he knew how and I admit he had many good qualities, but I don't know if I will ever be able to heal the wounds he directly and indirectly inflicted on me.

Fifteen years ago I decided to stay away from men, because I had obviously made bad choices in that arena. Instead, I focused on healing myself, getting to know myself, and starting to understand the "outside world"—the one we were taught to be so afraid of. Today I am happy and feel I have achieved some of those desperately longed-for goals. For me, the greatest sign of that healing is my readiness to experience a balanced, loving, monogamous relationship with a man.

Linda Beth

CHAPTER 13

1949

I WAS BORN SO QUICKLY in the wee hours of October 7, 1949, that Mother almost had to birth me with no assistance. Dad barely had time to get Dr. Ogden, who delivered most of Mama's children, and there was no time for the ether that was typically given. I was her eighth child out of thirteen.

My earliest recollection was what I would refer to many times as "the spanking." I was standing in the middle of a very large room. Daddy held my arm tightly while spanking me with a rolled-up newspaper.

"Stop crying!" he shouted in his big voice.

I was two and woke with an earache. Hearing me cry Daddy came instead of Mama and he began spanking me shouting, "Stop that crying. STOP IT NOW."

The earache wasn't as bad as disappointing Daddy. I tried so hard to stop crying, swallowing my tears and even though I held my whole body as tight as I could, it wouldn't stop jerking and he wouldn't stop spanking me.

My body betrayed me. I was horrified, humiliated, and exhausted. What I needed was a hug. I wanted to run away but Daddy's tight grip on my arm held me firmly in place and I wouldn't run away because I was an obedient daughter. Instead, I held myself as still as I could in silent shame. As a two-year-old, I made a decision to do whatever would please my parents and anyone else who was an authority figure.

When I was three our family was knelling in a prayer circle, we were praying for Doris who was only 13 months younger than I was, and my constant playmate. She was in an iron lung in the hospital. I cried as I heard Daddy plead with God for my sister's life. She did live and I helped

Linda and Doris.

her to regain the full use of her body. I became her protector. It upset me when she was punished for wetting her bed because I knew she didn't do it on purpose.

Soon after that, in 1953, the state of Arizona decided to raid a little town of polygamist families. The police broke into their homes in the wee hours of the morning to gather women and children into buses while arresting the men. Well-meaning people in Arizona perceived that they were rescuing these "poor women and children" and were waiting to adopt the children and give them "a good life." At least one of the women had her eight children taken away from her. It took many years and a lot of court battles for her to get them back.

The raid on that Arizona town had a major impact on us. Dad had spent time in prison before. He wasn't afraid for himself. But the threat of his children being scattered and his family torn apart was more than he could bear. My parents reacted to the implied threat by quietly gathering all of us children in the early-morning hours and taking us to the canyon until they could find a way to keep us safe.

My older sister woke me. I could feel the fear in her voice as she put me in the car saying, "Be very quiet. If we wake the neighbors the police will take us away, and we may never see our parents again."

We were home again in only a couple of days but that fear instilled in me a strong belief that I needed to be very quiet in order to stay safe. After that, I kept to myself in public school. I often had nightmares in which my sister and I hid in a covert under the street because we heard a siren, and we were sure they were looking for us so they could take us away. Even as an adult, I had nightmares of policemen coming to my door to take away my babies because I had chosen to live plural marriage.

When I was about twelve, I came into the room as Shauna was yelling and physically attacking Doris. Shauna was vicious when she was angry, so I stepped in between them to protect Doris who was terrified of Shauna. Shauna then lunged at me, claws bared in an attack. I turned to catch myself as I fell and hit my tooth on the bedpost. That tooth remained loose and to this day has a very weak root.

I experienced Shauna as the "scrappy one" in our family. She seemed to have a great need to be right or to win. She once used my brother, Steve, to "get" me and then would give a smug "gotcha grin." It took me many years to realize that whenever she was nice to me it was because she wanted something from me. I still don't always trust myself to know when she is nice to me whether if's genuine or whether she has a motive.

Betsy, being in charge of the housework, made a game of our chores. When washing dishes, she had someone wash, a rinse, several dryers and one to put the dishes away, an assembly line. Doing the laundry with a wringer washing machine and hanging the clothes outside to dry, we again had assigned tasks making the work go faster while talking and having fun. We could relax with Betsy while she taught us housecleaning. She would also take time to teach us the latest dance and once put on a Halloween party for all our friends using us girls as part of the spook alley.

When I was about thirteen, I moved in with Aunt Kate to help her run a rest home in her basement in Bountiful. Her son John was a very successful salesman who had a beautiful home nearby.

As I grew older I was a nanny and did some housekeeping for him. While driving me home to visit Mom one day John earnestly pleaded with me not to live plural marriage. He said that if I did, I would always be poor and unhappy. It was the first time I really questioned my father's lifestyle. After all, I was happy and felt safe and loved in my home. It was the outside world that frightened me.

After talking with John, though, I decided I needed to educate myself about the doctrine and put the question to God. In seeking to know whether I should pursue plural marriage, I prepared myself with fasting and prayer. As I knelt, pouring my heart out to God for some kind of answer, I suddenly felt an overwhelming confirmation. My answer was a definite yes. I knew plural marriage was right for me. I was so grateful to have received such a powerful answer. I knew I would live plural marriage, and it didn't matter to me if I were the first wife or a plural wife.

In June 1968 when I was eighteen and had just graduated from high school, I simply asked God to show me the man I was to marry. Three days later Dad asked me if I was interested in dating Gary Kelsch. I hardly knew Gary. All I knew was that my older sister Faye—one of my sisters from Aunt Vio's family—was his second wife. I reluctantly told Dad that I was interested.

Gary's first wife, Renee, called and invited me to Sunday dinner—a common way for a family to become acquainted with a potential new wife and for a single woman to get a feel for the family. I watched the family very closely, especially Gary. He seemed respectful of his wives and attentive and loving to his children. He even pitched in to help wherever he could instead of sitting in his chair giving orders, as was the custom in our family. I was impressed by his manner. I sensed he would be easy to live with.

A few days later, Faye told me that Gary's beliefs were slightly different from Dad's. Gary would not pressure me in any way about coming into his family. The door was open, and it would have to be completely my decision. I would have to make the next move if it felt right to me. As she spoke about him, I knew that what I felt wasn't just an attraction. I'd had that many times. It was the "knowing".

The next day, Gary came to where I worked operating a till to exchange new quarters for solid silver ones. We had a chance to talk one on one. The more I was with him, the more I felt drawn to him. I let him know that I had made a decision, and I needed to let my parents know.

Dad was pleased. Gary's father, Louis Kelsch, was a dear friend of whom Dad thought highly. Dad wanted Gary and I to go see Grandpa Barlow and get his blessing. One Friday morning, Gary took time off work to keep his appointment with Grandpa and me. To my surprise, he came without his other wives—and he gave me our first kiss.

"Were you planning on a big wedding?" he asked.

"No way." I responded. "I helped my sister and my best friend with their weddings, and it was way more work than I want."

He said, "Good, 'cause if you did, I probably wouldn't come. When would you like to do the ceremony?"

"Whenever you'd like." I told him.

"How about tonight?"

That night, after our marriage vows, I gave my body and my whole heart to this man. I knew I could trust him with both.

I assumed that I would grow to love my husband more as our marriage progressed. I was surprised and pleased at how quickly that happened. I also assumed there would be the same camaraderie between me and Gary's other wives as I saw with my three mothers. They took care of each other and were kind and respectful to each other.

My life, in fact, would look nothing like my dream life. It was difficult for them to even look at me, so happy and eager to be a "good wife," while they were feeling betrayed inside. I also quickly learned that my ideal of sharing the children as "another mother" was not accepted by the other two women in our family.

I had enjoyed my childhood so much that I dreamed of being in a large family of my own. That ideal was very important to me. But things didn't work out as I had planned—a reminder of my feelings that something was wrong with my body.

I became pregnant right away and spent nine months elated with the expectation of having my own little soul to love and care for. I began my labor normally and we called the naturopath who delivered many of the babies born to plural wives. He sent his assistant to care for me at home. I had anticipated having a wonderful natural birth. After three days of labor I began to worry, the pain in my cervix was becoming unbearable. I also couldn't feel my baby moving anymore. Finally on the sixth day the naturopath came with his nurse/wife and they tried so hard to get me to push this baby out. Then on the seventh day I heard through my delirium, "We need to take her to the hospital."

He said, "We can't, she's a plural wife, they'll lock her husband up."

But they did finally take me to the hospital. My first child, Jeremy, was a full-term stillborn, after a full week of labor. The cord prolapsed during labor, cutting off his life support. He was extracted vaginally three days after he died following many hours of my trying to push him out. No one would let me see him. I didn't understand why, and I was too weak to stand up for myself.

In my culture, a baby who did not "breathe the breath of life" was not counted. No name was given and there was no burial. The birth was simply dismissed as a sad event, a mistake. I was expected to just get over it and try for another baby. I found the best OBGYN I could for the rest of the pregnancies I had.

Natalie came about two years later, at twenty-eight weeks gestation, weighing 2 pounds 1 ounce. She lived ten days in the newborn intensive care unit. She was healthy and had a lot of spunk. One day as I was leaving after a visit, I overheard her nurse call the doctor to see if she should feed Natalie. The milk she had extracted from Natalie's stomach was pink. Without examining her, the doctor gave the go-ahead to feed her. I later received the phone call that she was gone.

How could this have happened? Why did I leave her? Maybe if I had stayed, she would still be alive. Gary and I felt numb and heartbroken. We spent the rest of the day looking for something to bury her in and arranging for her burial. I couldn't find anything tiny enough in which to bury Natalie. She weighed only one and a half pounds when she died, and I could put my wedding band on her tiny wrist. I decided to buy some material and make her dress. As grief-stricken as I felt, at least I could bury this baby.

I had to try again, and within a few months was expecting. I got big really fast, and one day felt movement up near the rib cage and down by the pelvis simultaneously. I knew the baby couldn't be that big, but it was just a passing thought. I was working a sit-down job, so when I started spotting—as I had done with the other two pregnancies—I asked Gary if he thought I should stop work and take it easy at home. His comment was, "My sister works up until the day she has her baby."

About a week later, I was at work when I felt I needed to use the bathroom. I discovered it was the baby's head presenting. I panicked!

When the doctor examined me, he said that the amniotic sac had broken and the baby would probably come soon. I reasoned with the doctor that if I stayed still in bed, the sac might mend and we could save the baby. He said, "Not likely, but we'll keep you for the night and check things in the morning. If I don't bring the baby now, you risk developing an infection that could render you unable to ever have another baby."

I spent the night pleading with God to let me keep this baby. I was taught to "submit" to His will, so I comforted myself knowing that whatever happened was His will. In the morning the test showed that things were getting worse, so I submitted to what I believed was God's will. Maria was born alive. There was this beautiful, fully formed, nine-ounce baby on my tummy gasping for breath for about fifteen minutes. When I asked what would be done with my baby, the nurse tried to console me by telling me they would baptize her before "disposing" of her. My heart sank into the depths of despair. I didn't think it could get any worse. But it did.

Back in my room, I felt another urge to use the bathroom. The nurse brought a bedpan. I was shocked when another baby came out. This one was a stillborn boy whom I would later name Matthew.

I begged Gary not to take me home. Faye was running a daycare, and the chaos felt overwhelming to me. My Aunt Barbara lived across the street, and no one was home at her house. She gave me permission to go there and sleep all day. I learned the value of stillness that day, and would eventually use it as a powerful tool for healing.

I felt so much guilt, shame, and worthlessness. I couldn't face anyone. I built an extra-thick wall around my heart to survive. I resented Renee's complaining about having babies too close together. She resented my freedom to just be with Gary and the closeness that was evident from the pain we shared.

Faye had been very sympathetic and attentive. However, my state of depression after the twins put a strain on our relationship.

One day Gary came home from work. He had privately heard from each of us our "side of the story." But Faye and I were not speaking with each other unless absolutely necessary. He knew we loved each other, and he saw the big picture. He sat the two of us down together and said, "The air in this house is so thick you could cut it with a knife. I know you both want your own home now, but I don't think that will open up for you until you become friends again."

Gary was very focused on running his cabinet business. One way I could stay close to him and keep myself occupied and out of the house was to work at the cabinet shop. It was my best escape, and I didn't have to be with other people's babies all day. This move created a rift in the family, but it was the only way I felt valued.

The following May when I discovered I was in the early stages of pregnancy, we decided I should try bed rest for the whole pregnancy. As she had been during my earlier pregnancies, Faye was amazing. This time she insisted I sleep in her bedroom upstairs. She was intent on doing everything for me except bathroom privileges so I could have a normal, healthy baby.

Garrett was born the following February in1974. Everything was stacked against him, yet he powered through it. His cord was not only wrapped around his neck but it was tied in a double knot—something few babies survive. Garrett successfully confronted insurmountable odds. I held my breath for the first twenty-four hours after his birth while he was in isolation from getting meconium in his lungs.

Finally, the doctor brought my miracle baby—my normal, healthy boy—into my room. In that moment, I finally felt fulfilled as a woman. No one but God Himself could come between my baby and me. Three months later Faye and I had our own homes near each other, and I began building my own little world of happiness.

One of Gary's brothers had invested in some land in the Park City area. It was pretty desolate looking, but it was ours. All three families put the funds together to build a cabin on this piece of land on the very top of a hill in Silver Creek Junction. As we were cleaning up one Sunday evening to go home, I found Gary out on the deck gazing across the valley to the beautiful mountains on the other side.

I said, "You're having a hard time wanting to go home."

"I am," he responded. "When we were kids we had a lot of room to run without neighbors and fences. It makes me sad when I see my children hanging over the fence and confined to a little yard in the city. Up here, they could have more freedom to run without offending the neighbors. I want that for my children."

With that, Gary and his brothers and two sisters began buying up property adjacent to the cabin site.

Faye and I each had a baby girl in September 1975. We named them Carrie and Connie and raised them as twins. My pregnancy and birth with Connie was the first and only one I experienced as completely normal and healthy. There were no threats, no bed rest, and no complications at the birth. What a blessing to have two beautiful, healthy children. I was sure the struggle to have children was over.

How wrong I was.

I started out with Noah in the winter of 1976. Early in the pregnancy, I began cramping and bleeding profusely. Faye let me and my two babies move in with her so I could be on bed rest for two weeks to save this baby. It worked, and Noah was born one month late, healthy and happy. He grew to be such a comfort to me, and I'd never been happier.

In January 1979 I'd been in bed for a week trying to prevent another miscarriage. Faye's children were old enough now to come over and assist me during the day. One night, as Gary was leaving to go to Faye's after his nightly visit to check on me, I had a really bad feeling that I should not be alone that night. How glad I am that I listened to that prompting. Gary took me with him. After the baby passed, Gary had to call the ambulance to save my life.

When I returned home empty-handed, I looked in on my three sleeping babies and felt grateful I had babies to come home to this time. I fell to my knees and begged God to show me what I needed to learn so that I wouldn't have to keep doing this. The word that came in loud and clear was surrender. I would come to learn the power of surrender on the path to joy and true happiness.

By August 1979, we had all moved into our new homes in Silver Creek Junction. Among four men, there were ten homes filled with many children. Each wife had her own beautiful, brand-new home. Groceries and large groups of people had to be brought in with snow cats during the winter months before the roads were plowed. It was quite an adventure, a different way to live than any of us had experienced before.

The Park City school district provided us with curriculum and materials for the winter months when the children were not able to make it through the snow to school. I had been taking classes on how to teach children and had already taught Garrett preschool. We decided to create a private school with all the families in the community who wanted that. I chose to teach kindergarten so that I could teach my own children.

I conceived again and started spotting. Bed rest had worked with Garrett, so I took the high-school-age class and taught them at home from the couch. When I was four months along, I went to the doctor for a checkup. He thought I was too big and wanted to do an ultrasound to see if there were twins again. I stopped in at my sister Bonnie's house to visit while I was in the city. Suddenly I began to bleed—a lot.

With my obstetric history, Gary didn't want to chance me going home while the pregnancy was so fragile. Bonnie offered us her bed until I could stabilize.

I did everything possible to keep this baby, including complete bed rest, but after a month I went into labor and delivered Aaron at twenty-six weeks. He did not survive.

That night, I pleaded with Gary to take my little boy home and bury him under a tree. I couldn't bear the thought of another baby being "disposed of." He was stillborn, so I didn't expect anyone else to count him, but if I could bury this baby and keep him close, I could count him in my heart. Gary said, "Just let the hospital do what they normally do. I don't think they will let us have him."

I was too weak to fight. I just crawled into a hole and told myself I should be grateful for the three children I had at home, alive and well. I was so angry—angry with myself for my defective body, angry with God for being so cruel, and angry with everyone for dismissing my babies so easily, as if nothing had happened. At the same time, I felt ashamed at my failure.

In my desperation to understand what kept going wrong with me, I got involved in midwifery training and began assisting midwives. I needed to make some sense of it all. I needed answers.

For the next year I tried desperately to conceive again. Finally I went to a fertility specialist to find out why I had not been able to conceive. The tests showed a two-fold problem: my Fallopian tubes were blocked with a tremendous amount of scar tissue, and there weren't many places in my womb for an embryo to attach. Basically, I was told there wasn't any chance of conceiving again.

I was devastated. Having many children of my own just wasn't an option. I seemed to have no choice but to "surrender" to the inevitable. I was around many children—I worked with sweet children every day at the school and was surrounded by women with multiple children. I petitioned God to show me my purpose. If I wasn't to have a big family like the other women, what did I come here to do?

In answer to my desires to find my purpose, I buried myself for the next fifteen years in service to the people of my community, even becoming the principal of the private school we had established. I was trying to achieve anything that might possibly be recognized and valued. I would be there for the children who sort of fell through the cracks. I knew I had the capacity to love and care for many.

I knew it the night I conceived my last baby. It was electrifying and terrifying at the same time. When I started the spotting that was usually the signal for bed rest, I was determined I was not going to endure bed rest only to have it end badly. I made up my mind I would simply surrender to what was. I would not form any attachments to this baby.

This pregnancy was the beginning of my training for the profound peace I enjoy today. This angel in my womb came to teach me the art of letting go—of knowing through experience the power and perfection of God in my life. Many times the fear of losing the baby occurred. Each time, I let it go and relaxed into the peace that if this baby belonged in my life, she would stay.

Jessica was born March 29, 1982, two weeks overdue. When I finally got to take her home after three weeks in Primary Childrens Hospital for tachycardia, I saw her as the gift of God to me for my willingness to surrender to His will. It was the beginning of my awareness to change the things I can and let go of the things I can't.

I began to wonder about the after-life and my babies who had gone there. I studied everything I could get my hands on and began to want it for myself. I had let go of the limitations of the structure of religion and wholeheartedly embraced the ideal of unconditional love as taught by Jesus. I began letting go of judgments, finally finding a sense of peace within and listening to the still, small voice of God in my meditations.

I spent the next couple of years in intensive training and staffing retreats. My life took on meaning beyond anything I could have imagined.

I grew confident in my purpose and determined to work through any fear that got in the way. I felt and understood God was with me.

Beginning in January 2000, I became a spokesperson for those who were living polygamy; I took part in helping to shape legislation and even did an interview during the 2002 Winter Olympics.

Most of the time, I was greeted with acceptance, gratitude, and openness. In 2005, I announced to a gathering of leaders from various polygamous communities that, "We have built the bridge, and it is now up to you to cross it. You need to form a coalition and work together so the people and the justice system trust you to turn in the abusers in your midst."

It was a milestone in the history of the underground polygamous culture, to have leaders from nearly all the polygamist factions come together. The veil of secrecy that sheltered abuse needed to come to an end.

I was then asked by the state to support a plural wife who had her children taken from her. When it was finished, I felt complete in my healing around polygamy. I was exhausted, and felt it was time to retire—but the biggest challenge in my life lay ahead.

In the spring of 2006, Gary went to the hospital for a simple procedure on his heart. He had undergone open-heart surgery in 1999, and the doctors now decided he needed another open-heart surgery. This time he was in the intensive care unit for three weeks with no guarantee he would get well.

Gary signaled to me that he wanted to speak to his son, Louis, about family concerns. When that was settled, he seemed to relax. The next morning he was improving. Later, when he was stronger, he shared an out-of-body experience he had that morning. When he finally got out of the intensive care unit, some of his first words were, "I am not the same man I used to be." His mind had been opened.

Gary retired, to my delight, and I felt so much gratitude for his life and for our life together. I've learned that the gift of facing death is the courage to live life more fully. As we learn an ever-increasing level of letting go of judgments, attachments, worries about the future, and trusting the process of life—living in gratitude for every moment and everything that shows up in our life—we experience a joy and happiness that is richer and deeper than anything we had ever imagined.

As I reflect on my childhood, I realize that my decision to choose plural marriage was heavily influenced by my upbringing—not by any pressure or the words that my father preached to us, but by the sheer joy I experienced as part of a plural family. I watched my three mothers interact in a loving way, especially as they took care of each other while Dad was in prison. They consistently helped each other, and I never heard them gossip about each other or trash on each other. I had big sisters who filled in when Mother felt overwhelmed, and I never lacked for care or attention. I was surrounded by loving siblings and always felt safe within my family.

As for my father, I feel a lot of gratitude for his legacy of courage, relationship to God and his faith. I always looked forward to seeing my dad. He worked hard and did a lot of fun things with us whenever he could. I saw him as honorable in the life he chose. I wanted a family like his.

My choice to live plural marriage was absolutely the right one for me. Though I no longer believe in the religious aspects of my lifestyle, I am confident that I made the right choice and am very happy in my marriage to a very good, kind, and loving man of impeccable integrity.

Our family is very diverse in our beliefs and lifestyles but I've never seen a more loving family than ours. We gather often to celebrate our love for each other and our devotion to our family—and those things are much more important than any particular religious belief or lifestyle. When it comes right down to it, I am as happy as I choose to be, and I choose to be very happy in the family I have helped create.

I also have a very happy relationship with the family in which I grew up. My parents and siblings were very supportive of my choice of lifestyle, and my sisters and I meet often to celebrate our love. Differences sometimes arise because of the various ways in which we have chosen to live our lives, but we always seem to be able to work through them. Rather than resent the ways in which we differ from each other, we respect those differences and share in loving support of each other, an attitude that enables each of us to feel peace and joy.

Evelyn Roberta

~

CHAPTER 14

1950

M Y FATHER, ALBERT BARLOW, had thirty-four children in his large plural family; I was his twenty-ninth. I was the seventh born to Vio Fraser. My father named me Evelyn Roberta.

For me, growing up was always an adventure. There were plenty of siblings to share in whatever was happening at any given time. I didn't have a daddy around a lot like most of my friends did, but I really didn't think about it much—I was too busy just being a little girl in what I thought was a normal family. I knew I was loved, and always knew that no matter what I needed, someone was there for me. That assurance brought me a great deal of comfort as I was growing up.

Daddy was a big presence in my life. He was strict and generally expected perfection from the members of his family. But more than anything, I felt his love and to me he was the best dad a girl could have. It seemed like Mama was uncomfortable giving me hugs and kisses, but I always knew she loved and cared for me. She took me on bus rides to downtown Salt Lake City; we shopped for school clothes, got our hair permed together, and stopped for a hot dog at the Kress dime store where Mama's sister Zola worked. Mama always let everyone know that I was her "baby girl."

My sisters always told me I was their cute little baby sister who brought joy to our family. Ramona, my oldest sister, was my caretaker until I was about five or six. She gave me dolls, took me for rides on the family horse, dressed me up, and styled my hair. After Ramona got married, Laura and Faye stepped into her role and continued to give me love and attention.

Laura taught me how to do the latest teenage dances, including the shuffle and the bop, throwing me over her shoulder and swinging me around until I was so dizzy I couldn't stand. Faye told me stories and let me sleep with her. I really felt like I was a little princess.

When I was about three, Mama went out for the evening and left Laura to care for me and my other siblings. Mama told Laura we could all have a gum ball for a treat after the chores were done. Shortly after Laura had given me a gumball, I started to choke. I was looking into the kitchen and saw Laura come running toward me, she looked scared and she was yelling as I was choking.

I learned later she pounded me on the back then put me down and tried to call Mama, but our phone at that time was a party line and no one was willing to give her access to call out. Her only thought was to pray in desperation for help. No sooner had she finished praying than she saw my older brother's car coming down the road. She rushed out to the car, threw my limp body into my brother's arms, and yelled that I had a gumball lodged in my throat. My brother, David quickly tipped me over and flipped out the gum. He then said, "Laura, I wasn't planning on coming over here but I had a very strong feeling come over me that I should check on you kids." I remember none of that.

I have mixed memories about my father. Some are pleasant, like when I was young Daddy often came home from work and handed my little brother and me his lunch pail, having made sure there was food or some kind of treat left in it for us to share.

But some of those memories are frightening. For example, one evening when I was about seven, I saw Daddy chasing Mama around the table as he yelled at her. I stood in the kitchen doorway and cried out for them to stop. As soon as she heard me cry out, Mama ran over to me, slapped me on the back and yelled at me to "get out and close the door behind you."

Faye came to my rescue, hugging me and reassuring me that Mama loved me and didn't mean to hurt me. I now realize Mama was only trying to prevent me from seeing their fight and the way my father was treating her.

On my ninth birthday, shortly after Dad was put in prison for practicing plural marriage, I went with Aunt Katie to visit him. I didn't understand why he had to leave us, and I was overwhelmed with sadness and confusion when I saw the prison bars and the guards standing around us. Dad gave me a big hug saying, "I'm doing alright, don't be afraid. Heavenly Father will always protect me."

Even though the prison atmosphere was scary, I always looked forward to visiting Dad during the years of his imprisonment. He tried his best with what little he had to make the surroundings as pleasant as possible.

He always made sure there was Postum (our favorite hot drink) and crackers, or cookies for us children when we arrived. Even though he was incarcerated, he used our visits as opportunities to teach us lessons about the gospel and taught us how to behave ourselves while we were there.

During the time Dad was in prison, Mom was left to be the protector and provider for her children. She tried the best she knew how to support and care for all of us. Shortly after he left, I had one of the most dramatic and disturbing memories of my young life.

My sister Susan's husband, Gene, was an alcoholic, and he became very violent when he was drinking. Susan had just given birth to a sweet baby girl and was staying at our house to be cared for by Mom. One evening during Susan's stay, Gene came to our house drunk and demanded to see his wife and baby. Knowing Gene's history of violence, Mom wouldn't allow him into the house. Instead, she locked the doors shouting, "You come back when you're sober!"

He was not going to be denied by something as simple as a locked door. He used his fist to break the glass window in the front door, reached through the broken window, and unlocked the door. Yelling and screaming, my mother and my sister Laura tried desperately to hold the door shut, doing whatever they could to keep Gene from entering the house and harming Susan and the baby. I was standing on the couch and crying. My mother's leg was bleeding. I just knew Gene was going to hurt or even kill all of us.

Gene managed to get into to the house. Mom called Mr. Christiansen, our wonderful next-door neighbor, to come and settle Gene down.

Somehow the nightmare all ended but I was so frightened by that experience, I was sure I hated Gene. I hated his drinking, I hated his smoking, and I hated everything about him. Even at my young age I knew I didn't want to have or do anything that reminded me of Gene, who in my mind was an awful man. This experience, as well as many others I saw or experienced with Gene, happened because he was under the influence of alcohol—and those experiences became a big part of shaping what I did and didn't want in my life.

The saddest experience of my life occurred just after my thirteenth birthday. My sister Ramona had entrusted me to take her two boys—five-year-old Jeff and four-year-old Dennis—to the circus. Afterward, I was to catch a bus and meet her at a department store uptown. The boys and I had a great time watching the circus and enjoying a picnic on the lawn; then we headed to meet Ramona as planned.

In order to get to the bus stop, we had to cross busy State Street. Waiting for the light to change, I told both of the boys they needed to hold on to me while we crossed the street. The instant the light changed, Dennis was so excited to try to beat us across the street that he let go of me and darted into the street. At that very instant, I saw that an oncoming car was not stopping for the red light. I yelled at Dennis to stop, but it was too late. The car hit his little body and dragged him down the street. I was so frightened that all I could do was scream and cry and hold Jeff so he wouldn't get hurt.

Dennis survived the terrible accident, but because his head was injured, he sustained a permanent handicap. For years I couldn't even bring myself to talk about it. I tried to block it completely from my memory and blamed myself for what happened. It was so difficult for me to see him in his hospital bed. I wanted to make him better but I didn't know how. I just knew Ramona would never trust with me with her children again—but even with all the heartache and trial Ramona was going through as a result of the accident, she never once made me feel like it was my fault. Instead, she did everything she could to help me through the hurt. I truly believe the Lord was there by my side helping and loving me through the entire experience.

Dad was released from prison when I was thirteen. My love and respect for him really grew from that time forward. He treated me like I was his favorite girl, showing me love and affection and taking me to church meetings and school events whenever possible. I felt so special to Dad, even though I never remember him calling me by name. To him, I was his "slim."

Dad made sure his family was together as much as possible. He took us on camping trips, rides in the canyons, and picnics in the park. He also spent part of Easter Sunday with us at the State Capitol Building, rolling eggs—and us—down the hills. He held Sunday school with his family every Sunday, and we started each meeting with singing hymns. One of my favorite memories was singing the hymns of the LDS Church while Aunt Maurine played her old "player" piano. Dad spent time teaching us of the prophets, reading scriptures, and always having family prayer. I was most captivated with the lessons he taught about our Savior's love and His atonement. Dad told me if I truly believe in my Savior and pray, asking Him with true intent for any need, righteous desire, or help, He would hear and answer my prayers.

One of my fondest memories is the time we went on a daddy-daughter date. We went to dinner and then to a dance at my school. At fourteen, I was so excited; Dad taught me how to do the fox trot, and I was so proud to show off my handsome father to my friends for the first time.

Some of my favorite memories are of the times I spent with my Aunt Maurine's family. Her daughters (my sisters) Linda, Doris and Shauna were my best friends, and Bonnie and Barbara were my cute little sisters. Whenever I got the chance to stay at their home for the weekend, it was pure joy. If I couldn't get one of my brothers to drive me to Aunt Maurine's house, I caught the bus. I had such wonderful times at the big house taking part in Halloween parties, delivering newspapers, doing laundry with the ringer washer, and playing night games in the back yard.

Shauna and I didn't always get along very well. We were both very stubborn and liked getting our own way. There was a kind of underlying tension in our little squabbles and an unspoken understanding between us not to push each other too far. I think jealousy played a part in our estranged relationship, but at that time in our lives, we didn't really recognize why or how these feelings existed.

That strained relationship with Shauna came to a head just after Dad returned from prison. He took his whole family on a camp out. All of us girls shared a tent. We had a great time laughing, telling jokes, and talking about girl stuff. The next morning we woke to the smell of a campfire and breakfast. I was still cold after I ate, so I went back to the tent and snuggled into the bedding to get warm. Not long after I went back to the tent, Shauna came in and wanted to join me.

Being the feisty girls that we were, we started fighting over the blankets. One thing led to another, and we started to fight. When I realized Shauna had pulled out a chunk of my hair, I was so angry that I hit her in the face, giving her a bloody nose. With both of us screaming and crying, hair flying and the tent rocking, dad thought a wild animal was in the tent with us—and he came to our rescue. To his surprise, he saw it was only his sweet little girls fighting like wildcats. That made him madder than a hornet—he pulled us apart, spanked me hard, and threw Shauna in the cold creek to wash the blood off her face. He scolded both of us and told us that we were to never fight like that again.

It surprised me when some of the other sisters congratulated me on "beating Shauna up." I was aware that Doris and Linda were afraid of Shauna but never could understand why.

During the ride home, Shauna told me she was sorry for pulling my hair out. My head was throbbing so badly, I didn't believe her. It took me quite a while to really forgive her. Eventually, however, we became loving sisters and even friends.

Beginning at the young age of twelve or thirteen, I began praying that the Lord would send me a man to marry who didn't smoke or drink and who loved Jesus Christ. Just before I turned fifteen, I met a sweet young man named Steve. My sisters always told me that most boys wanted only one thing, and they warned me against letting Steve get too close. So at first

I was afraid of him because I didn't trust boys in general. The more I got to know Steve, I knew there was something special about this cute guy. I knew the Lord heard and answered my prayers by bringing him into my life.

My belief in prayer and the warnings of my sisters about men came together in a horrifying experience I had when I was sixteen. I was walking home from school one afternoon on a little-traveled path with fields on both sides of the road. Very little traffic ever used that road. I was strolling along thinking about my boyfriend and not really paying much attention to what was going on around me. A little more than a mile from home, I looked up and noticed a car parked on the side of the hill about a half mile up the road. I felt extremely uneasy but I didn't know why.

As I got closer to the car, I noticed four men inside. Seeing them just sitting there caused a chill to race through my body. I thought about what my older sisters had warned me about, including the wretched things some men would do to a young girl if given a chance. I was so frightened and didn't know if I should run the other way or cross the road and keep walking. But I realized there were no homes to which I could run for protection, and I couldn't see another person in sight that could help me.

I knew I was in real danger, but suddenly I remembered what Dad had taught me, to ask God in the name of Jesus Christ to protect me whenever I was in danger. Right then, I truly believed with all my heart that God would hear and answer my prayer. Calling on my faith, I started to pray harder than I had ever done before. I prayed over and over, asking in the Lord's name that these men would not touch me.

Just as I walked between the car and the field, one of the men opened the car door, jumped out, and demanded that I get in the car. My blood ran cold; as I knew he could grab me at any time and pull me into the car. But I kept walking as fast as I could, continuing to silently pray; I did not make any eye contact with the man, but simply looked straight ahead and acted as if he wasn't there.

I had nearly walked past the car when the man started walking after me, yelling and swearing at me and telling me to get in the car. He was so close behind me that I could hear him breathing. Then a miracle happened. The driver leaned out the window and said, "Just forget it!"

The man behind me swore again and said, "No, I won't forget it."

At that the driver got out of the car, yelling at the man following me, and said, "I told you to forget it. Let's go."

The man following me swore again, turned around, and climbed back in the car without ever having touched me. The men in the car drove off. When I knew they were some distance from me, I started to shake and cry, all the time thanking the Lord for hearing my prayers. I knew without a doubt that nothing other than my Savior's protecting love could have prevented those men from taking me that day. I know my life was spared because of Him. That day I gained an undying testimony that would stay with me for the rest of my life: my Savior lives, and He hears and answers prayers.

At sixteen, I knew I was in love. My dream was to be married forever to the man I loved, to raise our children, and to live in a cute little house with a white picket fence. Steve reassured me that he loved me and knew I was meant for him, but he said he wouldn't marry me unless I was willing to live plural marriage.

My first thought was, why is this so important to know before we get married? I had been taught that living the law of plural marriage was one of Gods' commandments. Our parents lived it and some of my siblings lived it, so how hard could it be? Isn't that what the Lord wants for us? So my answer to Steve at that time was a simple of course I will, not knowing what the future would bring. So at the tender age of sixteen, I agreed to marry my only love.

Steve and I had been married for a little more than three years when we decided to live plural marriage. It was not a decision that was pushed on me by my parents or by Steve. My parents taught me what they believed to be the true gospel of Jesus Christ, and plural marriage was part of that. It was something I had accepted after much observation and thought, not simply because I blindly accepted what my parents did.

When Steve and I decided to live plural marriage, I thought I was going to be the best, most giving, most understanding, and most loving sister-wife anyone could have. I had watched my mother's relationship with her sister-wives, and it was clear that she loved them. She was always willing to do whatever she could to be helpful and kind. Mother worked together with both of them, and she and Maurine were the best of friends. These three women provided a good example of love toward one another within a plural marriage. All three women had their faults, of course, but they never gave up on what they had committed to and they lived within their plural marriage to the best of their ability. Their example has continued to impact my life, and when I consented to bring another woman into our marriage, I thought I would be just like the women I had watched and admired as I grew up.

But then reality hit me, and I didn't know if plural marriage was really something I could do—or even something I wanted to do. I needed to know for myself without a shadow of a doubt that this was the Lord's will for me. I needed my own testimony and could not simply rely on my husband's testimony. So I studied and prayed and asked the Lord for an answer, all the time afraid to find out that His answer would be yes.

The Lord did give me my answer—an unwavering testimony so strong that it has sustained me throughout my life. I have never since doubted that living the law of plural marriage was His will for me. I have had trials, and living in a plural marriage has sometimes been very hard, but the blessings have been numerous in comparison. Additionally, my trust in and love of the Savior gave me the courage and strength to live the lifestyle He asked me to live. I never felt coerced and knew I could leave at any time, but knew that leaving would be turning my back on the powerful testimony the Lord had given me. If I had my entire life to live over again, I would make exactly the same choice. The experiences that have resulted from that choice have made me the woman I am today.

As a result of my decision to live plural marriage, I have experienced more happiness, joy, and love than I could have ever imagined as that young girl so many years ago. The Lord has given me so many blessings. I have ten wonderful children, thirty-nine grandchildren, two beautiful great-grandchildren (with the hope of more in the future), and a husband who loves me with all his heart.

I have benefited from a wonderful relationship with my parents and my siblings. Some of my brothers and sisters did not agree with the priesthood group I chose to follow, but I never felt rejected or criticized. As far as I am concerned, my relationship with my siblings is the best it has ever been. I have been shown nothing but respect, kindness, and love by my sisters, and I love them dearly. I have gained strength from their experiences and have greater understanding as a result of the choices we have all made, even though those choices have differed.

When it comes right down to it, everything really goes back to my father and his tremendous influence in our home and on my life. He wasn't perfect by any means. He made a lot of mistakes, as we all do. For example the way he treated my mother, but even through that, I knew that he loved her.

My memory of my father is and always will be of his courage and determination. He never gave up on what he knew to be right before the Lord. The trials he endured would have caused most men to walk away and leave behind everything they had worked for, and travel the easy road instead.

I don't say that lightly. I have personally seen a lot of men abandon their polygamous lifestyle, and I have seen firsthand the subsequent destruction and sorrow it has caused their families. No matter how tough things got, my father never turned his back on what he knew to be right and on us as his family. I always knew that Father loved his family, including me, more than life itself.

I am thankful for the family I have been given, everyone has good times and sad times, regardless of the lifestyle he or she chooses, and I am no exception—but we make our own happiness. The joy I have in my life right now comes from the things I've gained through my experiences, and I am convinced that my joy would not be as profound had I chosen any other way of life.

Vio's five daughters. Top left: Laura, Ramona, Susan, Faye; Bottom: Evelyn.

Doris Alberta

CHAPTER 15

1950

I WAS BORN at the old Salt Lake County Hospital on December 12, 1950, the ninth child of my mother's thirteen children and almost the tail end of my father's thirty-four children. I was the only one of Dad's children to be born in a hospital.

In 1953, when I was two, Dad was preparing to leave the house when I went to Mom complaining of a tummy ache. I tried to eat the dry toast she gave me but I just gagged on it. Mom wanted me to take another bite, but I gagged again and could not swallow it. She then gave me some milk, but I wasn't able to swallow that either. As it dribbled out of my mouth, I was having a hard time standing up.

Mama laid me on the couch and sent someone to catch Daddy before he left. I could feel the fear in her voice. Dad noticed that I was not closing my right eye and my right arm and leg were not moving as I cried. He asked his friend who was at the house, to help give me a blessing of healing. He and Mom took me to the old Salt Lake County Hospital.

The doctor and nurse took me away, telling my parents they had to leave. I felt a deep panic and fear and started thrashing and screaming. The nurse had to call for three more people to hold me down while they put a needle in me. One of them even sat on me and I felt a deep rage. I needed my Mom and my Dad to protect me from these awful people.

The polio paralyzed the entire right side of my body; I clearly remember being in an iron lung, a machine that was used to help polio victims breathe. After I had spent some time in the hospital, the doctors told my parents there were three strains of polio and I had the worst kind—Bulbar. They said they were sorry, but there was nothing more they could do for me and they did not expect me to survive.

Dad called one of his best friends, Morris Kunz, to come and help him administer another priesthood blessing. Morris "rebuked" the disease and commanded it, in the name of Jesus Christ, to leave my body. He blessed me that I would heal and would become a mother in Israel. From that moment the polio stopped its destructive path and I began to heal.

I was transferred to Shriner's Hospital, and after what seemed like an eternity but was only three weeks, I went home. I crawled for a while and was soon able to walk again. I continued to heal until I regained the use of the right side of my body—all but the muscles on the right side of my face. Dad told me that the resulting crooked smile was God's way of reminding me of the power of the priesthood. I was a miracle baby, and I felt special to God.

One month before I got sick, a salesman had come to the door selling insurance for the "five dread diseases," one of which was polio. Even though he had never before purchased any kind of health insurance, Dad bought that policy—and it covered the cost of all of my medical bills. I know that was no coincidence.

Dad was the disciplinarian in our home and was strict about some things. When he was angry, all of us children learned to scatter and find something to do that kept us out of sight. He could also be fun-loving and kind. Often the older kids were in charge of all the younger kids and sometimes they weren't very kind, often mimicking Dad's behavior. Once Ginny was being mean to Steven for wetting his pants and that worried me because I often wet my pants.

Once I witnessed Betsy hitting Bonnie for not doing her "chore." As I saw Betsy hitting Bonnie I said, "I'll do it for her."

She responded, "No, she has to mind," and she kept hitting her. I was afraid of Betsy when she was mad but, like Dad, she was also the creator of most of the fun we had at home. Sometimes she would take us to see her friend Iris and I knew she was proud of us.

By the time I was turning five, I was still wetting the bed. I have wondered if my stay in the hospital and the ravages of the polio somehow affected me, because I also had a hard time not wetting my pants during the day. We wore dresses most of the times back then, so no one could tell until I started to smell bad and was told to take a bath.

Everyone thought the odor was from my wetting the bed at night, but I knew different—and so did my sister and best friend, Linda, who was 13 months older than I. She watched me several times sitting hard on my heel, pretending to tie my shoe or fix my buckle, and I told her what was happening. Linda never left me when she saw I was having a dilemma, and I've always appreciated her love and loyalty.

Wetting during the day was bad, but I hated the bed-wetting worse. I tried various things—including prayer—but nothing seemed to work. One day Dad came up with his own style of discipline in an effort to help. He said, "Every time your bed is wet in the morning, your mother will put you in the bathtub naked and run cold water over your head."

I knew it was Dad's order so I hated him every time I stripped in front of Mama and got into the tub. The last time it happened, I was sobbing so hard and asked, "Why does Dad hate me so much?"

Mom let Dad have all the blame, responding, "I'm sorry I have to do this."

She must have told Dad that the cold-water showers weren't working, because I never had to go through that again. From then on, every time I woke up wet in the night, I had to deal with it myself. Once my big sister Ginny came home from a date and saw me wet, cold, and barely awake. "Why don't you get some dry clothes on and come and sleep with me?" she said.

Looking down, I mumbled, "I might wet again."

"I'm sure it will be fine, I would love to have you come and snuggle with me."

I woke up clean, dry, and wrapped in the arms of someone who loved me. Mom came into Ginny's room the next morning and seeing me there, smiled. She was as happy as I was. By the time I grew into puberty, I finally gained some control over the wetting.

One night, when I was about eight, several of us were out playing hide and seek. I was hiding by the back fence in the bamboo Mom was so proud of.

I saw a man come walking down the alley that was behind our property. I was afraid at first, I was going to run and find some of the other kids until I realized it was a neighbor from two houses behind the alley. His wife was a nighttime nurse and his two kids played at our house a lot.

I thought he was coming to get them so I spoke to him and offered to go find them for him. He said, "No, I want to talk to you about something. I have something at my house I want to give you. Come with me and we'll get it."

I went with him easily, trusting. He wasn't a stranger and my little sister Barbara played with his little girl at his house all the time. I was chatting with him as I followed him home, asking "What do you have for me?" as we went in the front door.

It was dark inside and I was going to wait politely by the front door when he said, "Its back here in the kid's room, come on."

I didn't feel comfortable but I was curious so I followed him through the kitchen into the back bedroom. There was a single bed and a chair that I can still see. He sat on the chair as he pulled me toward him.

I was getting nervous and asked him what he had. He said "I'm going to pull down your pants but I'm not going to hurt you. " I was so scared I couldn't move. I've often asked myself why I didn't run. I guess every victim behaves differently particularly at eight years old.

What he did created sensations I'd never felt before and I started praying to Heavenly Father to protect me. I was praying so hard yet I felt so ashamed that these sensations I was having felt good to my body. I had tears silently rolling down my cheeks.

I thought maybe God wouldn't want to take care of me because I knew what this man was doing was wrong and I must be a very wicked girl for my body to like the sensations. I kept praying anyway and told Heavenly Father I was so sorry.

After a while (probably only 10 minutes, but it seemed like an hour), the man got up, told me to stay there while he went in the bathroom. I was so scared I was shaking real bad. Why didn't I run? I don't know. I ask myself again even now.

The man came out of the bathroom and stood at the side of my head. He asked, "Do you want to taste this?"

I vigorously shook my head no. I had a huge lump in my throat and couldn't talk, tears still streaming down my cheeks. He zipped up his pants and told me I could pull up my pants if I wanted to.

He walked me out to the sidewalk and said, "Before I let you go you must promise me you will never tell anyone what we just did."

I would have promised anything at that point. His left hand was in the pocket of his sweater and he was pointing to me with it telling me I better keep my promise. I visualized a gun in there, pointed at me even though I never saw a gun and he never mentioned one.

I was backing away from him and promising never to tell anyone. As soon as there was 10 or 15 feet between us I turned and ran back down the alley, around the south side of the house to the front of our house and up on the porch. Mom was reading a book while Barbara, Bonnie, and the neighbor man's little girl were coloring. The man had asked me to send his 2 kids home so I did.

Haven, my brother, asked me where I'd been hiding because they couldn't find me. I made up a few places, which he accepted and then he praised me for hiding so well. He asked, "Why did you come in now?"

"I'm tired. I don't want to play anymore."

I went up to my room, got ready for bed and knelt down to pray. I told Heavenly Father I was so sorry for being a bad girl, crying some more and I thanked him for protecting me from being hurt. I was so glad that the man didn't make me taste his "thing".

No one suspected any thing and I kept my promise to keep it a secret for over a year. I would never go past his house again if I was alone and I told Mom she shouldn't let Barbara go over there to play. She asked me why and I didn't tell her. I had made a promise and in our family "a promise is a promise," like being taught never to lie or steal.

I had been agonizing over every detail in my head and feeling even more ashamed because that man probably had no gun and I kept berating myself over and over and over again for allowing myself to be his victim. I went over every moment when I could have run away and didn't. It was eating me up inside.

Even now as I write it down, I shed new tears. Not for any pain, there was none, but for the shame, humiliation, and guilt that I felt. I was pretty sure that anyone who found out my secret wouldn't see anything good in me. They would think I was a very wicked little girl and not worthy of their love.

My sister Linda and I were very close. She was my best friend and finally, after a year, I decided to take a chance on telling her to see if she would reject me or hate me.

So one day while Linda and I were out for recess at school, I told her I had a secret that I promised not to tell but it was a really big secret and if I told her she must promise to keep it secret. She promised, so I told her. She asked me why I didn't run, but I could tell she still loved me.

It helped a lot to be able to tell her but about six months later she told my big sister Betsy while they were in her room discussing how important it is to tell someone when something bad happens to you. Linda came running to find me saying that Betsy wanted to talk to me about my "secret." I was so mad at Linda for telling and now Betsy wanted me to tell her. There were some of the other kids hanging around to listen as well.

I was so ashamed, but Betsy said, "It isn't you that is bad, it's that man. You have to tell Mom."

I started to cry saying, "NO, I CAN'T!" I was so afraid Mom wouldn't love me anymore. How could I risk that?

Betsy said, "You tell her or I will."

I knew she meant it and I figured even if Betsy told, Mom would ask me about it anyway. Betsy took me to Mom's room where she was reading a book. Betsy said, "Mom, Doris has something to tell you," and she shooed the other kids out and shut the door.

I still remember how hard it was to talk about it to my mother, looking down at Mom's hands the whole time, answering her few quiet questions. When I was through telling her I looked up and saw her crying. I was crying too and I asked, "Are you crying because you don't love me anymore? I guess God doesn't love me either does He? I know I'm very bad because I knew what that man was doing was wrong but it felt good to my body."

Mom touched my shoulder, tucked my hair behind my ear and said, "I do love you, I'm just sad you didn't tell me sooner because I could have made that bad man go to jail. God does love you and I'm so glad that you weren't hurt more."

I'm sure glad Dad wasn't there that day. I really don't know how he would have reacted. He and I never did talk about it. I'm thankful and grateful my two loving sisters interfered and told my secret. More than anything, talking to Mom helped me to know that I was loved and helped me believe in myself.

While Dad was in prison for practicing polygamy, Mom got two big paper routes to earn extra money. She put them in my brother's name so she wouldn't compromise the money she received from state welfare. She explained to all of us kids how much she needed our help to make the deliveries in the morning before school. Someone stayed home with the youngest children, and the rest of us got up at five every morning to deliver papers before school.

One day Mom heard a report on the news about a pack of dogs that had been attacking people in the area where our paper routes were. To make us feel more secure, she sent Linda and me to do our delivery streets together. It was scary walking down that dark street with no people, no cars driving by, and loaded down with so many papers we knew we couldn't defend ourselves if there was a problem.

One morning we were at the last house on one street when we spotted a pack of six or seven dogs running rapidly in our direction, snarling and barking. Terrified, we were too far from Mom or the car, and the bags of papers were still too full and heavy for us to run. The last house had a tiny porch out front with a small railing on it. That was our only option. We hurried up onto the porch as the dogs came up the driveway. We huddled together, closed our eyes, and prayed that Heavenly Father would protect us.

Slowly we opened our eyes. The dogs, just three steps away from us, acted like they couldn't see us and had lost our scent. They circled a bit before running around the house to the next street. We quickly thanked God and hurried to find Mom. We wanted to make sure the dogs didn't get her. That morning I learned again that God is real and He does answer our prayers.

By the time I was a teen in junior high school Dad was out of prison and doing everything he could to control his daughters. The mini skirt had become popular and it was at least three inches above the knee. One morning as Linda, Shauna and I were leaving for school Dad stopped us and began lecturing me on how short my skirt was (barely above the knee), "Why don't you do what Linda and Shauna do? Their skirts are below the knee."

Surprised I looked at Shauna who was always into the latest fashion and sure enough her skirt was below the knee. Linda was no surprise. She always did what Dad wanted. We soon left for school and as we were out of sight of the house Shauna asked me to hold her books. She proceeded to pull her skirt up, tuck in her shirt, zip up the skirt and said, "I don't know why you're so stupid, and he doesn't have to know what we do at school."

Shauna was always on top of what and who was in. She bought clothes at the "right" stores. Sometimes she would look at me and say something like, "Why don't you wear this?" or "Why don't you do this with your hair?" I usually liked the way I looked when I followed her suggestions and tried to take more care with the way I looked. I appreciated her for that.

Once I asked her, "Can I walk home with you?" School was about a mile from our house.

"I don't know, well, yes, I guess," she said and then I walked behind the four of them. Her friends were popular. I didn't really fit in with them. I didn't ask again.

Around January 1968, I began in earnest to search and study the scriptures with fasting and prayer. First of all, I wanted to find out what I truly believed about plural marriage. Was it right? More important, I wanted to know if it was right for me. I intentionally did not seek Dad's advice or counsel, because the only influence I wanted on my decision was that of my Heavenly Father. Through that process, I became certain I wanted to live plural marriage. So I took the obvious next step. I prayed a lot about whom I was meant to marry. I was seventeen years old.

In June, Quin asked Dad if I could go out with him and Betsy. Betsy treated me so well, and her children—a four-year-old boy and two-year-old girl, with another expected in August—were used to me because I sometimes tended them. I felt so comfortable with the four of them that it felt like I was home. I was kind of nervous about the jealousy that might come between us as sisters, and I expressed that concern to Betsy. She immediately stated, "You never have to worry about that, I can hardly wait to share him."

Within a few weeks, Quin proposed marriage and I accepted.

Being the right decision for me does not mean it was easy. Betsy was my big sister and often the boss of me when I was growing up. So I allowed

Betsy to talk me into marrying Quin before I was ready: I wanted to finish my last year of high school and I thought we should wait until Betsy had given birth to her baby (I came into the family three weeks before her due date) and I thought it would be better if we waited until we could all live in a house together. With Quin and Betsy and their children living in a tiny one-bedroom apartment I would have to continue to live at Mother's.

I was confident about my choice to live plural marriage, but I experienced a lot of anxiety as I thought about marrying into Quin and Betsy's family. I was afraid Betsy would grow to hate me or that jealousy would come between us. I was afraid that Quin would never grow to love me. I was afraid I wouldn't fit into their circle of friends. Their friends were married adults, while my friends were young, single, and still dating. I was afraid that Quin's family would not accept or welcome me. And in my heart of hearts, I was afraid of becoming a plural wife who was unhappy or mistreated, because I had seen many of those kinds of women.

Quin picked me up on the day we were to be married. He had made an appointment with Louis to perform the ceremony on Friday, July 12, 1968. The ceremony was to be performed in Louis's home with the blinds drawn and no witnesses—there wasn't even a ring for my finger. Louis had spent more than seven years in the state prison, half of it for performing plural marriage ceremonies. Once he got out of prison, Louis kept very secretive about marriages he performed, but he didn't stop. He had even secretly and carefully solemnized several marriages during visiting hours while he was still in prison.

Soon Quin did buy a home big enough for all of us. The most frequent visitors to our home were my cousin, Dale, Quin's sister, Carol, and my best friend, Ann who was Dale's plural wife. Ann became like another sister to me, I was even closer to her than to most of my sisters.

I did not marry for love, but for a principle I believed in. But I was falling in love with Quin, and I learned how to be a good wife and mother as I watched Betsy. I felt that I had a good relationship with both of them most of the time. All of us lived together for almost a year when Betsy asked Mom if Quin and I could rent two of her empty upstairs rooms and make one of the rooms into a kitchen for me. After that, we lived apart off and on for many years. I had a lot to learn about living "the Principle," and a great deal to learn about Quin's quick temper, his insecurities, and his way of showing his love. As it turned out, I also had a lot to learn about myself.

I was pregnant with my second child when Quin physically abused me the first time. I had blatantly embarrassed him in front of others regarding his "authority" as the head of the family, and he struck out as a result. I was stunned and confused. I wasn't sure I wanted to stay with him, and I said so.

I didn't hear from him for three days. I started to wonder if he would come back at all. When I told Mom what happened, she suggested that if I start with an apology for what I did wrong, and then we might be able to work things out from there. Even though I didn't want him to think that striking me was acceptable behavior in any situation, I called him, and he grudgingly accepted my apology.

My second child, Jessica Lynn, was born on April 6, 1972. Jessica was an easy baby to care for but she was fussy if I laid her on her back or her stomach. I found that if I laid her on her side and put a pillow or blanket behind her, she slept well.

I started going to Al-anon with Ginny and Betsy. I had a good reason to attend because Quin drank a lot—but going to Al-anon was not about his drinking; it was about me. I was having a difficult time understanding my temper and my inner rage. I also had a lot to learn about men and relationships.

On Friday, May 6, Jessica got sick with pneumonia when she was only five weeks old. She was in intensive care for about three days. Six days later I brought her home from the hospital with strict instructions to bring her into the office the next week for a checkup. I took her in exactly one week later on Friday, May 19. The doctor checked her lungs very carefully and said, "I'm surprised her lungs sound so clear this soon after being that sick."

The following Thursday night, six days after Jessica saw the doctor, Quin and I had a quiet night at home watching television with our two little ones. The children settled easily, as usual, and at about 1:30 am. Jessica woke up for her regular feeding. I sat with her on the side of my bed, as was my habit, but she was acting a little odd. She wouldn't nurse but definitely wanted to be held. She wasn't crying in pain, just fussing for me to hold her. I was puzzled, wondering what to do. My eyelids were heavy and I longed for more sleep. I talked to her and cuddled her for a bit, then finally laid her on her side and propped the blanket against her back—but she still fussed. I lay with my arm over the side of the tiny crib and stroked her cheek, talking softly and lovingly to her. She calmed down and I went back to sleep.

The next morning Quin got up for work while it was still dark. Not wanting to wake the kids and me, he turned on the light in the walk-in closet. Glancing at the tiny crib, he thought Jessica didn't look right. He went to her, turned her over, and then yelled, "Doris, our baby's dead! OUR BABY'S DEAD." He groaned, "Why didn't I wake up for her?"

I jumped up, looked at the baby, and began to wail and moan. Quin stepped outside the door at the top of the stairs and cried in a strangled voice to Mom, "Maurine, our baby is dead."

Mom ran up the stairs and into our room. She quickly realized that the baby was dead and suggested we place the blanket over her. As soon as Jessica was covered, little Dardi woke up in her larger crib, fussing a little at all the commotion. Mom agreed to watch Dardi while Quin and I took Jessica to the emergency room at Holy Cross Hospital, where she had been born. There was no 911 to call.

The attending physician asked us a few questions while checking Jessica's vitals, and then he gently told us what we already knew: Jessica Lynn Kunz passed away on May 26, 1972. He told us that Sudden Infant Death Syndrome (SIDS) appeared to be the cause of death. We arranged for him to send the baby to Larkin Mortuary. We buried her on May 30, and I was glad to have so many friends and a large, loving family to get me through this horrible ordeal.

Quin stayed with me for almost a week and felt he needed to go to Betsy's that night. I told him I thought I'd be okay and encouraged him to go. As soon as he was out the front door, I couldn't hold back my tears of anguish. I couldn't stand being alone, and I hated this room where our little Jessica had left us. I felt conflicted. I knew Betsy needed him too, and I didn't want to be selfish. I was still crying when the phone rang. "Have you been crying?" Quin asked.

"Yes."

"Betsy said we should bring you and Dardi to stay at her house for a few days. Would you like that?" Quin asked.

"Oh yes!" I said.

"Pack enough to stay for the week, and we'll see how it goes from there."

I felt so grateful to Betsy for that.

I wouldn't stay in my bedroom without Quin after that. Whenever I was alone I started to cry, so I began staying with other plural wives every other night when Quin was not with me.

At my six-week checkup with the doctor, he expressed his condolences and handed me a pamphlet with information on SIDS to help me understand a little more about what had happened. The pamphlet said that if you have one child die with SIDS, there is a greater chance of another child dying from the same thing. I wanted more children, but didn't know how I could face the possibility of another SIDS baby.

I have always been thankful and grateful for my belief that Jessica is alive with God and that I will see her one day in heaven. I am also grateful that several things helped me see the Lord's hand in Jessica's life and in her passing. First, she was born on the sixth of April, which I believe is the true birth date of our Lord, Jesus Christ. Second, she was under a doctor's care shortly before her death, so she didn't have to be mutilated by an autopsy and the authorities had no reason to suspect any child neglect. Third, Quin was with me and Mom was home when we found Jessica dead, so I didn't have to deal with everything alone. Fourth, she had no suffering or pain— she simply went back "home" to our Father in Heaven. And last, but just as important, I had Dardi to fill my empty arms.

By the middle of summer Quin's father heard about my aversion to staying in my room alone and asked if I would like to live in one of his empty apartments. I was thrilled. I had been married four years, and this would be the first time I had a real place of my own.

I got a job to help with the expenses, and within a month I realized I was pregnant again. I prayed that the Lord would give me the strength to continue with this pregnancy without living in constant fear of SIDS. When Boaz was born I chose a different doctor, a different hospital, and different details surrounding my delivery. I needed it all to be different, and the Lord gave me a boy instead of another girl. His love is so apparent. The first few weeks of Boaz's life were pretty scary for Quin and me as we woke in the night, fearing our baby was dead. But Boaz was a deep sleeper and seemed oblivious to the many times we poked and nudged him to make sure he was still breathing. His life was very healing for us.

One night when Quin had fallen asleep next to me, he had a dream. A beautiful young girl came to him in the dream and said, "I'm okay, Daddy, don't worry about me." Jessica was telling him not to grieve so much because she was very happy.

There were many tumultuous years of marriage and many additions to our family when one day Quin came home only slightly drunk and said he wanted to talk to Betsy and me. The three of us sat in the living room, and he told us he knew he was the cause of much of our unhappiness. He said he knew he needed to make some changes and wanted us to tell him what he could do to make our lives easier and more pleasant.

Betsy asked that we have family prayer every night, and he agreed. She then asked that we spend more time with the kids and less time out. He also agreed to that. She asked that he not drink every night; again he agreed. I asked that we not have television on every night. He agreed. He also agreed to a handful of other things. For the short time he complied with all his promises, it didn't seem as crowded for us with three adults and fifteen children in our seven-bedroom, two-bathroom Taylorsville home.

Late in the summer of 1983, I had quit smoking and was pregnant with my ninth child when I received a wonderful job offer from a previous employer. After getting Betsy's agreement to tend my younger children and Quin's okay to accept the job, I started working, and it turned into a wonderful opportunity. I was able to travel and take a couple of kids with me many times. I was also welcome to take my new baby to work with me. I received a lot of praise and respect, which I would desperately need later.

Dale, Kelsch who was also my cousin, bought a nice boat and invited us to go boating several times. After one such trip in September 1984, Ann—Dale's wife and my best friend—who was due with her ninth child, called me from her mother-in-law's home. She was in a lot of pain, but it wasn't from labor.

"What's wrong?" I asked.

"It's my kidneys," she replied. "The doctor has given me some pain pills and told me to go home and rest."

"Let me know if I can help," I told her.

Two days later I learned that Ann was dead and that her baby boy had not made it. Even the death of my own baby never prepared me for the depth of my grieving for Ann. She was buried with her perfect, beautiful baby boy in her arms. Her death left a huge hole in my heart for many years.

During the next year, Betsy became somewhat distant from me and quite argumentative with Quin. I was still grieving for Ann but I couldn't talk to Quin about my struggle. He was worried about Betsy and wouldn't talk about anything else. I was feeling more and more like the old, battered shoe that gets tossed into the corner.

Betsy's primary struggle was that she wanted her own place—but she also wanted Quin to quit drinking. She felt he was an alcoholic and that he needed to quit drinking completely. He traded the equity in our home in Taylorsville for a duplex, and when we moved into the duplex, Betsy no longer wanted to tend my children. A month later, Betsy had Quin served with divorce papers, letting me know that it had nothing to do with me.

That was the beginning of the most difficult years of my life. Quin could not let go peacefully. He was with me every night but was obsessed with Betsy—where she was, who she was with, what was happening with her children, how to prove that he was right and she was wrong. I was afraid of what the future held for our children, and Betsy became a stranger to me.

I now had the responsibility of my own children and most of Betsy's as well. Quin and I were able to move into a large home next door to his parents and close to mine. It had a huge yard at the end of the street and was so safe for the children. It was a major fixer-upper, but Quin was great with his hands and did some beautiful things to it.

I felt very alone throughout this ordeal; Quin, still obsessed with Betsy, did some thoughtless things that took me years to get over. I often wondered if he would ever get over her and acknowledge me for my loyalty to him. I wondered if I would ever be a priority in his life. During this period he even tried to get custody of Betsy's smallest children, which cost a lot of money. The one positive thing that came out of it was that I became Quin's legal wife.

After six girls we finally had another boy, born on July 19, 1991—my thirteenth healthy, normal child. He was about a week old when I was finally feeling well enough to come downstairs one afternoon. Quin and the teens came home from work and most of us were sitting in the living room while two of my girls were trying to put something together for dinner. Quin made a remark about me getting off my lazy butt to make dinner, which started an argument that ended with him slapping my face. I was embarrassed that all the kids witnessed the abuse, but I was also mad as hell!

He stomped out the door, yelling at me to be gone by the time he got home from work the next day. I wasn't especially startled—I can't even count how many times he yelled at me in anger to "Get the hell out."

I really didn't know what to do. I took the seven youngest children and left for more than a week, staying at Linda's and pondering what I should do. I was so sad that I didn't feel love from him, but I was even sadder that I didn't feel any love for him. How did it get to this? I couldn't live with physical abuse, and if Quin didn't apologize, would that mean he believed he did nothing wrong? Would he do it again?

I still had no answers, but I took my children home and did two things. First, I got down on my knees and asked the Lord to help me find something in Quin to love and respect. I needed to have that if I was ever going to find happiness with him. I also asked God to help Quin find something in me to love and respect—something that would prevent more of this behavior in the future.

Second, I talked with Quin—he needed to understand that I would leave if he ever struck me again. We didn't talk much and we both walked on eggshells for a while, but before long my prayers were answered. I began to see the man I had loved come shining through.

Quin was different with the kids too. Now I came home from a function to find the teens wrapped up in a movie and Quin was pacing the floor with the colicky baby. He helped more with the meals, doing breakfast and Dutch-oven cooking many nights and most weekends. A newer, better love seemed to kindle from the ashes for both of us.

Between home schooling, working, birthing fourteen children, working in the back rooms of a local grocery store, helping our parents until their deaths, seeing the marriages and deaths of our children, and running a home overflowing with children, I have had a full life. Quin has been at my side for all of it. He has become the friend and lover I always hoped to have. I now have a thriving herbal business, which is my passion, and I recognize more than ever that God has been good to me.

Looking back on all that has happened, I chose plural marriage before I ever left home, and I chose it because it was what I believed—not simply because Dad told me it was right. I had always been a person who carefully thought things through, prayed, and used my agency in making choices, and those were the factors that had the greatest impact on my decision to live plural marriage.

My relationship with my father had a lot of ups and downs. My memories of him from when I was young are wonderful; he always had a smile, a hug or kiss, and time to play cards with me. He loved to play hide-and-seek with us while he dressed in the morning, to take us for an ice cream cone, or to take us camping. The way he acted made me feel special and loved.

That changed as I got older. He was much more strict and demanding; he insisted that I be "good" so the Lord wouldn't punish me. He said that "outsiders"—those who didn't share his beliefs—were not to be trusted and were not acceptable people with whom to socialize. He often gave me lectures about the dangers of becoming popular in school. And that's not all: He sometimes touched me inappropriately—kissing me on the mouth or touching me too close to my breast—which left me confused about boundaries.

In trying to arrive at a decision about whether to live plural marriage, I took a lot of opportunities to observe my mother and her sister-wives. Watching Mom, Aunt Kate, and Aunt Vio demonstrated more than anything else that there is both good and bad in living plural marriage. All three of them did some things that were selfless and giving, and all three did some things that were selfish and thoughtless. After all, they were human, and I truly believe all three of them did the best they knew how.

I also had plenty of opportunities to watch how Dad treated his wives. During the years I was growing up, he had a "my way or the highway" attitude, something that actually made me feel sorry for all his wives. I especially hated the way he treated Aunt Vio when I was younger (though he later came to love her dearly). Watching his interactions with his wives really didn't impact my decision about whether I wanted to live plural marriage—like most young people, I was convinced things would be different for me. Ironically, I married a man who had many of the same attitudes Dad did.

Despite my very real fears, I clung to the knowledge that I was to live plural marriage, and I relented to the pressure to get married before I felt I should, which is my only regret. I resented my father so much by the time I married that I avoided him as much as possible for the first few years. I knew he was proud of me for choosing plural marriage and proud of the fact that I would likely have lots of babies, but he didn't know the first thing about how I was feeling. I wasn't even sure he cared. As long as I was making the "right choices"—his choices—he was satisfied.

My fears about entering plural marriage with a sister-wife who was my sister turned out to be legitimate. My relationship with Betsy was strained from the moment I said, "Yes," a period spanning more than 22 years. Sometimes she was thoughtful, kind, helpful, loving, and much more— the perfect female companion. I loved those times. But other times she was the complete opposite: jealous, competitive, demanding, selfish, and manipulative. During those times I felt hurt and confused. I rarely knew where I stood. Even after she left our marriage, she occasionally chewed me out.

I do have to say, though, that Quin taught me more than anyone in my entire life about how to stand up for myself and speak my truth. Linda is the one who helped me learn what it feels to be "present," and those are lessons that have been invaluable to me and have molded my life.

Betsy left our marriage almost thirty years ago. We made a few attempts to get another wife to join our family, but none of those worked out; as a result, I am not living a plural marriage lifestyle now. That doesn't take away from the fact that I still believe in the lifelong commitment I made all those years ago, and I'm completely confident I made the right choice for me. I'm happy, I feel complete.

At this point in my life, I have the love and support of all my children—something not all mothers can truthfully say. Quin has become a good companion, a good provider, and has taught me a lot about effective communication. He was also amazingly patient and supportive during my long journey through menopause.

Thankfully, the long-term strain between Betsy and me did not negatively affect my relationship with my other siblings. I've had a great relationship with most of them, something that has had very little to do with my choice of lifestyle. I did have one sister who, along with her husband, tried very hard to talk me out of plural marriage. Other than that, things have gone fairly smoothly.

Later in Dad's life, things came full circle: He became more open, accepting, and loving and less preachy. I spent a lot of time with him during those later years and I came to understand many things about him that I had never fully appreciated. As I reflect on him, I am grateful for his belief that marriage is a lifelong commitment, for the ways in which he worked so hard to support his large family, and for the years he spent in prison defending his lifestyle. He lived those lonely years behind bars so I could call him Dad. More than anything, I am grateful that he taught me to gain a personal relationship with my Heavenly Father and Jesus Christ.

Shauna Lynn

CHAPTER 16

1952

M Y FIRST NAME IS SHAUNA. My last name depends on which period of my life I am writing about. I was married, widowed, married, married again and then divorced. I am now living with an American Indian who is a member of the Ute Tribe. We live on a beautiful forty-acre ranch on the Ute Reservation in Fort Duchesne, Utah, in a house my son built for us.

Everyone asks where I get my drive, my confidence to go forward without questioning myself after all the adversity I've experienced. I never saw myself as driven. I did know I was different from my sisters—not better than, just different.

My memories as a small child are very vague—certainly nothing to write about. I do not remember any connection to or affection from any adult. In fact, I can't remember ever being held by an adult. At some point in my infancy, my mother shut down and became completely indifferent as I grew up. The only time I felt any affection from her was when she called me Dear. I never saw much of my dad; he was in prison for four years for practicing polygamy, but even when he was not in prison I avoided him.

I was my mother's tenth child—right in the middle of five little girls who were barely more than a year apart. I was the least favored—at least, that's how I felt.

The oldest of the five girls was adorable with curls and an irresistible smile. The second sister had polio as a child and needed a lot of care. The girl just younger than I was emotionally fragile; she was always hanging onto Mother, begging for her attention. The youngest sister had big, beautiful

The three children born after 1952 family photo: Bonnie, Shauna & Barbara.

eyes. Then there was me. I was bald with big ears, and such a loud, even shrill, cry, I am determined to be heard, by darn, because I have something important to say. I learned to make sure I was heard.

I have been told that Mother endured some of her most difficult struggles during her pregnancy with me and the two years following. Dad bought a ranch and took his first and second wives to help with that. He left Mother with boarders she had to feed and a day care filled with children for whom she had to care in addition to her own. She didn't see Dad much unless it was to take the money she earned and possibly get her pregnant.

I believe that as a result of her suffering during this time, I was a mature little spirit who was very aware as an infant. I knew what I wanted and demanded that I get it. There was one major problem: no one was listening to me. They didn't even want to listen because they were facing so many other demands.

I must have made myself louder and shriller in order to be heard. Guess where that got me? My mom's philosophy said it all, "Feed them, change them and if they still fuss, let them cry it out in the crib. Otherwise, you will spoil them."

I have a memory of standing in a crib crying to get out. Mom got pregnant when I was nine months old, so she weaned me. I assume that's when I received my first spanking from Dad, because if Mom couldn't handle us, she let Dad take over.

While Dad was in prison, Mother supplemented the small allowance she received from the state by getting some early morning newspaper routes in my brothers' names. So we delivered newspapers early in the morning. I was about seven when I had to start helping to deliver newspapers at five in the morning. In the winter my hands were so cold, and on the way home I would always cry about it. No one thought to get me a hat or gloves or to even button up my coat. That kind of nurturing simply wasn't available to me. To this day I tense up whenever I go out in the cold, and I have to tell myself to just relax.

When we got back home from delivering newspapers, I went back to bed. I had to get myself off to school. I was always late and rarely had my hair combed. In second or third grade, a new girl came to my class; she often fixed me up by buttoning my dress or combing my hair when I came to school looking like an orphan. Once I accidentally came to school with my pajama bottoms on under my dress. No wonder no one would play with me as a child.

I was a very angry little girl being left in that crib so often. I made a promise to myself: I will show them, I don't need them. I will be somebody when I get out of here. I will never again be confined or stopped by anyone.

My sisters just older than me say that when I got old enough to stand up for myself they were scared of me. I was reasonable unless I felt anyone try to confine me or control me. If they did, I beat them up.

At Christmastime we played a lot of games and had special treats, and some of the older kids would come home and spend time with us. Mom even seemed happy at this time. One Christmas I received a music box just like Betsy's. I loved it. Another year I received a little buggy and a "dancing rabbit" that was as tall as I was and I loved dancing with my rabbit. I felt free and special.

I remember taking care of Bonnie sometimes, helping her to look nice, the kind of nurturing I wanted for myself. Bonnie hung onto Mom a lot and would say often, "I love you," to Mom. I watched her do that and knew I wanted Mom to love me but I tell Mom I loved her.

My brother, Steve, was always nice to me but that's about the only good memory I have. Most of my memories are a blur of fighting between my parents or between my sisters and I.

When I was eleven Dad lined us all up to be baptized by Uncle Morris and I later kneeled in prayer and asked God to please give me a large family who were good people and a vision opened up to me of great men and women, I felt I was being shown my children. I knew I was going to have amazing children.

I remember living with Dad's first wife for almost a year when I was in seventh grade. She observed that I was always doing something—playing the accordion, knitting, sewing, painting, or doing anything else for which I had a passion. I thought my drive was a good thing and always felt very confident. Later in life I realized that what I felt was not always confidence. At times I have been so driven that I got in my own way and pushed too hard. Many times I have found myself in survival mode rather than in partnership with my Creator.

I felt my family didn't know me or recognize me for who I was. When I read about all that my mother went through, it was no wonder she was not emotionally available.

Once I was determined to get a reaction out of Mom, anything that would show she cared about me. I began pushing her buttons. She was "slow to anger" by nature so I had to go to great lengths to finally get a reaction out of her. She began slapping me and did so several times until all the rollers (curlers) I had in my hair fell to the floor. Then she began to cry, something I had never seen before, and she said, "I'm so sorry, I'm so sorry. You look so much like Vilate." (Vilate had married into a plural family and we had no contact with her.)

Looking back, I realize I had some learning disabilities that were not recognized in those days. I did not do well in school. It didn't help that Mom never asked about our progress or report cards. I couldn't figure out why I couldn't learn or be as smart as the rest of the students. I worked so hard, yet I struggled in every subject, and even more in reading and math. I could not follow more than two directions at a time, and the first two were "Get your pencil and paper out."I was lost after that, asking, "What did she say?"

All through school, I was unable to retain information. They didn't have the great programs they have today to help students who struggle my family didn't notice or try to support my learning. I was more than happy to drop out of school in the tenth grade to get married. I had been taught that women should not go to college or they would be exposed to the evils of the world—but even more than that, I hated school. The irony is that today I am very worldly and damn proud of it.

My only regret in life is that I didn't get to have a college experience in my youth. I choose to become a mother at a young age, and I have never regretted that.

I married my childhood sweetheart, Lynn Darger, when he was twenty-one. He was tall, well built and very handsome. We had been seeing each other at social functions for two years, and he proposed when I was sixteen. I asked Mom if I could marry Lynn, she said, "Absolutely not, you are way too young!"

I talked to Ginny and several others who were older than I was, insisting I was ready but they all agreed with Mom. I was already very independent. I had been working in the fabric department of a small department store and had recently been made manager of the fabric department.

I told Lynn, "The only way we can get married is to get permission from Dad—and that might be impossible because Mom made him promise to deny permission until I was at least seventeen." I knew Dad could over-ride Mom if he wanted to.

I decided to just leave it up to God, praying that if it was meant to be, Dad would say yes. If not, he would say no. Sure enough, when Lynn went to visit Dad to ask for my hand in marriage, he refused, saying Mom had insisted I wait until I was at least seventeen. Then Lynn said, with a grin, "I'm not leaving until we agree."

Dad smiled, they shook hands and sat down. Dad ended up giving in after Lynn told him about a dream he had. Dad realized that Lynn was a good man and he trusted Lynn's integrity. It helped that Lynn was the son of one of the men Dad had served time with in prison in 1945. Lynn's father was also arrested in 1955 at the same time Dad was.

I was married September 10, 1968, and I was expecting my first child at seventeen, exactly nine months later. I was the only one of Mother's daughters to have a lovely traditional wedding due to my sister Ruth. She had always adored her little sisters and so knocked herself out to provide me with the kind of wedding she had always wanted. I was a nervous wreck so she gave me a tranquilizer to settle my nerves and sadly the whole day is a blur to me. I blame the tranquilizer. The photographer was a neighbor, and he never did come up with any pictures, I don't even remember his excuse now.

Lynn was extremely intelligent, almost like a walking encyclopedia, even though he had been forced to quit school to help his family financially. However, he was an avid reader, giving him a very broad education. He resented his dad for that lack of education and for the many beatings he endured from his father. He lost his mother when he was twelve, and as one of several boys in a polygamous family he got lost in the shuffle and ended up having a traumatic youth.

After we were married I discovered Lynn's temper. My response only complicated things—instead of standing in my own power and letting him go, I felt responsible for his anger. Looking back I wonder if he was bipolar. At the time, I just knew he had crazy mood swings and eating habits, and I never knew which mood was going to show up. He was a good man in many ways and I loved him very much. When he was good he was so good, cheerful, kind, loving, talkative, social and respected by his family and mine. Actually no one ever saw the angry Lynn but our little family.

His rage would ignite at inopportune times, such as most holidays and birthdays—times when most families enjoyed relaxing. Unfortunately, it got worse with age. He started out as a very healthy and robust man but abused his health and became a serious diabetic but was in denial about it. He began to have serious health problems. I was raised with a healthy lifestyle and tried to cook healthy but Lynn liked to eat and would often buy unhealthy food loaded with fats and carbohydrates from the 7-11 before he came home to eat whatever I had prepared.

I had ten beautiful children with Lynn. He loved his children very much but was controlling and had a patriarchal mindset like my father that always sparked his temper. He kept a tight control on the family. If he had physically abused me I may have left him, but verbal abuse didn't register as unacceptable to me at the time.

Before my children started school I heard about some parenting classes through one of the high schools and began attending them. They introduced me to parenting books and a lending "library" of educational toys. I was so excited to be able to teach my children and even encouraged my nieces to join me in those parenting classes.

That's when I heard about the Step Parenting Program and eventually attended the Glen Doman Institute in Pennsylvania, they actually paid my way there three times. I began to sell the educational toys and became a sales manager and that company sent me to Detroit for training. I also attended some Montessori classes and then began to home-school my children after attending some home-school conferences. When I had a passion there was no stopping me, my children and their education was my passion at this time.

Lynn's rage seemed to get worse with each passing year. I knew he was the man that was meant for me, so I told myself I must have needed that conflict to keep me humble. I processed my feelings the best I could. Because we were both raised in plural families, I told God I did not want to live that lifestyle unless I had to. I also knew I needed to do it "right or be damned" (according to my father), if we did live that way.

I had been married to Lynn fourteen years when the day arrived; a young, beautiful girl approached her father about marrying into our family. When this happens the man is duty bound to accept the girl into his family. I was pregnant at the time with my seventh child and was confined to a wheelchair because of some muscle issues and I could not carry the weight of the pregnancy.

I was determined to make our plural marriage work and did my best to overcome the intense feelings that came up in me. I woke up every day determined to make the very best of my situation. For a few months I hurt so bad I thought I would go crazy. I cried so hard one night that I went into labor two weeks early. After, I decided I had to quit fighting the situation and instead make the other wife my best friend. You always want your best friend to have a great relationship with her husband, so that became my goal. I began to work on her relationship with Lynn rather than worrying about mine.

My husband tried hard to live this lifestyle better than he felt his dad had lived it. But with his rage disorder, one more woman put him over the edge and his temper got progressively worse. It is a lot of pressure for a man to have two women in the same house. As if that wasn't enough, she had two sisters down the road who wanted to marry him as well.

These three girls were not expecting a man with a temper, and Lynn knew he could not rage at these younger wives. As a result, he held them responsible for very little. He usually told me to have them do things then held me responsible for their actions. If they didn't do what he felt they should, he raged at me. He also held me responsible for the behavior of their children. It gave the other three wives confidence when he always exploded on me, never them. I was foolish for taking that kind of thing on, but I thought I had to be obedient to his demands. We were taught to be obedient to our husband and I really tried to be.

For the most part, all four of us worked hard to get along; we had a good relationship with each other and worked through a lot of things. I worked hard to overcome jealousy, thinking that would fix the problem. But Lynn's behavior was increasingly unreasonable. I extolled the great qualities of my husband and my sister wives to everyone, except sometimes Ginny because she had been in an abusive marriage and I knew she wouldn't judge me. However, God was aware of my struggles, He was my confidant.

Throughout these years we were homeschooling our growing family and with the help of Lynn's family we were able to purchase a large piece of ground in Herriman which was a small community at the foot of the Oquirrh mountains in the Salt Lake Valley. We built a much larger home and to help make ends meet I started a housecleaning business. I had my three sister-wives and my daughter to help me get this business off the ground. That worked for a while and then I started a ski jacket business and made all the jackets for the Brighten Ski Team.

I could not get permission in my heart to leave Lynn, but I was at the end of my rope. I felt I was going insane having to put up with his anger toward me. No matter what I did or how hard I tried to appease him, his behavior became increasingly worse and at last it was more than I could stand. One day after a horrific emotional incident that Lynn inflicted on me, I had taken all I could and asked God to take me. I am not the type to take my own life, but I told God that I did not want to keep living in such tumult.

When I told my husband what I had done, he started to cry. Knowing what a strong relationship I had with God, he said, "I am in trouble now."

Four days later Lynn woke me and said, "I was visited by a spirit (not a visible one) that told me to get my affairs in order." He spent more than two hours confiding in me about what God told him to do.

Not more than two weeks later, he was bitten by a brown recluse spider and he refused to get medical attention. We both had a strong distrust of the medical profession. He died six weeks later at the age of forty-nine from the spider bite and complications from his diabetes. All the while he refused to go to the hospital because he knew it was his time to go. He suffered greatly all that time, and I believe he became the man he always wanted to be. He never had the mental strength to accomplish that until he was compelled to on his deathbed. His suffering was purging that ugly rage of his like nothing I have ever seen. He kept saying, "I have to get this right," meaning preparing himself to meet the Savior.

I had to spend all my time with him because he would not let anyone else care for him. I slept a few hours early each morning. It's hard to describe what I was feeling at the time; I think I was just in survival mode. It was so difficult for the children; they couldn't come in and see him because he was in so much pain. They often sat outside the door listening to their dad in so much pain, waiting for me to come out. I ended up with an ulcer after Lynn died, but the experience was priceless and I gave him all the love I had to give. He had many good qualities and I loved him very much, but part of me was also relieved.

His death was very difficult but at the same time liberating. Ten months later, I became a plural wife to Lynn's best friend who I will call Mel. My daughter, Danielle, was also one of Mel's plural wives and had been for years. She had five children by him.

I proceeded to organize and establish a catering business. All the ventures I began were done in a building outside my large home so I didn't have to leave my children.

Mel was the total opposite of Lynn. At the time, I connected with Mel on a spiritual level, and he helped me heal after Lynn's death. Two years later I gave birth to a beautiful daughter I named Sarah. I was forty-nine years old. All of Mel's wives left him during the few years I was with him including my Danielle. Danielle met a man at my catering company and she left Mel, took her children and began a relationship with him. Mel eventually left me.

I invested everything I owned to start a business in downtown Salt Lake City. It was a wine bar, restaurant and catering company combined and required many long hours of my time. I was working away from home for the first time, leaving my children. Mel basically abandoned us by the time Sarah was five, and I worried about her a lot because I was working such long hours and had trouble getting her older siblings to watch her while I was at work.

Danielle had a very strong attachment to Sarah and eventually agreed to let Sarah live with her for the school year; as part of the agreement, I would come and get Sarah on the weekends as often as I could.

The following summer Danielle's husband called me about Sarah. He said, "I have a father's love for Sarah and I want to know what your plans are with her. Either leave her with us for good or take her for good.

Danielle was at Sarah's birth and had bonded with her immediately, so her attachment to Sarah was very natural. Also, Danielle's children were close to the same age as Sarah. I allowed Sarah to choose to be adopted by her sister, which she did.

It was the most difficult decision I have ever had to make, but I knew in my heart that her sister would provide a family that could give her stability—a family with a father who loved her and two mothers who would always love her for eternity. Not long afterward, she asked me if she could call me Grandma because other kids in school had only one mom, and she did not want to be different. I have been her grandmother ever since. That was the most difficult decision of my life, I understood then what unconditional love was. I loved her enough to give her up.

Meanwhile I met my third husband but soon knew that wouldn't work so we divorced and have remained friends. Then I met my Native American partner who I have learned so much from. I lost everything in my business but because of having that business I gained a relationship that has been very good for me. My involvement with him has given me the fulfillment of a prompting I had many years ago that I would be involved in the Native American Culture.

My choices regarding lifestyle have been diverse. As a result, I've had a wide range of experiences, and with each decision my only concern was that I live what was for my highest good and that I be able to live with integrity. In each case, I have learned what I needed to learn from that experience, and I am who I am today because of that.

Each of my decisions required courage of some kind, and I am grateful for the strength that inevitably resulted. It took great courage to share my husband with another woman after living a monogamous lifestyle for fifteen years. It took courage to give that woman what I wanted for myself. And it took tremendous courage to break all the religious traditions by which I had been bound once I decided to leave the polygamous lifestyle. I do not regret any of those decisions, and in each one I made the choice that was best for me at the time. I do have to say I am happy today to live without all the drama that came with plural marriage.

When I first left my plural marriage, some of my family and even some of my own children judged me harshly, but things have evened out and we enjoy a good relationship.

Now that I have experienced both the polygamous and monogamous lifestyles, I have a unique frame of reference from which to gauge my life experiences. Reflecting on all of it, the most difficult thing for me was my dysfunctional relationship with my father. The memories of my father are extremely conflicted. On the one hand, I remember him making the effort to give us crackers and tuna when we visited him in prison, something that required care and thoughtfulness in addition to meticulous planning. But after he was released from prison, he was so controlling that I had to hide the fact that I wore dresses above my knees, wore makeup, and had boyfriends. One of my greatest regrets is that he made us feel like education was bad and that we would be "worldly"—in other words, evil— if we went to college.

When I went through puberty I avoided my father because when he saw us he insisted that we kiss him—then he violated our trust by touching us inappropriately once we developed breasts. As a result, I never trusted him enough to get close to him.

I understand now that my father had some very difficult issues of his own, and I have been able to find a love for him in spite of his abuse. One of the reasons for my current state of peace and joy is that I was able to make things right with both my mother and my father after their deaths. Today I have great peace of mind, I don't feel driven and I enjoy my eleven children and all my grandchildren as they are all very amazing individuals.

Bonnie Gayle

~

CHAPTER 17

1953

I WAS BORN TO Maurine Owen and Albert Barlow on October 19, 1953—the eleventh child of my mother and the thirty-second child of my father. He was arrested when I was two years old, which began my distrust of "outsiders" including the government and the law. As my dad fought for his right to live his religion he was gone a lot and my mother was dealing with the overwhelming burdens of her large family. She relied heavily on the older children to help out with all that needed to be done and because I was so young I felt I was just one of my mother's many burdens.

I experienced physical, sexual, and emotional abuse from some siblings who were "in charge" a lot while my mother was busy or away. I always felt like an orphan and fantasized that a young couple that really wanted a little girl would find me.

I wish Mama and Daddy loved me, I guess no one can love me. There must be something wrong with me.

Doris was one sister who treated me good, she was always trying to teach me things. At Christmas she taught me how to wrap a present and how to put the bow on. I think she still tries to mother me sometimes. Christmas was fun because we played a lot of games together and every one seemed happy. Sometimes some of us would sit on the landing on the back stairs and play card games like Go Fish, War, and Crazy Eight. Maybe the landing on the back stairs was a place we would be out of the way. Sometimes we would play Jacks on the kitchen table or whatever games we had access to.

On the other hand Barbara seemed angry with me most of the time. I guess there's always a pecking order in families and Barbara didn't want to be on the bottom of that order, so that left me.

Why am I treated like a little kid? I'm almost the same age as Shauna? Will I ever be one of the big kids?

I remember one time when there were a lot of people at our house. The older kids were downstairs having a good time and several of the little kids were lying on top of the narrow banister pretending to be asleep. Jostling to get in on the fun, a sister and I fought for the same space. I climbed on, and soon after, either fell or was pushed and landed below, hitting my head on the radiator. I remember having a lot of confusion and a bad headache and even some nausea and vomiting.

Where is Mama, I need Mama, kids everywhere. I NEED MY MAMA!

Today I realize I had a concussion and attribute that incident to my being treated like I was stupid and clumsy much of my young life. I don't remember any adults being there.

Once I was at Aunt Vio's place and I accidentally dropped something and it broke. Aunt Vio screamed and I ran into the living room, very frightened Evelyn came and hugged me, reassuring me, "It's okay, don't be afraid."

I whispered, "She's mad at me."

"No, she isn't, she always does that, don't worry." She was always so kind and gentle with me.

Evelyn is actually the one who started me drawing horses, she taught me how to draw the head on a horse. Aunt Vio's family was always nice to me and I loved being at their house.

I think Aunt Vio's family loves me, I would be happy if I could live with them someday.

I was almost six when my father went to prison again. He referred to prison as "college," since he felt he was getting a higher education in exchange for maintaining his testimony of the "truthfulness of the gospel." I entered kindergarten that fall and my first day of school a sibling took me to the door of the classroom and said, "That's were you go," and walked off.

What if no one is in there? What if this is the wrong place for me? I just want to go home to Mom, but then she'll give me 'the look', and be upset with me.

Each year, the first day of school, I went alone. I felt awkward and terrified the first three years but the following years, I knew not to expect anything else. Each time there was a program at school where parents came I would wait and watch intently.

I just know Mama will come this time, she knows we're having a program. She'll be here. All the other parents are here, she's just gotta be here somewhere.

She never came.

I remember visiting my father in the prison cafeteria on Sundays, a time when his children were allowed to visit in a relaxed setting. We saw many of his "friends"—other convicts—sitting at other tables. My mother didn't get to visit him because she was not his legal wife, so she gave the older children notes to smuggle in to Dad. My parents had quite a stack of letters back and forth after almost four years of incarceration.

I learned more about drawing horses during those visits. I brought my best drawing to show Dad, and he corrected some of my clumsy lines. He also taught me a little about horses, their nature and habits, which he learned from being raised on a ranch. I knew I had the horse right one day when he looked it over carefully and then remarked gravely that there was only one thing missing in my drawing. Then he took the pencil and put a dark spot under the belly to show that the horse was a stud.

Why did he do that? I don't care if it's a boy or a girl. I'm not showing him my horses anymore.

I was embarrassed.

A new family moved in next door to us and they had a darling little girl just my age. Soon after they moved in, I went over to see if she would play with me. As the two of us were talking, her mother came out and asked where my dad was.

"In college," was my proud answer.

She asked what college he was attending.

"Oh, the Point of the Mountain," was my bright reply.

I wasn't allowed in her yard after that day. The "point of the mountain" was the location of the Utah State Prison.

Suddenly faced with being a single mom, it was necessary for Mother to make all the decisions and do what she felt was right. It was all up to her to figure out how to pay the bills, keep up the mortgage, feed the family and discipline the children.

Doris, Shauna and Linda were allowed to do things and go places that Mom considered Barbara and I too young to do. Once I pleaded with my mom to let me help with dinner. She looked at me for a minute and then said, "Go downstairs and get some potatoes and you can peel them.

Am I such a screw-up that she won't even let me help with supper? No one trusts me to handle anything. How am I gonna ever be one of the big kids if she won't teach me anything?

Over the years I began to feel more and more invisible, not just to my mother but also to everyone. Even Linda, Doris and Shauna would say, "You're too little!" as they shut me out of their activities. Sometimes I would feel them begin to yield to me, then Barbara would show up and want to be included and the door would shut on us both.

Why do I have to be tied to her? She won't even play with me. Why can't I be included with them?

When Dad came home from "college," there was a period of confusion that lasted for several years. I was unaware of the delicate dance of power and dominance that occurred in relationships and marriage. What I did see and comprehend was the incredible stress Mom carried and her frequent arguments with Dad. One day she came out of his library, sat down on the couch, and burst into tears right in front of me.

What did I do wrong? I'm always dong something wrong. I've been a butt-head today; that must be it. I'll just stay out of her way. I'm always doing something wrong. She doesn't want me around. She must hate me. I don't blame her.

When Dad came home from prison in 1963, his former place in the world was gone. It simply didn't exist for him anymore. We had continued to grow and progress in the four years he was gone, and he wanted us to go back in time—and he especially wanted Mom to go back. Obviously, she couldn't, nor do I think she wanted to. I often heard her complain about him to my adult siblings. As her resentments grew, so did Dad's confusion and insecurities. I developed some deep fears about marriage around this time.

I was still in the thrill of getting to know my dad again, but I felt cautious with him, because things were pretty unpredictable. But it was so good to see his handsome face, to smell his wonderful Old Spice aftershave, to see him all dressed up in his suit and tie for Sunday, and to hear his gentle chuckle. I had missed my daddy.

Once Dad invited me to go with him to work; I spent the day with him as he drove a big dump truck around for my uncle's construction company. He liked having me with him at that job site. He introduced me to the other men with whom he worked, and I knew he was proud of me as his little daughter.

The children who walked past to school pumped their arms at him as he drove by. That seemed odd to me, "Why are they doing that?"

He said, "They like to hear the big horn," and with a big grin on his face he asked, "Do you want to hear it?"

I shrugged and nodded as I watched him reach above him and pull a cord. A startlingly loud blast of noise erupted from the truck. The kids got excited and waved at us, and Dad chuckled. Later he hopped up on the caterpillar and showed me how the big tracks could turn back and forth, and he explained how those tracks were necessary for moving large amounts of dirt without getting stuck. It reminded me of the big army tanks I saw on TV.

Then he offered to let me try it for myself. He carefully fitted me with a hardhat while explaining safety. I didn't hear much. I was just so thrilled to climb up on that big seat and take those levers in my hands. He seemed to sense my excitement and gently encouraged me to turn to the left as I pressed down on the right brake. It took coordination. I held my breath. It was so amazing to me to be able to handle something so big and powerful. But my greatest thrill was that he trusted me, a little girl, to do it. He scoffed at that and said, "You can do anything if you put your mind to it."

Can I really? Are you sure? Yes, maybe I can even be a truck driver. My dad actually trusts me. I'm not just a little kid to him.

There were certainly many acts of kindness from my siblings as I grew older, some more than others. When I married and started my own family, I always looked to my siblings for approval and guidance more than I did my busy parents. As a child, I remember always being surrounded by family and family activities. One of my favorites was when Dad took us all up to the mountains to camp out. It was a big project to get us all there, but he seemed well prepared for anything that came along. I enjoyed being out in nature and roughing it. One of the best parts was when Dad pulled out his fifteen-inch cast-iron skillet and made us omelets so delicious they could not be matched in any restaurant.

I loved it when Dad took us all up into the mountains to camp. One of my most vivid memories from camping is of two sisters from different mothers who were close in age disagreeing more than usual. Whenever we girls disagreed, hair-pulling was the default weapon.

Suddenly we all heard squealing and snarling coming from one of the big army tents. The tent was swaying back and forth as these two sisters were having it out, and tufts of hair and hair curlers were flying out through the tent flap. Everyone stopped what he or she was doing and looked around for the source of the commotion.

Once it dawned on the adults what was happening, Dad took action. He called to the older brothers, who fetched a bucket of water from the nearby stream. Before I knew it, there stood two wet sisters gasping from the shock of the cold water. Problem solved.

Dad was a generous man who loved to fix things for people. I remember being in the basement with him in his tool room as he was fixing things.

He asked for me to hand him certain tools as he was working on an item. When I didn't know which tool he wanted, he patiently walked over and showed me the different tools and even demonstrated how they were used.

He is so smart, he can do anything. Why does he get so angry sometimes? To him I'm not a screw-up. He likes teaching me. He likes having me with him.

It was about this time that I was in the back seat of Ginny's car with her little ones. She had stopped to get all of us an ice cream cone. I usually got a kick out of sucking out the melting ice cream from the bottom of the cone. I liked the texture and the different approach to a common activity. Her children were watching me with wide eyes, so I showed off, thinking it was cool. When Ginny noticed what I had done I could tell she wasn't too happy. Then she said with a grin, "Just remember, what goes around, comes around." I didn't realize it then but now I do, my children also came up with different approaches to life and I had to clean up the mess.

I really enjoyed spending time with Ginny and her children. I felt so comfortable with them, and I knew she cared for me. Her kids were smart and fun to play with. I eventually tended them, too. My first experience with babies was with hers. She taught me how to calm a baby when crying by holding their tummy next to yours to warm it and soothe it. I was so amazed at how much Ginny knew and was willing to share with me but she waited till I asked her for it.

I'm so excited for my birthday, I get a party this year. I get to invite all my friends.

Then one evening before my birthday Mom said, "Bonnie, wouldn't you like to go to a nice restaurant for dinner on your birthday?"

What? What is she saying? She doesn't want to give me a party? Why would I want to go to a restaurant instead of having a party? She hates me.

"I guess," I shrugged.

I was rooming with Linda for awhile but we were not a good match so Mom cleared out one of the rooms in the basement. That was scary to me, there were a lot of scary bugs down there. So I would creep upstairs and sleep on the couch after everyone went to sleep. Dad caught me up there a couple of times and loudly declared to me, and later to Mother, "....that arrangement isn't working." So I became Shauna's roommate.

Shauna had a very bad temper and that would come out at Doris and Linda but she was always nice to me. I knew not to step on the tiger's tail. Mom had made a very special room for Shauna in the basement near the stairs. She painted the room, put up new curtains and a matching comforter for her bed, she even painted the bed to match. Shauna took me under her wing during the short time that I roomed with her. She taught me how to dress, sometimes looking at me when I was ready to leave the house and saying, "Um, why don't you try this blouse (or whatever I needed), it will look so nice with that skirt."

Shauna knew how to shop and what clothes were in style. Once she even let me wear her Lady Manhattan blouse. I felt so fine. I felt cared for and was glad to have her be a friend to me.

Then in one year five of Mom's kids were married which left just Barbara and me. I think Evelyn was even married that year. It was a shock to my system. Mom redid the corner room upstairs for me in avocado green and gold. She went to a lot of effort and money but by then I was one very rebellious teenager. It was too little too late. I was going to an "alternative school" and began trying some things. During that time I figured out what I wanted and what was not okay for me.

One day Dad took Barbara and me to lunch, which was so weird. He was very nice but let us know he knew we were doing "dope" and he proceeded to let us know how bad it was for us and he asked us to promise him we would not ever do it again. To my surprise Barbara agreed.

I didn't. Down the road Barbara caught me using pot and said, "Bonnie, we promised."

"I didn't promise." *They don't care about me; I don't f...ing care about them. Besides, I've been on my own enough, I can figure this out myself.*

Then the summer before I turned sixteen, I met a very nice-looking and muscular young fellow. I felt such an unusual draw to him and felt I would always be safe with him. He was a gentle guy, especially with children. I watched him take a misbehaving child and gently talk him out of it instead of using harshness, which I was used to seeing.

I want that kind of father for my children. They would feel so loved, and I would feel like they were safe.

I asked my older sister Ginny, "How do you know if someone is the right man for you?"

She didn't skip a beat with her reply: "Well, Bonnie, if you can imagine yourself sitting across the table from his unshaven mug every single morning and you think you could be happy with that for the rest of your life, he might be the right one for you."

Aw, yes, that feels really good.

Then she added, "Just remember—you'll be sleeping in the same bed with him night after night, too."

I felt very secure beside him. Once when I spent the night at my girlfriend's house, this same young man came over with some friends to visit. He ended up falling asleep on her front room floor. After everyone went to bed, I crept into the front room to look at his sleeping face. I just wanted to be near him. Throughout childhood, I suffered from insomnia and night terrors and could never sleep through the night. But I felt calm— and safe—when I was near this young man, Alan. I carefully sat down on the floor by his back, and soon ended up falling asleep on the floor behind him. I slept peacefully through the night.

The next morning I woke with a start as he suddenly jumped up and headed for the door. He was embarrassed that he had fallen asleep there. Even more, he was surprised to see me on the floor beside him.

In the spring just before I turned eighteen, Alan still didn't seem interested in marriage but I knew that we should be together. He seemed to like being with me, so his disinterest confused me. Years later, he told me that he heard my mother comment that she didn't want me to marry at sixteen as my older sister had done. What I interpreted as his disinterest was his attempt to regard my mother's feelings. That and the many other ways he expressed honor has held my esteem for him throughout the many years we've been together. As of this writing we have been married for forty-four years, and he is a loving, sweet man who is a vigilant protector of his children and wives.

Alan chose the way of his father (who also spent time in "college") and married two more sweet ladies. Sharing my husband was such a hard thing for me. My world seemed to have collapsed and I was sure I would never be happy again. Stepping into the world of plural marriage was like stepping into a different country where I didn't speak the language and didn't know my way around—in fact, couldn't even distinguish north from south. I was terribly confused and hurt for the first few years. Being raised in a plural family and seeing your parents, siblings, and relatives live it doesn't begin to prepare you for the actual smack-up-side-of-the-head reality of the situation. It's a huge commitment for all concerned, and the harsh reality of sharing your husband, and all that goes with being his wife, didn't go away.

About this time we had moved up near Park City with all three wives living in the same house, more of a duplex, but under the same roof. I wrote Mom a letter asking her to come up and see me. I knew she went to Linda's often but never stopped at my house. I was hoping she could help me with the struggle of living plural marriage. Soon after I sent the letter Linda came over to my house and was telling me what I needed to do. I resented her being so invasive in my affairs. She later indicated Mom told her I needed help and asked her to help me. I wasn't that close to Linda at the time to allow that.

Well, Mom, you did it again, push me off to one of your kids who doesn't really care about me. Believe me, I will never reach out to you again.

I turned to Ginny and she helped me to look in the mirror and figure out what I was doing to help or hurt the situation. She didn't live plural marriage but she did have an amazing understanding of psychology. I found that plural marriage is an intense and firm teacher of accountability and acceptance. You learn to discipline your mind, and you have to learn to mind your own business. Betsy taught me to laugh and be more positive, Doris taught me to enjoy food and people, Shauna taught me to crochet and Linda taught me how to embroider. Whenever my sisters got together at Ginny's we would exchange our latest insights about parenting and being a better person.

I have come to realize that in asking for the Comforter promised by our Savior, I have received more than I ever hoped for. I have come to know that a true testimony really does provide an anchor by which to live. And I have come to enjoy the perks of living this challenging discipline. I have chosen this way of life, and continue to choose it, because I have the freedom to follow what I believe to be true for me. Oh, wait, I hope to have that freedom.

I'm glad that I never felt obligated or forced into living plural marriage. Such a situation would be intolerable for me. We have always told our children that plural marriage isn't for everyone, and that they should only decide on it as a lifestyle if they really believe in it with all their hearts. We lost Alan's second wife to cancer, which is still hard on all of our family. I see her children having such a hard time with her gone. She left nine children.

As of this writing, I am the mother of eleven strong, independent children and the grandmother of thirty-nine sweet souls. Some people have looked down on me because of the size of my family, but there are many others who really appreciate the hard work and dedication it takes to raise such a family. What matters to me is that I love my beautiful family and that I am who I am because of those choices.

The story of my life you just read is really a third-party version. I felt like a "third-party version" for much of life; mostly because I couldn't seem to connect. I felt that the real me could never fully be completely seen. I felt that no one, no matter how close—husband, sister, parent, or friend—could see or hear all of me because they would never understand the real Bonnie, the weird version.

The story below reveals the weird version.

I was a bit of an 'odd duck' as a young child. I was always very aware of another world, and beings of from another dimension. It's hard enough for a child trying to figure out the world of adults—; add in my awareness and sensitivities, and it's easy to understand that my life was frightening and overwhelming.

I was quite young when I began seeing "angels." I mentioned it to a sibling and who told me they were "'bad'" spirits pretending to be angels. Even though I couldn't always see them, however, I could always sense them and knew where they were in the room. There were plenty of them around. The very worst occurred when I was alone, or during the night while everyone slept. I assumed that I must be very bad to have bad spirits near. I learned early not to talk about it. The need to straddle both worlds was a constant stress for me. They were always making noises.

As an adult, when my husband and I began practicing plural marriage, my husband suddenly had other places to stay for the night, I had to face "them" alone again. Him sleeping in someone else's bed didn't bother me nearly as much as my being alone and having to face all those spirits alone. It was intimidating until I finally confessed my strange dilemma to my husband. He listened patiently to my silent hysteria as I explained what had been happening my entire life....

"Have you given any thought to the possibility that these spirits aren't evil? Maybe they are family and friends that who love you." He spoke with a soft sincerity.

I froze. I stared at him. It began to dawn on me that he could be right—that what he said it could be the truth. Then he said, "Good-bye," and left for the night.

I was left with them again. That night wasn't near as stark and empty as the ones before had been,... but I still wasn't convinced. So I prayed. Soon after, I called my sister and mentor,, Ginny. I knew I could always turn to her; I trusted her. Without her knowing what my husband had said, she repeated much the same idea but added, "Maybe they are there to comfort you, pray for you. They will help you feel less lonely."

It wasn't long before I began to enjoy my "friends." I made the best of it, but still kept it pretty quiet. In the 80s and 90s, it was not that common to talk about the kind of world that I experienced—and on the few occasions that I did make that mistake, I was avoided.

Finally, I went to see a movie, The Sixth Sense, with my husband. It was a pretty spooky movie, and I could tell he wasn't enjoying it very much. It was real spooky. But for me, it was like seeing a home movie of my childhood; I cried throughout the entire movie.

It took me years to come to terms with my little secret. It was a huge burden to me. At some point I began to find people here and there who were also experiencing some kind of "dual reality." I learned from them how to manage my gifts. They also benefited from what I understood. I became comfortable. I began to relax and explore these my gifts instead of denying them.

I found friends that I could relate to. It was so nice to feel accepted. I no longer felt so out-of-place as I associated with these people. I learned from them how to, not only accept this odd part of me, but to see it as a gift that might help others as well...

I learned to see with more clarity and even to understand what I was seeing —and why I was seeing it. Finally... I started exploring every book I could find that explained the spiritual fluid that is not only in the body, but that surrounds it. I found it fascinating. In response to one book in particular, Alan gave me one of his looks and I knew to pay attention.

"I know you are excited about this information, but you have to realize that all of what you read might be someone ease's ideas," he said. . "I know you, Bon, and you are looking for the truth. I'm going to give you some advice, and you can choose to take it, or not.

"Truth always agrees," he continued. "It doesn't change. Some of this what you are reading might sound like truth, or look like truth, or even feel like truth, but if you want eternal truth, you will find it through our Heavenly Father, and nowhere else. I suggest you take that approach, and you will find what you are looking for."

That was the reminder I needed. I no longer feel that I'm cursed by this gift, but I feel it is a comfort and a blessing I can share. Several of my children are also sensitive in the same way I am. One of my sons has straddled two worlds since he was three years old. We walk this challenge together;, and I am happy that he has someone to walk it with. Only one or two out of my eleven children who have ventured to openly help others with their multi-dimensional gifts. The others choose to offer their sweet gifts in various, heartfelt ways because they all want to be truly helpful to any one of God's children that they encounter. I'm so proud of them all.

Plural marriage was not my original intention—in fact, I actively wanted to avoid plural marriage. Plural marriage looked like a very hard way of life. I wanted an uncomplicated monogamous relationship within the walls of a nice, cozy house. I wanted to enjoy a life of travel and excitement, and I wanted to work with horses.

I felt my mother was left to make it on her own a lot. She seemed to have relationships of mutual respect with her sister-wives but Mother was not chatty or friendly with them. Among my sisters, relationships seemed competitive and subversive. Also, I witnessed firsthand the nastiness that occurs between sister-wives when confronted by the complicated relationships in plural marriage. In fairness, though, my older sisters who were in monogamous marriages didn't seem much better off. Instead of drama between sister-wives, they endured drama between husband and wife. Throughout my adolescence I watched and listened as many of my monogamous sisters' husbands drank too much, committed adultery, were abusive, or were just plain absent. About the only positive "role models" of marriage I saw were on television, not exactly reality.

For the first few years of my marriage we didn't meet the unspoken expectations of living plural marriage by those who did. Once we invited another wife to join our family, my parents and siblings were very supportive of our decision. I didn't feel completely safe with plural marriage until I started to step up to life and make decisions for my children and myself. My husband always encouraged me in that, but I had to stop worrying about what other people thought of me or might be saying about me. Most of all, I had to stop focusing on what I perceived to be my failures.

Today, I am very happy as part of a plural marriage. I have learned so much about life, people, human nature, boundaries . . . the list is almost endless. Most important is that I've learned so much about me by living in plural marriage. I am the one who determines whether I come out of any given situation feeling powerless or standing in a place of compassion for others and myself. Every difficult situation requires me to strengthen some part of myself.

At first it startled me that my husband was not as strict as my father had been. Then I grew to appreciate the difference between them. My husband is far more relaxed with his children, far more relaxed with his wives, and much more accepting of how his wives express their needs. My husband is respectful of my choices, whereas my father would insist that he influence his wives' choices.

Dad continually voiced his pride in his families and owned who he was: a polygamous man. I am also proud to be who I am and to own my religion. That's not to say there haven't been difficult experiences. Being judged as uneducated or naive can be hard sometimes.

There are people who object to my religion, that doesn't bother me. The only ones who bother me are those who want to take away my freedom because of their own misunderstandings—the ones who assume I would commit fraud or that my husband and sons are sex abusers. Sadly, misinformed people still attach those kinds of things to my religion. As polygamists, my children and I are vulnerable to many forms of judgment that can isolate us from the community if we let it. I am much more compassionate toward people who are treated the same way because of the color of their skin.

Once I realized that I wasn't unlovable and did not deserve bad treatment, I began to heal the way I saw myself. I know that I am not only lovable but I'm not a screw-up. I'm a great cook, an accomplished artist, an involved mother and grandmother and I've been able to help many with my gifts. I also see now that I have a family that cares for me. I see that we are— a family of good, decent people that who grew up with dysfunctional behaviors. As adults we are doing our best to work these out and to help one another. As we work toward that healing,, I'm proud of my family, and my heritage.

Barbara Joyce

CHAPTER 18

1955

"I WANT NEW PARENTS!" I yelled, shaking with rage. At fifteen, I was feeling unexpressed pain, emptiness, and desperation. What I really wanted was to belong, to feel loved, to be held and comforted, and to be accepted, although I didn't know it at the time.

Instead of giving me any of those things, my father called the police and told them to come and get me. It felt like he was telling me, Go find those wonderful parents.

What he did say was, "Go pack your things."

This was like so many other things I had done—things I did without thinking and without being aware of the potential consequences. Feeling emotions was foreign to me. Or maybe it just didn't matter. What did I have to lose? I wouldn't have the answer to that question for a very long time.

When I left my parent's home in the fall of 1970, my father, Albert Edmund Barlow, was sixty-seven. My mother, Maurine Owen Barlow—father's third wife—was fifty-seven. My father had already raised thirty-one children, eleven of them from my mother. I was the last living child of both of them. For my parents it was all about the religion. For me it never was.

The home in which I grew up, a house built in the early 1900s, featured all the old craftsmanship: hardwood floors, beamed ceilings, French doors, a big bay window, built-in leaded-glass cabinets, stained-glass windows. It also had old radiators that could get hot enough to burn if you touched them and a monster steam heater in the basement.

Compared to many children, I had a very comfortable life. The neighbors and local schools knew my family name; we had lived there for decades. Our big house stood out in the neighborhood. All three of Dad's families were living in this house when the Utah state government eventually decided it needed to prosecute the polygamous community. It had been against Utah law to live plural marriage for over fifty years and the state of Utah decided it was time to enforce it.

In 1944, Utah state police rounded up men who were known to be practicing polygamy and put them in jail. The men who had been convicted were offered a release if they agreed to no longer live polygamy. Most of them signed the agreement, but a few refused.

The ones who signed had a variety of choices to make about their big families. Some moved out of the state, some moved out of the country. Some had only the first wife and her children carry his name, some moved their women and children into different homes so the schools and neighbors had less knowledge of them.

My father chose the last option. He moved his second and third wives into a friend's home. Being an open, honest person, Dad had a difficult time trying to hide his additional wives and children. He enjoyed having the whole family together, taking all his wives to the polygamist church and social gatherings, and claiming all of his children. He had worked hard to take care of them and to keep them together as a family over the years. He was very proud of his family and did not want to hide any of them.

However, my father admired men who stood up for their beliefs and "principles" (one of his favorite words) and he especially admired those men who had stayed in prison longer, not signing that paper. Dad eventually began to feel that he should have done the same, even if it meant being in prison again. He got his wish.

Dad was arrested again just a few months after I was born. He fought against going back to prison for several years spending a good deal of money for attorney fees. He eventually lost the battle and served a four year prison term beginning in 1959.

I was the 12th child my mother gave birth to and she was tired. At three years old, Ginny gave Bonnie and me a very short "Dutch" haircut, we looked like boys. Mom's only comment was, "When you're old enough to take care of your own hair you can grow it out."

At about three years old something happened that kept me from trusting the adults around me. I was standing next to Mom and Dad at the front door as they talked to a man they knew. They discussed the need for saving this food for the "last days". Then the man said, "I'd really like to see how you have your food storage set up. Do you mind if I take a look?"

"You bet," Dad responded, proud of what he had done for his family.

Can I take this pretty little girl with me?" The man said as he took hold of my hand.

Dad said, "Sure."

The man picked me up as we headed down the basement stairs into our huge dark basement, the small windows gave very little light. We passed the scary monster furnace next to the fruit room and through Dad's big shop and on to the last two rooms. In one room was the food storage where Dad stocked the room with 55 gallon drums filled with beans, rice and wheat—for the "last days" when everyone would be starving.

As the man stood there looking at the room full of drums, I could fill him put his hand up my dress. It felt icky and uncomfortable.

I felt frightened and bewildered. *But Dad had told this man he could take me with him and Mom was there too. Was that what my parents wanted? No one was supposed to touch my private parts. Was this OK or wasn't it OK? I was supposed to obey my Dad, I was not supposed to question him.* I couldn't resolve these questions. It felt like they had given me to that man. I never told anyone. *Daddy loves me, gives me to this man then Daddy is gone. Daddy does love me, doesn't he? Daddy is God, God isn't safe, safer to be by myself.*

I pulled away from everyone, too confused for my little girl to figure out what happened and why. I doubted everyone around me but mostly myself. This began the slow withdrawal from looking to my parents for what I needed to turning to my sisters. I no longer looked to my parents to protect me, keep me safe. I wouldn't understand why for many years.

While Dad was in prison Mom did whatever she could to earn money. When the older kids got a job they gave her half of what they earned, the state welfare gave her a small amount and she had paper routes. She worked hard to give us special days like Christmas. She may have had 'Secret Santa' help as well. One Christmas morning I found a small turntable and a few 45rpm records of Alvin and the Chipmunks. Bonnie and I listened to those records over and over for hours.

Mom must have been a music lover, we always had a turntable and sometimes in the evenings we played old albums; Moon River by Andy Williams, 16 Tons by Tennessee Ernie Ford and many more. I'm sure that's where my love of music came from.

One of my fun memories was when we were cleaning the house one day in the front room. Betsy, Bonnie and I had the couch near the bay windows pulled out and were vacuuming behind. It was raining pretty hard outside, which had darkened the day. Water was flooding down the curb gutters and onto the grass, which is unusual in this dry Utah climate. I love the summer rain that cools everything off from the summer hot-as-oven heat.

"Can we go outside and play in the rain? "I asked Betsy. I couldn't believe it when she said "Yes." Betsy even came out with us. We dropped the vacuum on the spot to have fun splashing and jumping in the rain as long as we wanted. We played hooky from work for a little while.

Mom studied the use of herbs and eating healthy based on the Word of Wisdom from our Mormon background. Dad provided a wheat grinder where we ground our own flour and made our own bread. With a family our size, that meant we had a large pan probably 2 ½ feet wide to mix the ingredients and let the dough rise. Then we filled the oven with the dough in loaf pans to bake. One batch of dough would make about fourteen loaves of bread, which lasted a week, then we did it all over again. This was always Betsy's job and it was a big job.

If we were lucky and Betsy was in a good mood she would break open one of the steaming loaves so we could each have some of the crust to slather butter and honey on, a real treat for us.

I wait and wait for him to come home. Even before he went to prison, he was gone most of the time. When he comes home, he fills up the house. There are so many people who want to talk to him, be with him, and love him. I wait and wait for him to notice me, hoping today I will have a little bit of his love. Maybe today he will call me his beautiful little girl.

I try so hard to be the best at home and school for him. It feels so good when he is proud of me. I write letters to him telling him how much I love him and how good I am doing in school but I never get any letters back.

Sometimes I do things I know I shouldn't.

When I was in second grade, I saw my sister, Ginny's purse wide open with a lot of quarters. I thought Mom had given them to her, I had heard them talking about her struggles. I knew it was money Ginny needed, she had three kids at the time and a husband who drank up much of his income.

I couldn't help myself, I took some of the quarters. Boy, did I have fun. I went to the corner store and got all the candy I wanted. I even gave Bonnie some of the candy. Big mistake, she told Mom I had candy, I was caught.

Mom knelt down so she could look me in the eye. "Will you tell me where you got the money for the candy?" she asked.

"In Ginny's purse," I whispered.

Why would you take Ginny's money?"

I shrugged, I felt terribly guilty about taking the money, but I couldn't tell her why I had done it. I didn't know why myself, really. I just wanted something that made me feel special, something I couldn't put into words. How could I say anything that might sound like she wasn't a good mom? She never yelled at us, and she worked so hard to take care of everyone.

She had the responsibility of making sure eight of us kids had a roof over our heads and food to eat. That was an especially hard job during the nearly four years Dad was in prison.

I don't remember much about Dad before he went to prison. "Daddy," we squealed as us three little girls ran into the prison cafeteria. He was sitting at the long picnic style tables made of aluminum tubing and plastic with attached benches.

"There are my beautiful little girls," was his reply as he hugged us. Next to him was a box of Ritz crackers and a bowl with canned tuna fish and Miracle Whip mixed together.

"Come, sit here with me, look what I have for you." Dad was a social person and having something to feed a guest was part of his family tradition. Even in prison he needed to provide that for all who visited him.

On one visit Daddy showed me a big charcoal drawing of me. "One of the men here saw your picture hanging in my work area. He drew this for you to take home."

Mom hung that drawing in the living room wall and I felt special whenever I saw it. It disappeared years later. I was quite disappointed that wasn't there once I had a home to put it in.

Being the youngest meant you had last pick, age gave seniority. When riding in the car, the window seat was the first choice for everyone, which meant I was always in the middle riding the hump. Ginny was taking us on a drive in her red convertible when I began to feel sick to my stomach. "I think I'm going to throw up," I said.

Doris responded, "Sure you are."

Ginny glanced back saying, "You'll be okay."

Within a few minutes I puked on the back of her seat, the floor, my lap and the girls next to me. From then on, if I said I was car sick I was immediately allowed to sit by the window. I upchucked more than once on the outside of a car. I also enjoyed the scenery from a better vantage point on our drives with that wonderful wind blowing in my face.

Despite Mother's good qualities, I loved her from a distance. I didn't ask much from her—I knew not to. It was my sisters who gave me baths, washed my hair, and told me what to do and when. I gave them a lot of grief, being a pain in the neck got me attention, even if begrudgingly. And it kept my sisters at a distance.

Mom made sure we ate healthy food and would pick up the fresh-from-the-farm milk from the dairy store and take some to Aunt Vio. She would try to get the 3 wives together once a week to talk about the "principle" (their religion). She delivered newspapers and was attending school to learn a trade paid for by state welfare. She was gone a lot. When she was home, usually in the morning, I would see her reading the paper with a cup of coffee and toast. I remember watching her, wishing I could talk to her, wishing she would ask me something about myself, talk to me about something.

I don't remember her holding me, talking to me, loving me. I always tried hard to be good. She was really nice and worked so hard. You never said anything bad about Mom, she was the best, and everyone thought so.

When I was old enough at seven, it was my job to do whatever Mom told me to do. One day she asked me to get a book from her bedroom. I didn't normally go into Mom's room. It was off limits. Having been given permission, I took the opportunity to look at everything there.

I was intrigued by so many personal items of Mom's and, even more so, of Dad's. In the closet his shoes were all in a row with wooden shoetrees in them. His belts and ties were hanging neatly on the closet door. As I scanned the room looking for Mom's book, I noticed her costume jewelry in a small box on her vanity. The pieces were not fancy but something with which she could dress up.

Then I saw chocolate. Wow—candy! We never got treats like that. So I helped myself to some. When I tasted it, though, it was bitter—not good at all. About that time Mom came looking for me.

"What are you doing, Dear?" she asked.

"Just looking for the book you wanted."

"What do you have in your hand?" She asked.

"Nothing," I lied, holding the chocolate behind my back.

She quietly said, "I would rather you take everything I have than lie to me."

Those words have affected my life in so many ways. Mom never said much to me. When she did, I listened.

About an hour after I tasted the chocolate, I found out it wasn't candy. It was actually Ex-Lax. I never touched it again.

Being in a large family, our snacks were found in the fruit cellar in the basement, usually a bag of carrots or a box of apples. We didn't go clothes shopping; my clothes all came from my sisters after they had outgrown them.

The dining area in our old house had a recessed section with big windows you could unlatch on the side and open, easy to yell at someone "Mom wants you". There were planter boxes lined with galvanized tin just below the windows with cabinets under the planter boxes. That was Mom's sewing room.

Mom had a beautiful old treadle sewing machine with shiny black paint and gold lettering over the cast iron body set into a dark wood grain cabinet. The lid would collapse onto the body, folding the machine down into the cabinet. Underneath was the cast iron foot treadle, big enough for both feet.

One day when Mom was sewing I had a feeling it was something special. My third grade teacher had given me a bag several weeks earlier and told me to give it to my mother. Mom called me and told me to try something on. She had made a dress for me! When the dress was done I was so proud of it. The material was gray seersucker and Mom had put big red buttons on it with red rick-rack down the front. "Wear this to school tomorrow," she told me.

I had never liked that teacher because she was mean. It was years later after I had thought about it I figured out my teacher had given that material to Mom so she would make that dress for me.

Every so often, we would find bags of used clothing on the porch when we came home. One day there was a large bag that included a very pretty dress. It was dark pink textured taffeta with a big sash around the waist that tied in the back, and included a short, matching bolero jacket. The minute I saw it I wanted it—and was thrilled to find that it was my size! I would be the first one in our family to get it instead of it being a hand-me-down from my sisters. I saved that dress for very special occasions and called it my party dress.

I could be pretty stubborn and learned to hold out for what I wanted. I soon found out what that trait would cost me.

In 1963, I was eight, and Dad had recently been released from prison. He immediately started having "Sunday school," where he taught us his religious beliefs using stories from the Bible and the Book of Moron. Attendance was mandatory.

One morning it was time for Sunday school and I was told to come down. I didn't respond. I was lying in bed in my underwear because I didn't have anything clean to wear. The only thing hanging in my closet was my pretty party dress, and I refused to wear that to Sunday school. Sunday school was not a special occasion.

Dad came upstairs and said, "Get dressed and come down to Sunday school."

"I only have my party dress to wear," I told him.

He had a rolled-up newspaper in his hand and began hitting me with it. I put my party dress on and headed downstairs, still sniffling from my beating. I learned that morning I had better obey my dad or I would pay the price. The only thing he wanted to hear was "Yes, Dad".

It was important to Dad that his whole family regularly got together. That meant many family parties at our house because there was plenty of room for our many siblings and their spouses to gather. During our parties, there might be a group in the dining room playing cards while others chatted in the living room. Occasionally I caught my mother's oldest son, Ed, smoking cigarettes on the front porch.

Ed had a sexy convertible sports car, which he liked to show off. One night he drove too fast down a canyon in Salt Lake. He had been drinking, and when the car rolled it dragged him down the paved road. He was lucky to survive.

When he was released from the hospital, he came straight to the old house so we could take care of him. His face, one shoulder, and one arm were bandaged. Ed was staying in an upstairs bedroom, and I was in charge of bringing him food, cleaning up after him, and generally doing the legwork for him.

During one of those errands, I saw his pack of cigarettes on the nightstand. I managed to sneak one of the cigarettes while Ed was asleep. I leaned out my bedroom window and, using my little box of wooden matches, I lit up. It was terrible! I didn't care to try that again for awhile. Later, while listening to lyrics from the Animals song "When I Was Young," I heard them sing, "I smoked my first cigarette at ten." I thought, Ha, I have you beat—I was nine.

At the age of ten, Linda told me Ginny wanted to talk to me. I came downstairs as requested and stopped in the doorway between the dining room and the big living room. There was Ginny surrounded by other siblings, my brother Ed was next to her. Ginny was looked up to and now that she was married we didn't see her very often.

Ginny looked at me and said, "You need to take more baths. If you don't, we will use a horse brush to scrub you down. It's a brush used to clean horses and it will scrub your skin off." Ed, who tended to be sarcastic anyway, laughed at what she said, they were a team. I already felt like no one liked me, that just added to it but it came from Ginny, whom I loved. I disappeared from them as fast as I could.

Being raised to be seen and not heard, I had not told anyone where my aversion to baths came from. At nine years old, I was in the bathtub with the door locked. My Dad pounded on the door, "What are you doing?" he asked.

"Taking a bath."

"Open the door," he demanded.

I jumped out of the tub, quickly unlocked the door and climbed back in the tub.

Dad said, "Don't turn around."

Next thing I knew he was in the bathtub behind me. I didn't dare move or say a word but I was feeling sick to my stomach. He finished his bath and got out closing the door behind him. There were no boundaries for Dad, he did whatever he wanted to do.

Our visits to Dad in prison were a rare treat but once he came home he was there a lot. He was sixty years old, an ex-con, and had a hard time getting steady work. His three wives had become self-sufficient, all with a steady income. So he focused on maintaining and repairing the big old house in which we lived. He also focused on what his young daughters were doing as opposed to Mom, who paid little attention to what we were doing.

He had set up a large middle room in the basement with a work bench. Tools were hanging from hooks on the wall and nails were sorted neatly in the baby jars whose lids he had nailed to a twirling rack. He filled each jar with different size nails, screws and bolts that could be screwed onto the lid —his own creation to organize them. He had proudly shown me this shop he had designed and built. I doubt I showed much appreciation for his efforts.

As his gopher, it was my job to retrieve tools left . . . somewhere. "Get me that wrench," he'd say. "It's probably in my car."

I had to learn quickly what the various tools looked like and try my best to find what he needed. If I came back without a tool he asked for, I might hear something like, "How can you be so stupid?" It wasn't much fun being his helper.

I was lucky when it came to my father's belittling. I was pretty sharp, and caught on quickly to what he wanted. Aunt Vio's son was not so lucky. I used to cringe when I heard Dad chewing on him. Ron was a big teddy bear like his mom. He had no idea how to defend himself; he wasn't so much a quick-witted person but he was a gentle soul with a generous heart. Dad would make comments like, "What's the matter with you?" "You are so stupid." "Can't you do anything right?"

I could feel the devastating blows to Ron's ego as Dad made it clear what a disappointment he was. He demanded more from his sons who were expected to marry multiple wives and raise large families. What Dad expected from his daughters was chastity, domestic duties and obedience.

One evening in 1967 at a family party, I was in the kitchen when Betsy and her husband Quin walked in from the back door. Betsy said, "Happy Birthday!" My birthday had been several days earlier. This party was not for my birthday but it felt good that Betsy remembered. I got a big smile on my face and said, "Thanks."

Betsy was wearing a pretty dress with a long beautiful shawl draped over her arms and her husband Quin was there with her. I couldn't help noticing the shawl and how happy she looked with her husband.

She said, "I didn't get you anything for your birthday, what would you like?"

I blurted out, "That shawl."

She didn't even hesitate, she took it off and gave it to me with a smile and walked into the other room to join the party.

That kind, generous gesture meant the world to me. I carried that shawl with me for 40 years before asking her if she wanted it back since I was finally ready to let it go. I don't think she remembered giving it to me but I have never forgotten.

Shauna at 15 had decided she was the style guru and told everyone how they should wear their hair, what clothes were in style and what brand to buy. Basically, if we looked like her, we passed her scrutiny. Doris and Linda wore their hair like hers, bangs slicked to the side and a bob that flipped out, usually a ribbon tied around with a bow on top. The three of them were a trio going most places together with Shauna as the leader.

Shauna also managed to get a job in a high end shoe and clothing store at the age of 16. We listened to her advice because she was quick to catch onto things and her style was much better than the old-fashioned polyg style sported by the groups we were allowed to socialize with.

Shauna also decided to get married at 16. Our sweet sister Ruthie, who had a large beautiful home in an expensive part of town offered to give her a wedding in the lovely back yard of her home. She and Shauna had become close.

It was a really big deal for me. Shauna had her young sisters as bridesmaids so someone made us all pretty, matching yellow dresses, our hair curled and darling shoes. There were flowers everywhere, the ceremony was a big, incredible party and I got to be a part of it. I felt very special and Ruthie treated us all with a loving kindness that I have never forgotten.

The polygamous community had decades-old connections and met together for church and occasionally for families to socialize. After Dad came home from prison, we began participating in the square dances that were held in the Murray Park activity hall. It was a single-story wood-framed building with a small kitchen area, a large long room with wooden floors, and a raised wooden stage the width of the hall. The entire room had chairs lining the walls where one could rest and watch the others dance.

Rosie, a man from this community of polygamous families, was the square dance caller, telling us which steps to take in each square dance song. He played Fox trots, waltzes and the Virginia Reel. He ended each evening with the kids doing the Bunny Hop. It was a place to let loose and meet other kids, and it was so much fun.

Dad loved to dance, taking turns with each one of his wives and daughters (his wives got extra turns). It took awhile to get a turn, but I loved it. It was a time the family could have fun together with the community of polygamists and where teenagers could meet "acceptable" kids to date or marry.

As a girl approaching puberty, I started getting Dad's 'talks,' "Who was that boy you were talking to?" "Those boys are only wanting one thing." "We are wicked by nature, you need to keep yourself pure." "You are disobedient and doing stupid things." "Stay away from those boys, you should be praying for God to guide you, not talking to some boy who is trying to take advantage of you." It went on for what seemed like hours.

During these talks I was not allowed to say one word as tears of frustration streamed down my face. What did I have to look forward to? I was attending public school but was not allowed to go to school activities—dances, basketball games, and nothing after school. Dad allowed no fraternizing at all.

In the seventh and eighth grades I had girlfriends from school with whom I would go shopping downtown, and sometimes I went to their houses. They were not allowed at my house for obvious reasons. I felt so different from all of them.

Watching Donna Reed as a child on our black-and-white TV gave me the idea I wanted that kind of family. There was a mom that loved and took care of everyone fixing them meals and talking to them. They had a dad that was nice and accepted the kids giving them good advice. Everyone seemed to love each other. The best part of all was that there were only two children. I figured that with two children, there would be lots of love to go around. That's what I wanted—not the kind of family I had grown up in, where I was at the end of a long line hoping there was something left for me.

At thirteen, I was sitting at our kitchen table with Mom and some of my sisters, talking. The other girls were sharing their dreams of marriage and family, including how many children they might have. One said ten, another one twelve. I spoke up, saying, "I only want two or three kids."

Mom turned to me and said, "Don't ever talk like that in front of my daughters again," giving me one of her stern looks. It was obvious she didn't want to know how I felt or why.

One by one, the sisters who had watched out for me left, following in Mom's footsteps by starting big families of their own. Eventually I was on my own in what I wanted for my life.

It was also at thirteen that I began spending every weekend at Quin & Betsy's house where we had drinking parties. The teenagers who gathered there were from approved polygamous families—the only people with whom I was allowed to socialize. I found the wildest kids in the polygamist culture to be friends with, and I did whatever they were doing. One of them was a girlfriend, Meg who lived just across the street from Betsy's house. Meg introduced me to many firsts—my first hickey, my first joint, my first dry hump, and the start of my addiction to cigarettes. I was finally stepping out of my parent's restrictions with gusto. Quin was a drinker and was happy to have us all at his house. He would put on his Marty Robbins albums, buy us liquor, fix us drinks, and tell us jokes. He loved to party.

It was during those weekends that I found out how much liquor I could hold before passing out. That education in handling my alcohol became valuable later in life. I was lucky—I learned how much alcohol I could tolerate while around boys from the "other families", boys who would never take advantage of me.

Eventually I got tired of doing the same thing every weekend—getting drunk and talking about marriage. My life was laid out for me. Marry one of those boys, have a big family, then die. That's all I could see. And, polygamy aside, I didn't want to marry any of those boys.

I was angry that my picture of life was not acceptable to my family because it did not include polygamy and a large family. I knew from a young age—thanks to television shows like "The Donna Reed Show," "Leave it to Beaver" and "My Three Sons"—that I wanted a two-parent marriage and two or three children. I wanted the life I saw on those shows.

Finally I was breaking every family rule I could get away with, pushing all the boundaries, and letting fly whatever teenage zinger I could. I was fourteen and all my older sisters but one were married to boys from polygamous families and were having babies. The one sister left at home, Bonnie, already had her man—of course, one from an approved family—picked out.

If you wanted Mom and Dad's approval, you were obedient. I was not.

The last beating I received was at age fourteen. I came home after one of my "fun nights out," I had stayed somewhere besides my sister's house.

In an unmistakably angry tone of voice, Dad demanded, "Where were you?"

With all the sarcasm, bitterness, and disdain I could muster, "I stayed at a friend's house," looking him straight in the eye.

A few of my siblings happened to be in the house at the time and were witnesses to what happened next. Dad whipped off his belt and started hitting me with it. He kept hitting me repeatedly as I rolled around on the floor screaming. But my screams didn't stop Dad. He kept hitting me. I found out later that Mom's youngest son, Steve, who was watching along with my other siblings, said something to Dad. At that point he stopped—but only long enough to close the door so my siblings could no longer watch. Then he came back and resumed the beating. I don't remember anything else after that—not how or when he stopped, where I went afterward, or how I felt.

My humiliation was complete. There was no one to protect me but myself, and the only way I could do that was to go inside myself where no one could reach me—someplace where it was safe, where the only thing that could touch me was my own misery.

Obviously, Dad's behavior did absolutely no good in winning me over to his way of life. Sometime after that, Dad and Mom took me to Zion's Canyon in southern Utah—just the three of us. That never happened in my family, and I am sure it was Dad's way of trying to somehow connect with me. Dad's idea of trying to have a good time with me on the trip involved coming up behind me and flipping my bra. What? Who would do that to a teenage girl who had recently developed breasts?

He was trying hard for the two of them. He had to. Mom never said much of anything to me. She didn't reach out and pretty much left me on my own once I made it clear I would not be following in her footsteps. She set an example, which was her way. She was not much of a talker.

One night when just Mom and I were at home, she asked if I wanted to get a hamburger. I jumped at the chance—she had never done anything remotely like that before.

We drove to the drive-in in silence, we sat in the car eating in silence, and we drove home in silence. That was so weird! *Did she want to spend time with me? Was she too tired to cook after working all day? Would she feel guilty buying herself something but not getting anything for me?* I never could quite figure that out.

I had been skipping school all through ninth grade. I didn't care about school. I couldn't socialize there, and my parents didn't care whether I got an education. In my parents' world, all a woman needed to do was get married, have babies, and live polygamy. It was an odd situation, because both my parents were educated. My mother's parents had been school teachers. My father worked his entire life to educate himself after leaving school in the eighth grade to earn money. Yet when I asked if they would sign me out of school, they readily agreed. I never did attend high school.

Things gradually got worse for me at home, and I spent a lot of time trying to escape. I escaped by getting drunk on the weekends and reading when at my parents' house. I read novels, mostly Reader's Digest condensed books—Mom had plenty of them. During the week when I couldn't be at my sister's house, I read all night and slept all day, living on lemonade and popcorn. Dad said often that God gave us free agency but Dad did the opposite, doing everything he could to control our lives.

I must have been pretty depressed. It took six months after quitting school before I finally blew up. About six months before I turned sixteen, Bonnie's friend called to ask if I wanted to go on a blind date. I told her I would. Anything was better than what I had in front of me. Being the brutally honest type, I told my father I wanted to go on the date. Most of my siblings told Dad what he wanted to hear, then did what they wanted when he wasn't looking. Some of the others were obedient, humble daughters, which was the best way to get along with Dad. I was neither.

We got into a big argument over the date. That's when I yelled that I wanted new parents.

"Pack your things," he said.

It took only three or four paper grocery bags to hold all my personal belongings. As I was walking from room to room upstairs gathering up my toothbrush, clothes, and other things, I walked past Mom's room and saw her sitting there in the dark. She kind of stood up once as I passed by. I didn't say anything to her, and I was angry that she didn't say a word to me.

Dad didn't tell me where I was going—I found out when I saw the policeman standing downstairs after I finished packing. While I was riding in the squad car, the police officer was harshly telling me that I should respect my parents and Yada, Yada, Yada.

I turned to him and quietly asked, "Did you know my father is a polygamist and expects me to live polygamy?"

"No." He was quiet the rest of the way to the detention center.

At detention, I was relieved of my possessions and locked into a small, glass-enclosed cell/room. No one talked to me. I had no idea what would happen to me. I knew I was in trouble. I knew I didn't want to live at my parents' house, yet I had no idea where I would end up other than maybe a foster home. I actually hoped I would end up in a foster home. I had an image of an ideal foster home in my mind, where everyone would be nice to me and like me.

After about four hours, a woman unlocked the door and told me to follow her. We walked to an office where a woman was behind a desk. My parents were sitting in front of it. I sat down next to my mom in the only available seat. My parents didn't say anything to me.

The woman told me I would go live with my sister, the same sister at whose house I had been getting drunk for years—the same house at which I had gone to parties full of boys to whom I was related or who were looking for compliant wives.

I moved into Betsy's basement bedroom. She had three young children yet was still willing to let a teenager with a big attitude live with her.

At fifteen, it was difficult finding a job. Everywhere I went had a minimum age requirement of sixteen. Not only that, I was limited to where I could get by walking or taking the bus. I was pretty discouraged by the time I learned of a government program that would pay my tuition to a trade school and pay $0.85 cents an hour while attending.

As soon as I turned sixteen in 1971, the age required for the program, I began attending classes at Trade Tech (now Salt Lake Community

College). I was given the chance to finish all course study required by the state at my own pace and then take the GED test to get my high school diploma. I could then study whatever trade I chose.

It was the seventies, and secretarial work was one of the main jobs available to women. That sounded to me like a job where women had to serve men—the very thing I resented.

I took a semester of photography, then one studying printing. Neither one seemed to open any doors to a career, so I ended up taking the secretarial course. The school offered a course of study and a certificate when you finished. They even helped you find a job. So I learned typing, shorthand, ten-key by touch, etiquette, how to dress for the office, and everything else a woman might need to know to succeed as a secretary.

There I was sixteen and had not been allowed to date "outside" men, nor had I attended high school with the opportunity to learn the ropes with teens my own age. I was quite naïve and suddenly in a big school full of men of all ages, from older teenagers to veterans returning from Vietnam. Because secretarial training was the only female-oriented course of study, women were in the distinct minority. Everything else was geared for men—courses like mechanics, carpentry, and plumbing—so there were men everywhere. It was a smorgasbord for me with my new-found freedom. There were also plenty of drugs to be freely had.

I had no guidance to navigate this new world. I had moved out of my sister's house into the first of many apartments. It was a very lonely time for me. Once I had left my family, they also left me. I rarely received phone calls or visits, and there was no family in my life. The direction I had chosen cost me dearly. My willfulness in doing what I wanted with my life brought me utter loneliness, and there was no going back.

My first job out of school in 1973 was at an architecture firm. After receiving a few decent paychecks, I purchased what I thought were the cutest outfits possible that I wore to work and when I went out to bars. One in particular I still remember was a tight bell bottom paired with a midriff peasant blouse. I didn't realize I was sending mixed messages, but I loved the attention I received.

It didn't take long for the owner to make me an offer, Mike asked me into his office. "I have a weekend planned at a resort, there will be a couple of clients there, would you like to come?"

It didn't sound like a place I would have many choices, "No, I don't think so."

Then one Friday Mike asked, "Would you stay late tonight? I have a meeting and I want you to stay and help."

There was a kitchen close to the conference room with liquor supplies. I took the drink orders and served the first round of drinks. Five or six men and I were all sitting around the conference table when Mike asked, "Would you make me another drink, Barbara?"

When I walked back into the conference room with the drink, all of the men were watching me. One of them was standing on the table with his pants down around his ankles and his everything showing, grinning at me. I gave Mike his drink and simply sat down saying nothing, no reaction. Bob, who was on the table, sheepishly pulled up his pants and got down. The meeting ended soon after. And so did my job, I gave notice the next week finally accepting that I was not in a job that was good for me.

Soon I was lucky enough to land a job with the Utah State Historical Society. As a bonus, they were then located in the incredibly beautiful Utah Governor's Mansion. I worked for the man in charge of finding historical places to nominate for the National Historical Register. The people I worked with felt like a caring family. They were mostly older (which at that time to me would have been forties and older) and took an interest in me.

"What do you want to do with your life if you don't like being a secretary?" Margaret asked.

"I want to run a business," was my reply.

"Well maybe you should go to college then," she said.

Jerry was reading a business journal, he pointed to a picture. "You could join the Air Force, they provide money for college through the GI Bill." So that's exactly what I did.

When Dad found out he asked me, "Are you joining the Air Force to reject your family?" All I could say was, "No". There was no explaining if he didn't understand by now.

Before I left for the military Mom said, "You can have a farewell party at the house."

"Really? Who can I invite?"

"Whoever you'd like to invite," she said.

"Anyone I want?" I asked with surprise.

I invited everyone I knew, from polyg families, friends from school and boys I had dated. I have pictures of my favorite silky blouse and black onyx earrings an old boyfriend had given me. Dad was not at the party, I'm not sure how she pulled that off but it made me very happy having a special party for me.

I was stationed first in Biloxi, Mississippi; next I received a transfer to Fayetteville, North Carolina. I had to get a transfer out of Mississippi before they had a chance to discharge me.

The squadron commander in Biloxi pulled me into his office, "You've been going off base with a black man, and you can't do that here. I'm getting complaints from the locals."

It felt similar to my father's dictates, it didn't make sense to me. Why wouldn't I date a black man? Being the rebel I was, I didn't stop.

I had also gone to a local bar in broad daylight and was sitting at the bar having a beer. I hadn't been there long when the young man sitting next to me stood up and yelled, "The South will rise again!"

He could tell I wasn't from the area by my lack of southern drawl. I left the bar soon after that. As I continued to date whoever I wanted, I began getting written up for small things, trash in the trash can, cigarettes in the ashtray, etc. I finally realized the military was not going to tolerate me making my own choices.

I met a man who was permanently stationed at Pope Air Force Base in North Carolina but was temporarily training in Biloxi. We had hit it off and I asked him if we could get married so I could transfer out. He agreed. Things went well for a short time but, of course, eventually got messy. I was way out of my element and really struggled to live the military life. I barely made it through to my discharge but managed to gain my military benefits that helped pay for college.

I had done it! It was 1976 and I could now enroll in college. I chose a small, private, liberal arts college in Utah—Westminster College, which was small enough that it kind of felt like the high school I had never attended. Westminster accepted transfer credits from Trade Tech and the Air Force, which reduced the time required to finish my degree to two and a half years. I was both surprised and thrilled.

While working my way through college, Ginny invited me to dinner. "Mom and Hazel will be coming too," she told me. As the four of us were visiting before dinner I began sharing my opinion on raising children. "Spanking children isn't necessary. You can teach children by talking to them, physical punishment is cruel. It was very hard for me when Dad whipped me."

I heard one quick comment from Hazel in reply, "If dad beat you, you must have deserved it."

I completely dissolved into tears. What I wanted to hear from my mother was that Dad shouldn't have beaten me. Instead I felt blame for my beatings.

Ginny said to Hazel, "No child deserves to be beaten." Ginny had fixed a wonderful meal for us and it ended up a disaster. I had no appetite and left.

I hoped getting a degree would make a big difference in my life— not only paving the way for a good-paying job, but hopefully, I would fit in better with the "outside" world elevated to the upper status a college degree seemed to provide. But more important, was the possibility that my family might think more of me. (I am the only one of Dad's children who attended and have a four-year college degree.) Of course that was a long shot considering I had parents who signed me out of school after ninth grade because they didn't care whether I was educated.

Throughout my teenage years and until I had my first child, I survived the best I could. I was on my own emotionally, financially, and physically. I did a lot of self-destructive things, including abusing drugs and acting out sexually. There was no one there to tell me not to, no one there to see what I was doing with my life. There was no one there but me. I was lost and had to learn by trial and error.

* * *

I am cooking Christmas dinner, although it's not what I would call traditional. I'm serving ribs, potatoes and gravy, and Brussels sprouts.

Untraditional is what I would call this Christmas of 2009. In sunny southern California at my sons' apartment, we have no snow, no Christmas decorations, no Christmas music, and no unwrapping gifts. Who needs it? Christmas is too commercial anyway. When it comes right down to it, every day can be Christmas.

I have become too comfortable with my life. It's time to rough it with the younger generation. I left my down pillows and comforter behind, as well as my big, soft couch with pillow footrest. Chairs and tables—who needs 'em? Coffee cups, well-stocked clothes closet . . . thank goodness it's only for two weeks!

Darice, our amazing daughter, whom I live with in Kansas City, is wading through the biggest snowstorm in a very long time. I've been trying to be sympathetic, but it's hard when I am on my walk enjoying the beautiful flowers blooming, birds singing, and sunshine warming me thrrough the window. I am pleased with myself that I have managed not to gloat.

My seventeen-year-old son helped me take the ribs out of the hot oven. The wooden dish rack became the tray onto which we scooted the ribs. I used a plastic fork to mash the potatoes, a plastic spoon to scoop gravy onto the potatoes. I had a choice—serve the food with a plastic cup or a paper plate. The boys will not be living here long, so are not investing their money in household goods. Besides that, they have very little money to spend right now.

Our teenager needed to see us be nice to each other. Our children hadn't experienced much of that in the past.

Their father, my ex-husband, moved out here with his significant other, a woman who did not want the boys living in her house. Ash had some legal issues so she wouldn't allow him to enter her home. The boys found an apartment to rent a couple of miles from their father.

Kiyan, the oldest, would tell his brother "You need to pick that up. Look at this mess in the kitchen, I'm not going to clean it." "Who drank my juice? That is a special apple juice that clears my sinuses." "Where is my hair brush? I paid $35 for that because it massages my scalp."

Detailed, precise and a bit anal, he has just graduated from University of Utah in Political Science and planned to live out here with his dad after finishing school. Our teenager was included at the last minute because of his legal issues. Ash has always hated school, is street smart, and takes each moment as it comes.

"Oh, that brush, it might be in my bathroom, or "What's the big deal? it's apple juice."

"Are you wearing a T-shirt?" I ask Ash, "You can't wear that to a job interview."

With ten years between them, it has been very interesting to have the two of them living together. Sound like a recipe for disaster? Maybe.

It is strange watching their dad play chess with Kiyan, arm-wrestle with Ash, and take Ash to a job interview. After so many years of hostility— especially after the divorce—this is a totally different picture. We are treating each other with respect. It's kind of like we are old friends and we know each other quite well. With our newfound age and wisdom, not to mention the nearly five years we've been apart, there is finally peace—at least in front of the boys.

I've made friends with my anger, sadness, and pain. I've learned how to feel it, talk about it, and let it go. I'm learning to change my old behavior patterns that have kept me in my own vicious cycle. Now I can listen to what my ex is saying without reacting. He may be pulling strings and playing things to his best advantage. I can't blame him, I've done my share of that.

I no longer fall for it, though. I no longer need him for anything, and I no longer want anything from him. It's very interesting seeing it now, when I am aware of what he is doing. It's much better and easier just letting things happen, not trying to control how it happens.

I do feel sadness that our oldest son is still in the middle of it all— thinking that disrespecting me may somehow enable him to gain some ground with his dad. I'm sorry that he needs his dad's love that badly. How do I make up for all the years my children lived with fighting and chaos?

* * *

The first time in I saw my children's father, I wasn't that impressed. He was living in my apartment building, and a friend took me to his apartment.

Then, when I was at my favorite club waiting to meet a man I was dating, I saw looking at me a strikingly dark, handsome man wearing a black leather jacket and jeans, and a button-down white shirt open enough to show his dark, hairy chest. I was mesmerized. He asked me to dance, and at one point he kissed my hand. I was blown away.

My date for the evening came as this interesting man and I were on our third or fourth dance together. I rudely ignored the man I had been dating as he stood there waiting for me.

An exotic Persian man, Harris and I quickly become intensely involved. He was quite possessive and made sure I wasn't dating anyone else.

We met in 1979, right in the middle of the Iran hostage situation, and my friends made it clear they weren't comfortable in social settings with him. A friend invited me to a party but said it would be best if I didn't bring Harris.

He and I were crossing a street close to downtown Salt Lake City one evening when a man in a vehicle waiting at the light yelled, "F--k Iran!" I was shocked but Harris was not fazed.

We were living together when I took him to my parents' house for the first time. He didn't make crude comments to me as other guys had after I told them about my polygamist background. In fact, he was very comfortable and respectful to my parents.

A couple of months after I had been living with Harris, Mom spoke to me privately about a man who was asking about marrying me. She explained, "He wants a second wife because his first wife can't have any more children and they want a large family. He doesn't care that you've been wild (meaning I was no longer a virgin), because he has been, too."

The man who asked to marry me—I'll call him "Curt"—was my father's grandson from his first wife. Think about that one. I didn't know what to say. I did tell Harris about it, though.

The next time I went to my parents' home with Harris, Curt just happened to be there. There was some head-butting and testosterone flying around the room during that visit, and I enjoyed the moment. But plural marriage went against everything I believed was possible for my life, and I knew it was not for me.

That spring when I was 25, the federal government was trying to deport anyone from Iran who was in America on a visa. That included Harris, who had a court date and a notice to leave the country. I didn't want him to leave, so I suggested that we get married. I didn't especially want a husband but had begun to want children. I had gotten quite comfortable with Harris, and figured things would be fine. He was six years younger than me. His parents had sent him to America before he turned 18 to keep him out of the military in Iran and they were helping him out financially. Harris was attending high school while I was in college. He was quite good-looking but still, he was a teenager and not that easy to live with.

Harris and I would regularly visit my parent's house. I would go downstairs in the split level home my mother shared with Aunt Vio who lived upstairs. Aunt Kate had passed by this time.

While I visited with Mother, Harris would play chess with my father upstairs. This went on for several years before Harris and I were talking and I said, "Dad knows I don't want to live polygamy after everything that's happened."

Harris shook his head, "He talks to me about getting another wife every time we play chess."

"He what?"

"Your dad has been doing that for years."

As the shock of that wore off I became really angry and began ranting, "How can Dad completely disregard what he knows I want for myself? Does he have such little respect for my life, my decisions and what I have fought for? My husband taking another wife would mean the end of my marriage, how can my father possibly think his religion is more important? Will he never respect my choices?" I was the mother of two children and in my thirties by then.

The next time I saw Dad I expressed my anger, "You have been talking to Harris all this time about polygamy where I couldn't hear you? You did this behind my back?"

His reply was a little sheepish but still stubborn, "This is the true and chosen principle that God has given us," all I heard after that was blah, blah, blah. That was the end of me spending any time with him. I would visit my mother and show respect for my father but gave up any thoughts of a relationship.

When my first child was born in 1982, I was truly afraid of screwing things up. I had no idea how to take care of a baby—not only how to give physical care, but also how to nurture, love, and bond with him. I loved him and all my children until I thought my heart would burst, but I did not know how to show it.

My husband and I stumbled through marriage and parenthood, butting heads, clashing, and fighting regularly. I had learned how to protect myself from attacks but not how to show love. I was able to stand up to the most imposing personalities and I could work hard for hours without a break but I was afraid to show any softness or vulnerability.

Harris was also a great host, a long-time tradition in his culture. He made all his guests feel very comfortable by making sure they had anything they might want, giving special attention to details, engaging in interesting conversation, making jokes, and interacting with them.

Coming from the background I did, this was all new to me. In my experience, people in my family watched out for themselves and took care of themselves. It was every man for himself—every girl for herself really, since the girls were instructed to take care of the brothers and father. My husband was often offended by the way I talked to him. He was quite suave and polite, and I did not understand the finesse he expected. He was offended when I didn't cater to our guests and children. His mother had spent every moment of her life catering to her family, cooking or cleaning or sewing clothing for them and never allowing herself to relax. All I knew is that I felt like a servant growing up, and I was determined not to be a servant to anyone ever again.

A year after we moved to Kansas City, I took a job as bookkeeper at a shop that carried furniture, wall art, custom floral arrangements, lamps, vases, antiques imported from Europe, and a lot more. All the employees other than me were interior decorators, and the shop was a home that the owner—I'll call her "Gina"—had beautifully remodeled. I had no idea where this job would eventually lead me.

There was a cafe in one wing of the house with big windows along three walls looking out onto the landscape. The large yard was surrounded by trees that made you feel as though you were out in the country even though we were in the middle of suburbia. The cafe brought a lot of traffic to the shop, and Gina, who owned both the shop and the property, depended on the customers from the cafe. The cafe was open six days a week for lunch only and catered at private events outside of that. I hadn't worked there long when Gina came upstairs to the office. "The owner of the cafe has given a thirty-day notice," she said, visibly distraught. "I have called the owners of several local restaurants, and none wants to open a business here." I talked to her about it for a bit then let it go. That night I couldn't help but think about our conversation.

When I saw Gina the next day, she again started talking about the cafe closing and how badly it would affect her business.

"I could do it," I heard myself saying, though I wasn't at all sure I could. Gina knew Harris had many years of experience managing hotels and restaurants and she wanted him to sign on as a consultant. He agreed to that even though he was already managing a hotel, working long hours with a lot of responsibility. It took the first week to negotiate and finalize the lease. I was glad my husband was involved with that.

A year later, Harris lost his hotel manager position, so he joined me at the cafe cooking while I continued to operator the cafe. Harris is a really great cook—I would call him a chef—and he took the food quality to a new and delicious level. Working together initially went pretty well. He worked a lot less hours and was there every day to prepare the food and clean up afterwards. However, the issues in our marriage became more exaggerated once we were living and working together.

For the first time, I felt like I had done something with which people were impressed. I could scarcely take in all the positive attention I received from my customers and it felt quite different to what I felt inside. The cafe became my escape from the fighting and turmoil of my marriage. I sometimes went there in the evening after it was closed. It was a quiet, peaceful place where I could relax and enjoy the beauty of my surroundings. I had worked very hard to create that environment, and it was gratifying to sit quietly and take it in. I used the time to reflect on the day's events, conversations, and conflicts in a place where I felt good about myself—a first for me. I could turn on soothing music, have a good cry, or enjoy a glass of wine.

I joined my first church when we moved to Kansas City. This church's focus was on our own behavior and how we change ourselves instead of focusing on what someone else was doing wrong. There were a number of classes on how to improve our lives. The church was filled with loving, kind people who were ready to support me in ways I very much needed, and it provided the community support I had wanted in my life.

Initially my husband joined me at church and enthusiastically talked about how to change our relationship. We even went to several different counselors. It soon became apparent that he did not really want anything to change. He had been the good cop to my bad cop. He had been the provider who was generous with money while I had to figure out how to pay for everything at the end of the month. When he pointed out my shortcomings, I had no defense. I already felt unlovable, and his criticism only served to reinforce that. I spent a lot of time beating myself up. I didn't like who I was and desperately wanted to change that.

My relationship with Mother was always cordial; she never raised her voice to me. In fact, she said very little, and when she did talk, I simply listened. Because I had not followed her path and embraced her beliefs, she saw that as me rejecting her.

Mother controlled her children by her approval or disapproval. If you did as she did, she approved of you—something she conveyed in very subtle ways. You knew where you stood by how much she talked to you when the women were together. If you were in her good graces, she pointed out what you or your family had been doing, asked you to do things for her, and invited you to go places with her.

Mother seemed to pull away from me even more following my father's death. She told me she couldn't write me anymore. She didn't call me for years. On the rare occasions I did see her, she made clear which daughters understood her or had a better house than I did. I felt abandoned and unlovable.

I loved Mother dearly and did what I could to maintain a relationship with her. I had not given up on her changing the way she felt about me. I had not given up on gaining her love and approval. And I had not given up on making her proud of me.

In 2001, mom passed away unexpectedly. After hearing the news, I initially felt fine. I was good at doing that. On the surface I felt nothing was wrong; I continued filling my responsibilities at the café and caring for my children, arranging to travel to Utah for the funeral. I was just fine through the morgue preparation, the viewing, and the funeral services. Things weren't as good as they looked, however, my capable, respectful self felt a profound disconnection from my family through all of it.

As my sisters and I were riding in the limousine to the burial site, they began discussing meeting at Mother's house afterward to divvy up her few possessions. As I listened, I began getting irritated. How could they talk about her possessions like that, with no respect? She had just passed! Then I began feeling claustrophobic. I just wanted to get out of that car.

As soon as the limo stopped, I jumped out and burst into tears, sobbing uncontrollably. My brother Steve held me for a while, but my sobbing didn't stop—it continued throughout the burial.

Somewhere deep inside of me, I realized there was no longer any hope of ever changing my relationship with her. As her coffin was lowered into the ground and covered with soil, so was the possibility that I would ever gain her love and approval.

As it became clear to my husband that I would continue to reach outside my marriage for change, he became more confrontational, more provoking, and more determined to get me to engage as I always had. He didn't like where I was headed. I could defend, retaliate, remain silent, or walk away, and I did all of those things. It was a constant challenge to walk the talk, to change my own behavior within that relationship.

As we worked together at the cafe, our differences and how we handled those differences spilled over at times with unprofessional outbursts. Business had grown to a peak just before the terrorist attacks of 9/11 and never recovered from the abrupt drop in business afterward. As our income slowly decreased, our turmoil increased.

I was miserable, our three precious children were miserable and acting out, the café was limping along, and our marriage was a nightmare. We couldn't even go out to dinner without a fight erupting, so we no longer enjoyed that activity together. I knew this man would never leave me. I also knew it would get very ugly if I left—and would remain miserable if I didn't leave. I was terrified of being on my own, and really reluctant to be alone again.

In 2005, I finally decided I had to leave for me and for my children. I had to believe my life could be better, that I could be happy, that I could feel truly loved, and that I could have peace in my life. Or maybe I just couldn't live with the constant conflict any longer.

I moved to Lawrence, where our oldest son was attending Kansas University hoping it would be good for our youngest son to be near his older brother. However, that left our very capable daughter in Kansas City by herself at the tender age of eighteen. I looked for a job and filed for divorce.

After living in Lawrence for a year, I was feeling a bit lonely and I was very ready for something different, a better relationship than I had experienced in my marriage. In walked a man who was everything I had disliked and judged to be wrong: Republican, country, and NRA member who owned guns. Despite all that, he was nice, polite, and so different from what I had experienced with men.

As he continued to show up and talk to me daily, I realized that I couldn't discard what God had put in my path. Our relationship was off and on for several years and he was very good for me. I learned a lot about myself. However, in the end I wanted more from the relationship than he was able to give me and I divorced him. We are still friends, but he is no longer a part of my family.

Throughout this relationship and the divorce, Darice has been a strong, steady support for me, helping me learn to stand on my own in a healthy way, expecting no less than my best. What a blessing she has been.

I'm discovering how to nurture and find peace in whatever my life holds. I've done a lot of soul searching, analyzing, and learning whatever I can about myself, and those who have been in my life and still are.

Growing up, I did not have a spiritual connection, foundation, or belief. I've changed that, and I think that is the biggest and best change in my life. Today I keep my spiritual beliefs close to me. I believe that someone or something greater than myself loves and cares about me and will help me get through whatever is in front of me.

I had several nicknames growing up. My teddy bear of a half-brother Ron called me Babs. Mother's children called me Spoiled or Spoiled Brat. My father's oldest children, those from his first wife, called me The Baby. Dad used Sis when addressing his daughters, including me—probably because it was easier than remembering the right name. (Mother would say, "Betsy, Bonnie, Barbara!" in exasperation when needing to talk to one of us.) I also remember my father occasionally calling me The Caboose, an endearing memory for me.

There were a lot of difficulties between my father and I, mainly due to the abuse. I experienced abuse at his hands. Most of the time, I couldn't bear to be around him. Now though, from the perspective of an older and wiser woman, I see that he cared and loved me deeply. Coming to that realization has taken time and it has brought a sense of peace and happiness.

Clearly, polygamy was never for me. Even as a little girl I thought 'this is BS, you can't be serious!' I knew something was off kilter, that none of it made much sense and the only way to live with myself was to follow what was true to me.

The molesting when I was very young began my questioning what I was told to do. And I no longer trusted the adults that I loved. With my father gone most of my childhood and Mother absent if not physically but in most other ways, I was on my own to figure things out—and I did.

My choice to go against the family rules required courage, it required strength and independence. I was a free spirit in an environment that frowned on it. I was also a willful child at a young age with no clear limits or boundaries. I survived being at the bottom of this huge number of people by fighting for what I wanted.

Dad was a different father after prison and that is the father I knew the best. He had little patience, love or kindness for a daughter who was used to making herself loudly heard, we butt heads and hard. I was determined that I would never be under a man's thumb, that I would have equality as a woman, that I would take care of myself and not need a man.

There was never a doubt about living monogamy for me. I couldn't have lived with myself otherwise.

My mother resented my father and the experiences she had as a plural wife by the time I came along. Mostly what I heard from her were the difficulties in her marriage. When thinking about my father's and mother's relationship, I swore I would never let a man tell me what to do, who to vote for, how to live my life or what to believe.

Choosing monogamy came at a great cost, a civil relationship with my father and acceptance by my mother. It was made clear from my parents not to talk about anything different than what they wanted and believed.

That conditioning carried over into my relationship with siblings. What I heard regularly from my sisters was how hard it is to live polygamy, how much that challenges and teaches them. The implication was polygamists are special and better than everyone else because they can handle more.

I was definitely listening to, 'Life is harder for us therefore we are better'. I managed to make my life very difficult when it didn't need to be in the hopes of measuring up.

While on a visit at Shauna's house in 1985, talking with her and her three sister wives about all their children, one of them asked me, "Barbara, why did you only have three children?"

My automatic response was, "Because I'm selfish." I very much wanted to be a part of my family and I felt that what it required was making myself less.

I eventually left the family, their lifestyle and went my own way. I still maintained contact over the years and relationships with the ones I felt safe being myself with. If I didn't feel respected, I wouldn't spend time with them. After our parents passed, the family changed a lot. Polygamy no longer holds the status it did.

I have come to understand my father was only human and I can now appreciate his strengths and weaknesses. He is always present in my thoughts and I am grateful to be a part of the unique, loving family he created.

Maurine's daughters. Top, left to right: Linda, Betsy, Ginny; Bottom, left to right: Shauna, Doris, Barbara, Bonnie.

Epilogue

This book has been a once in a lifetime experience. With the honest open stories from each sister, they have brought us to our knees many times as we shared their pain, their uniqueness and their joy.

For each person reading this story, it has only been made possible through divine intervention. We prayed through many hours of not knowing how or what to do with what we were given. Through these individual stories and the life experiences each one brings to the book, we are family because of the choices our Father and Mothers made. We are family through thick and thin. We may not always talk to each other, we may have better relationships with one sibling than another but we will always come together as family.

Family Tree

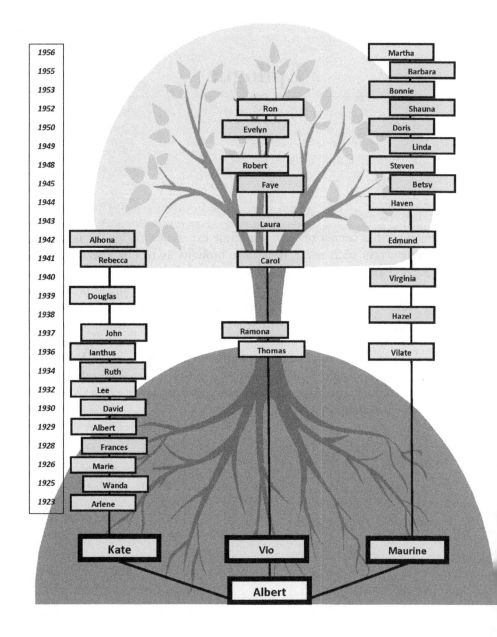

1956			Martha
1955			Barbara
1953			Bonnie
1952		Ron	Shauna
1950		Evelyn	Doris
1949			Linda
1948		Robert	Steven
1945		Faye	Betsy
1944			Haven
1943		Laura	
1942	Alhona		Edmund
1941	Rebecca	Carol	
1940			Virginia
1939	Douglas		
1938			Hazel
1937	John	Ramona	
1936	Ianthus	Thomas	Vilate
1934	Ruth		
1932	Lee		
1930	David		
1929	Albert		
1928	Frances		
1926	Marie		
1925	Wanda		
1923	Arlene		

Kate   **Vio**   **Maurine**

Albert

Acknowledgments

Over three years ago, many of the sisters were at a retreat in St. George Utah and I, Virginia, had the idea that it would be fun to have each sister write their story and have them all in one book. We are all so different and our lives were each so unique. After I pleaded, provoked and persisted I had all but one story. But by then I was tired, emotionally drained from reading about so much grief that I had not know about and was ready to quit. It had only been eighteen months.

Barbara realized what was happening to me and offered to help. I gratefully dropped it in her lap. She worked so hard from then on to completion, without her, there would be no book.

First we want to thank our sisters for being generous with their stories. It has been so much fun working with them. We have bonded while working on their stories and they shared some things that are not in the book.

We want to thank Darice Graham, Barbara's talented daughter, for her professionalism. I was amazed at how she moves into the corners of the situation.

We're grateful for the financial support of several of the sisters and the many who offered. The sisters have shown great enthusiasm and support of the many requests we had of them. Several grand kids provided needed support; Cameron Jacobson is one of them that finalized the cover for us. Diana Miranda was a key part of the final editing, thank you.

Virginia & Barbara 2003.

About the Authors

This is Virginia B Webb's second book. She was born the 16th child of her father's 34 and her mother's 13 children. She gave birth to eleven children and then divorced. After getting some college under her belt she remarried eight years later. Her father, Albert Barlow kept prodding her to write his story and eventually she agreed on the condition that he would just tell her stories but not dictate how she would write the book. That book was called "Wildcats, Wagons, Wives and Wardens" and was enjoyed by most of her family. After she turned seventy she had the idea to convince her living sisters to write/tell their stories for her and she would put those stories in a book. "Seventeen Sisters" is the result of that effort and would not have happened if her baby sister hadn't stepped in to take on the huge job of getting it into print.

Barbara Barlow grew up in the polygamous culture being 33rd and last child living in her family. After joining the Air Force to put herself through college in Salt Lake City, Barbara Barlow went on to become a business owner and leader in a community of spiritual growth-minded people while living in Kansas City. She returned to Salt Lake City to help write and publish Seventeen Sisters, a joint venture with her sister Virginia Webb where she still lives today.

To contact the authors, email address: seventeensisterstelltheirstory@gmail.com

Or visit our FB page https://www.facebook.com/pages/Seventeen-Sisters-Tell-Their-Story/1607592646175842

Made in the USA
Coppell, TX
31 May 2023

17547225R00134